I0800206

IMAGES
of America

NEWPORT

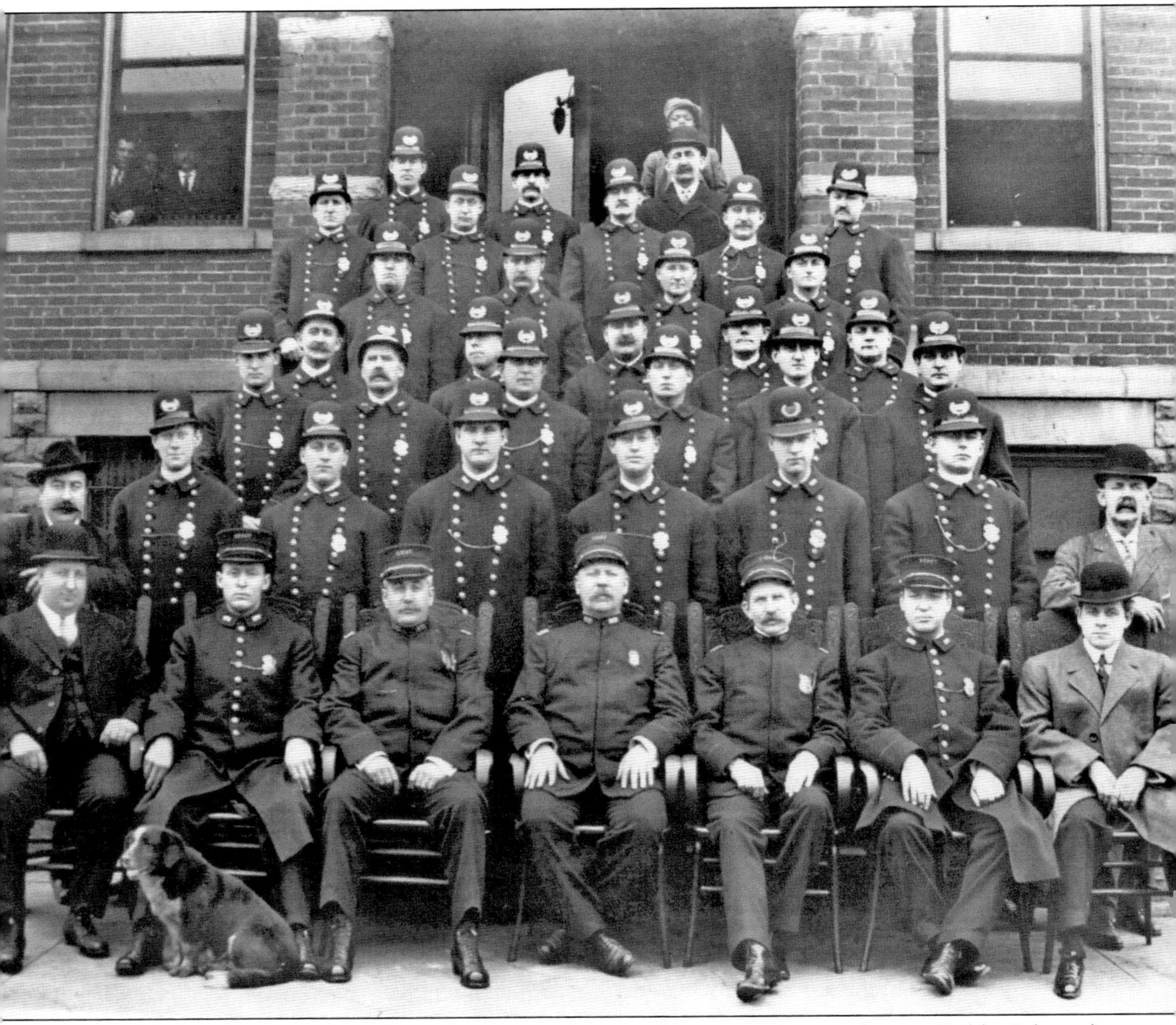

Pictured is the Newport Police Department, *c.* 1900. (Courtesy Kenton County Public Library.)

IMAGES
of America

NEWPORT

Judy L. Neff and Peggy Wiedemann Harris

ARCADIA
PUBLISHING

ISBN 978-0-7385-1728-5

Published by Arcadia Publishing
Charleston, South Carolina

Printed in the United States of America

Library of Congress Catalog Card Number: 2004109378

For all general information contact Arcadia Publishing at:
Telephone 843-853-2070
Fax 843-853-0044
E-mail sales@arcadiapublishing.com
For customer service and orders:
Toll-Free 1-888-313-2665

Visit us on the internet at www.arcadiapublishing.com

Dedicated to my late mother Alma who always was, and still is, the inspiration for everything I do . . . and to Rachel and Sophia who own my heart forever. –JLN.

Dedicated to my brother Carl Wiedemann Jr., Rhonda, Carla, Derek, and all my friends. I am blessed to have all of you in my life. –PWH.

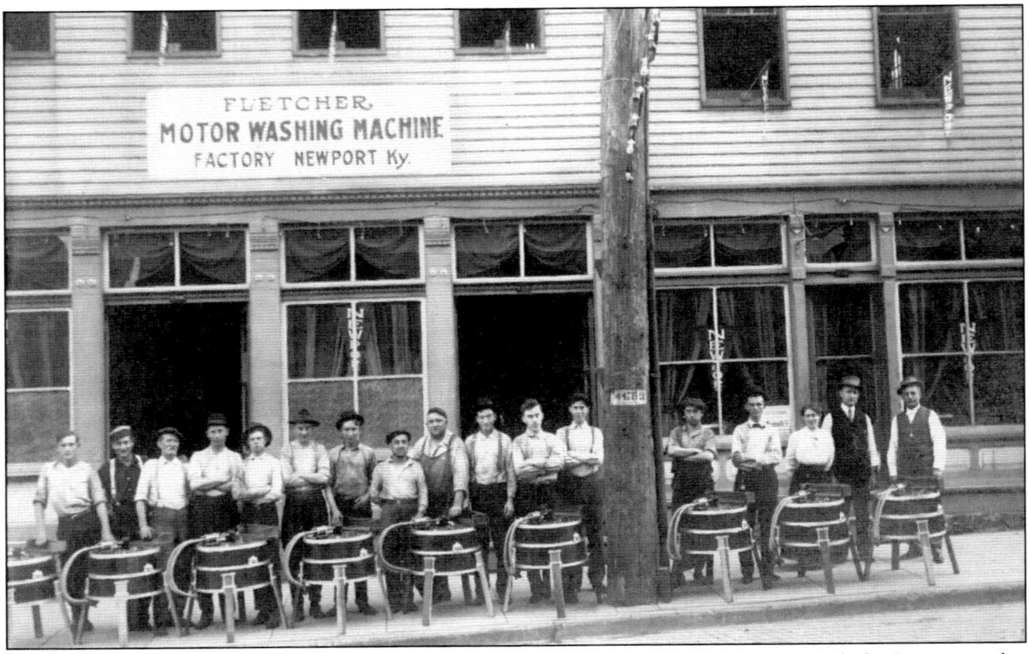

The Fletcher Washing Machine Company operated at 108 to 112 East Eighth Street under the direction of John B. Fletcher, president and manager. Incorporated in 1905, the company had the capacity to produce 3,000 motors per month that were shipped throughout the United States. (Courtesy Ross Raleigh.)

CONTENTS

ACKNOWLEDGMENTS

The Newport edition of *Images of America* represents the amalgamation of historical images from a wide variety of sources. We are indebted not only to the institutions and organizations housing such special collections, but also to each generous individual who reached into his or her closet to retrieve a family photo album for this purpose.

We owe a special thanks to the Kenton County Public Library and the Campbell County Historical Society for unselfishly allowing us access to their extensive collections. Also, as technical difficulties often attempted to inhibit our efforts, a deserving recognition goes to Ed Knue for his many hours of assistance with such issues. We would also like to acknowledge Prof. Barry Andersen and Frances McQueen of the College of Arts and Sciences at Northern Kentucky University for their expertise and assistance in the reproduction of glass slides.

Foremost in our gratitude are those individuals before us who were gifted with the foresight to save and maintain the historic images presented. Without their efforts at preservation, coupled with their selflessness and willingness to share, much of the material seen here could have been lost to time, and this book would not exist.

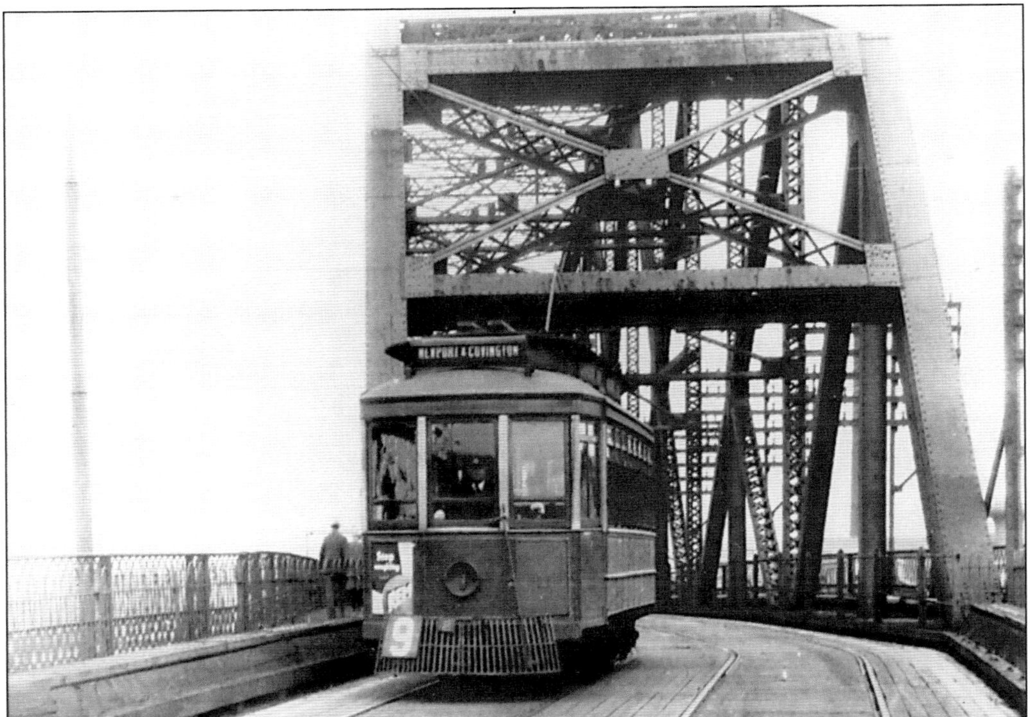

A streetcar crosses the Eleventh Street Bridge (Shortway Bridge) in the early 1920s. (Courtesy Special Collections and Archives, University of Kentucky Libraries.)

INTRODUCTION

Before Kentucky was admitted to the Union as the 15th state in 1792, the area including modern-day Newport was part of the Commonwealth of Virginia. The Taylor family of Virginia would become most significant to Newport's history. After the Revolutionary War, it was a practice of the government to reward citizens for their military service with land grants or patents. Such was the case with Col. James Taylor of Caroline County, Virginia; his service entitled him to a 1,500-acre parcel of land. While originally explored, surveyed, and named by Colonel Taylor's son Hubbard, it was his fifth child, also named James Taylor, who would later become responsible for the naissance of Newport, Kentucky. Their father never settled here.

Besides being a courageous pioneer and major landowner, Gen. James Taylor (son of Col. James Taylor) was a successful entrepreneur and invested in many of Newport's early businesses, including a sawmill and the Newport Bank. He was also politically active and immensely patriotic. Early on, he sold four acres of his land to the government for $1, upon which he convinced them to build the Newport Barracks. The presence of this facility would markedly change and accelerate the development of Newport. It is because of the barracks' establishment here that Newport overflows with military history.

Although founded and named in 1791, Newport was not officially incorporated until 1795. In 1800, the population totaled 106 persons; an increase to 234 citizens was seen in 1810.

Immigration visibly sculpted the face of early Newport and influenced the businesses and neighborhoods that would evolve. Although German immigrants comprised the largest ethnic representation, Newport would see more diversity with the arrival of various other groups, including Irish, British, and Italian families.

Obstacles were plentiful for the city, including the early isolation imposed by yet unbridged rivers and the ravages of a succession of floods. Many early businesses positioned themselves on the riverfront, only to have the indifferent river leave them in ruins. Later, the assiduous multi-decade grip of syndicate control became a well-publicized crisis for Newport. A little known fact is that Newport citizens had waged a war against gambling much earlier than the 1960s. A *Kentucky Post* article in 1916 discussed the "Committee of Ten" and their intention to rid the city of professional gamblers. A much larger and stronger "Committee of 500" would arise in the 1960s and begin the process that finally purged Newport of its corrupt reputation. Knowledge of the city's corruption and gambling had become widespread, and even U.S. Atty. Gen. Robert F. Kennedy became involved in the clean up.

Currently, Newport is flourishing and stands victorious over all of these substantial obstacles. The improper reputation and corruption have left town, but the excitement and adventure have returned to the streets of Newport. People are once again coming from other cities to visit the area and experience Newport. Historic properties are enthusiastically being renovated and preserved. Citizens are again proud to call Newport their home.

In looking back at the images contained in this book, the changes that have taken place in just over 200 years are astonishing. Clearly, Hubbard and James Taylor could have never known what would grow from the seeds they planted here when they claimed the wilderness as their own not so long ago. The authors hope you enjoy this trip into Newport's alluring and noteworthy past! We hope we have compiled a photographic portrayal of Newport that this extraordinary city truly deserves.

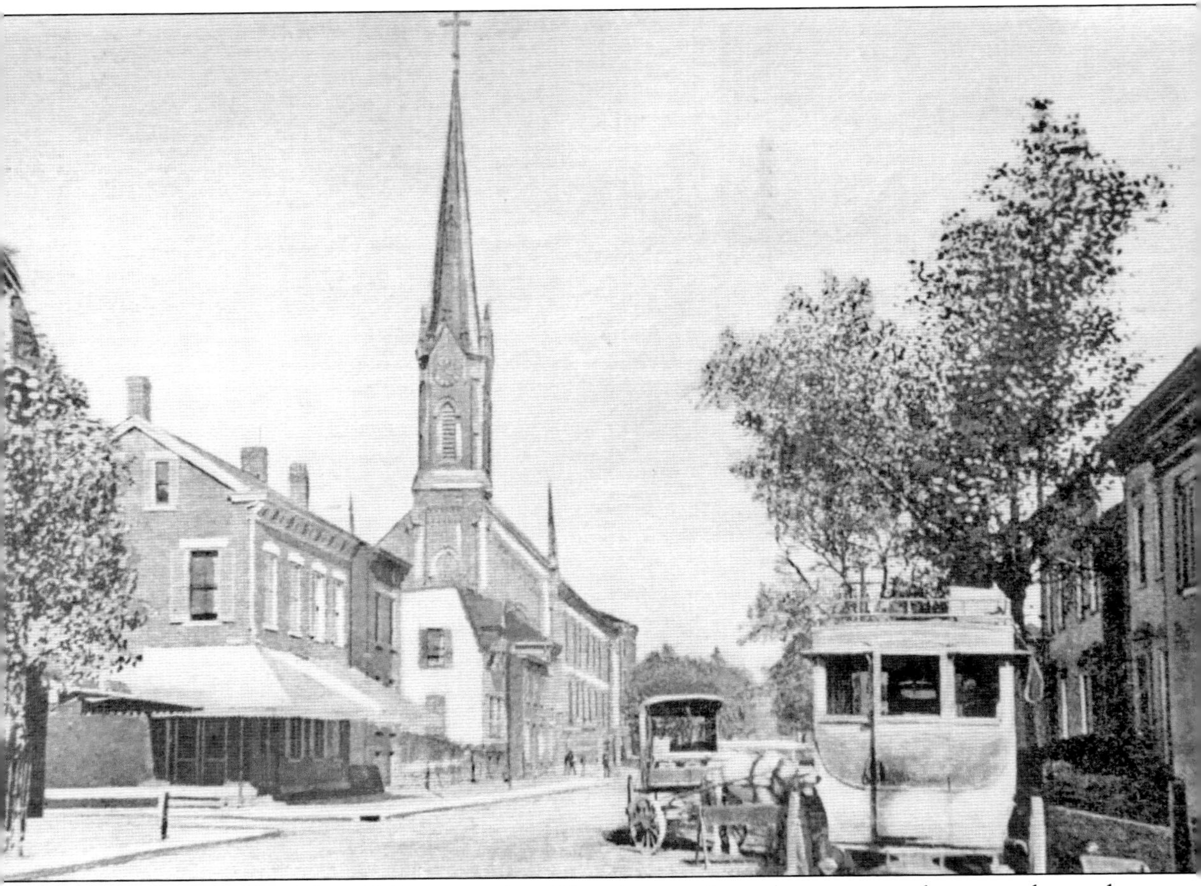

This early view of the old Saint Stephen Church was taken when stagecoaches were the mode of transportation. Stagecoaches would be replaced by horse cars, which were passenger cars pulled by horses along two iron rails. Electric streetcars would eventually replace them. This structure on Harris Street (later Ninth Street) was built in 1858. Saint Stephen Parish would later move to 825 Washington Avenue in 1938. (Courtesy Earl Clark Collection.)

One

BUSINESSES

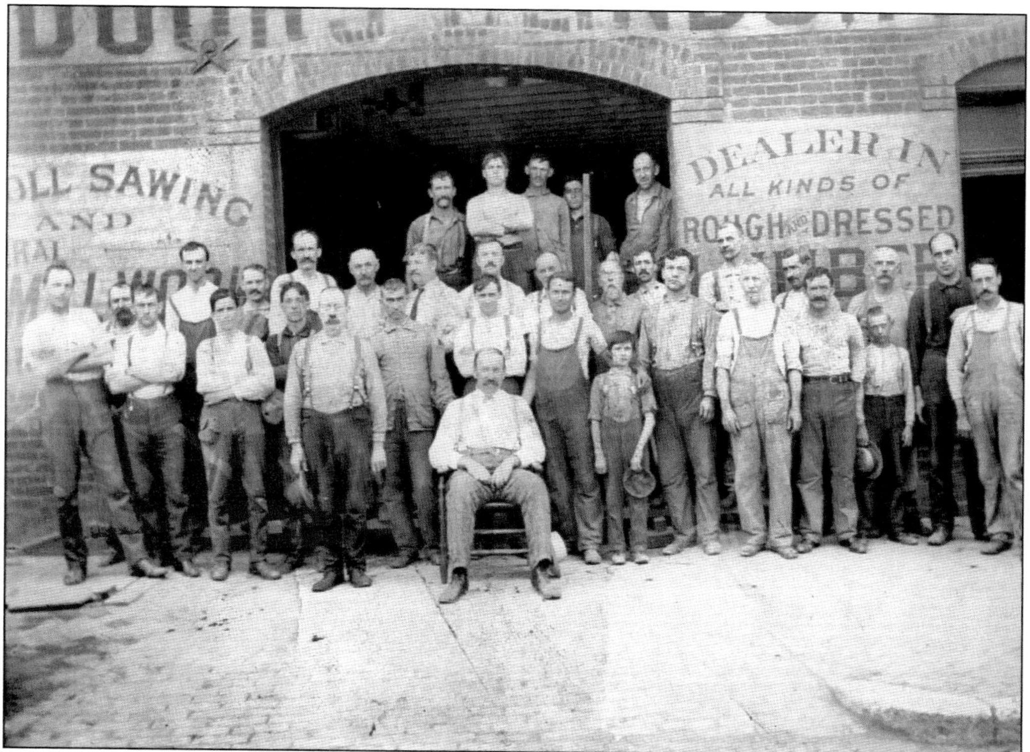

Fred Miller operated a lumber mill at 1028 Monmouth Street. It was destroyed by fire in August of 1916 with a loss estimated at $65,000. (Courtesy Campbell County Historical Society.)

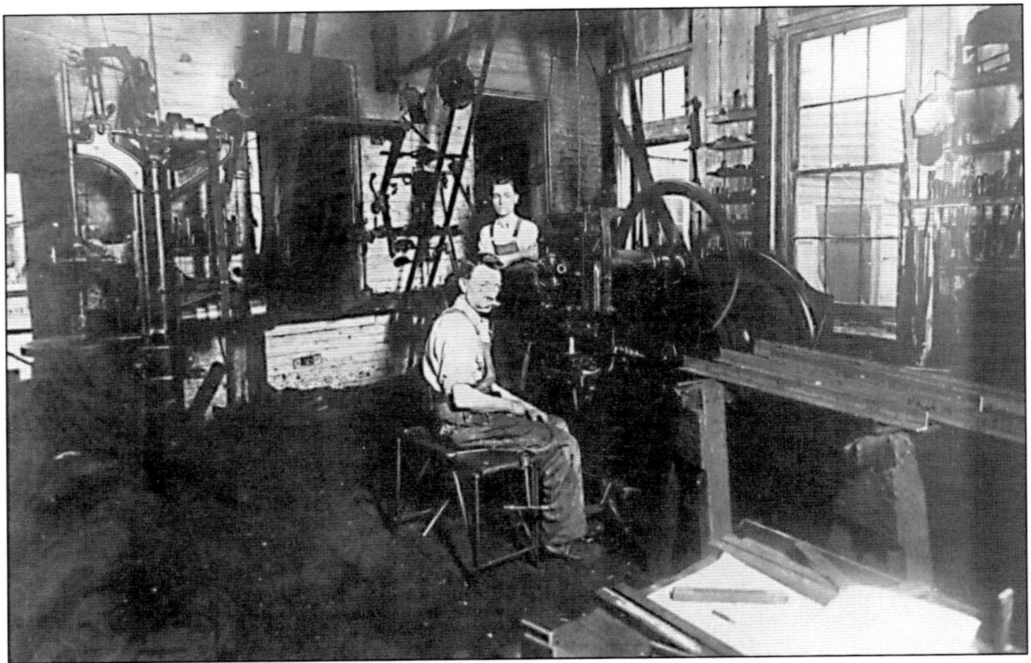

Work proceeded by hand inside the shop at Buecker Machine and Iron Works, c. 1918. Standing in the back is third generation owner Ernst V. Buecker. Buecker Machine and Iron Works has existed as a family-owned business for five generations. Founded in 1858 by Ernst Buecker who emigrated from Germany, the business is primarily known for ornamental iron work. Brother and sister team David Buecker and Linda Buecker Velten now carry on as fifth-generation owners. (Courtesy Buecker Iron Works.)

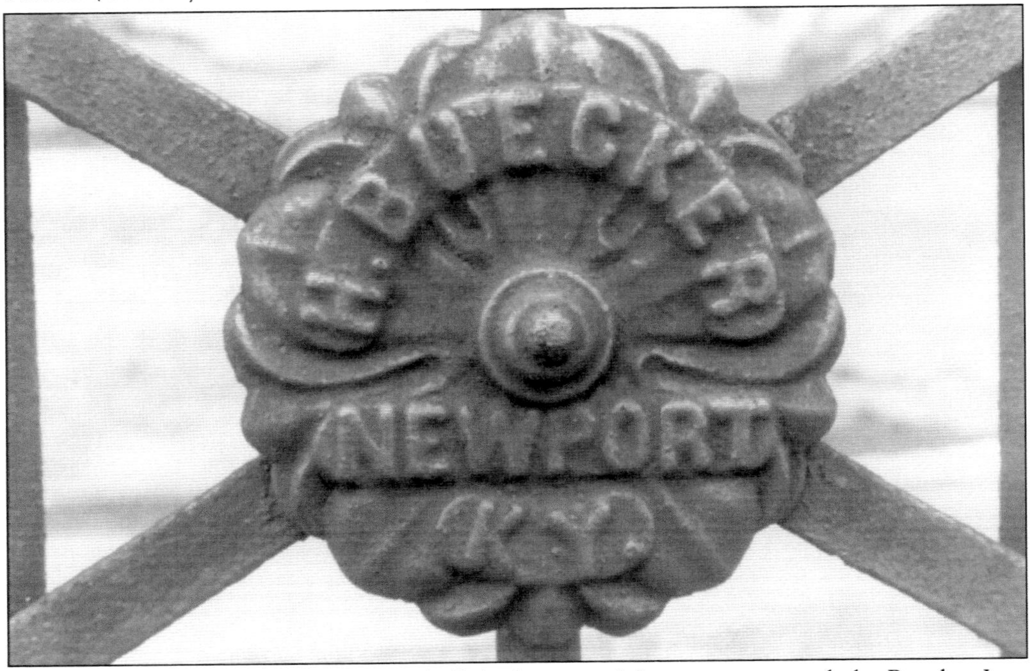

This signature cast iron medallion embellished many of the iron gates made by Buecker Iron Works. (Courtesy Buecker Iron Works.)

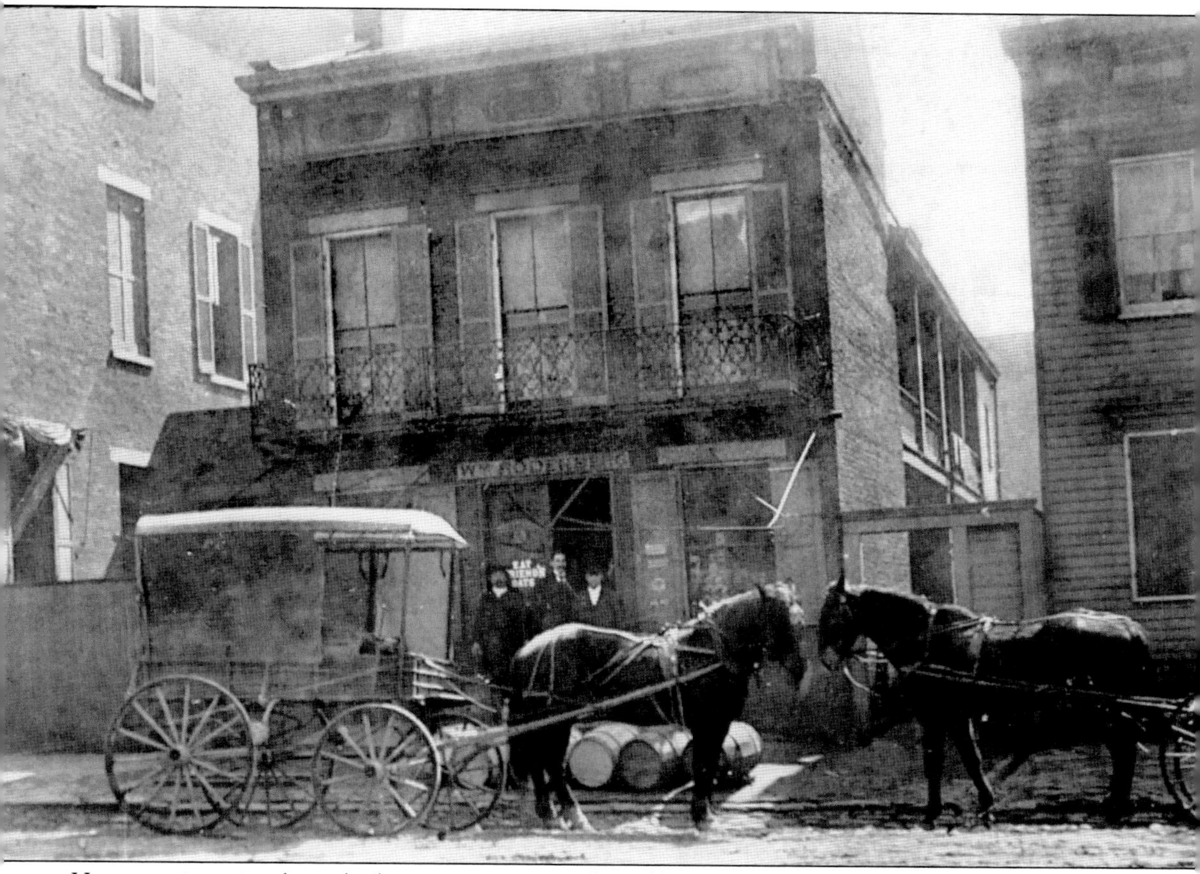

Horses wait patiently with their carriages outside William Rodenberg's grocery store on West Sixth Street, near York Street. Mr. Rodenberg was also a member of the Newport City Council. (Courtesy Campbell County Historical Society.)

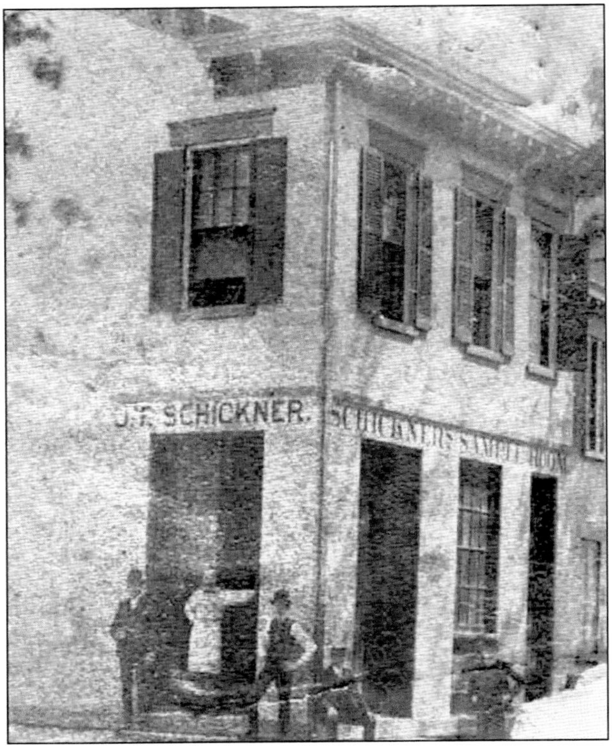

Jacob Schickner's Sample House was located on the southeast corner of Bellevue (later Fourth) and York Streets, which is the site the World Peace Bell currently occupies. Mr. Schickner would also later open another saloon at the Midway in Ft. Thomas. (Courtesy Susan Braun Smith.)

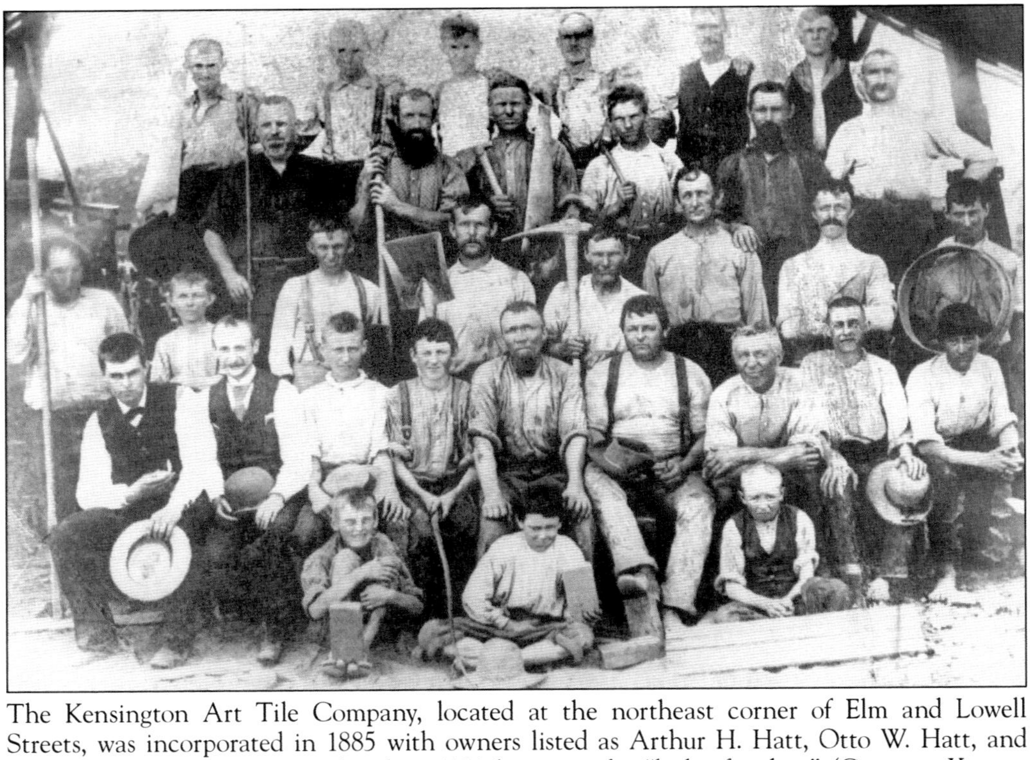

The Kensington Art Tile Company, located at the northeast corner of Elm and Lowell Streets, was incorporated in 1885 with owners listed as Arthur H. Hatt, Otto W. Hatt, and R.W. Nelson. The company closed in 1891 because of a "lack of orders." (Courtesy Kenton County Public Library.)

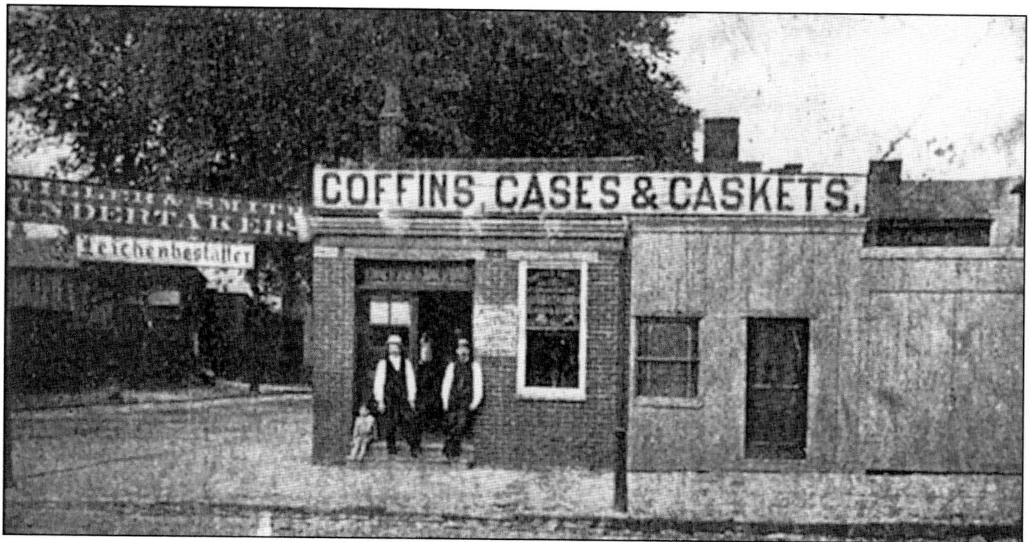

This undertaking business at the northwest corner of Madison (later Fifth) and Monmouth Streets was founded by E.A. Miller. During this time, caskets were made by hand; family members often brought in a piece of string to indicate the required length and width of the coffin. Charles A. Smith, his grandson, was an apprentice and continued the business after Mr. Miller's death. One hundred and five years of family management would end when the business was sold to Erschell Funeral Homes. The sign seen in the left side of the picture states "leichenbestatter," the German word meaning undertaker. (Courtesy Virginia Bennett.)

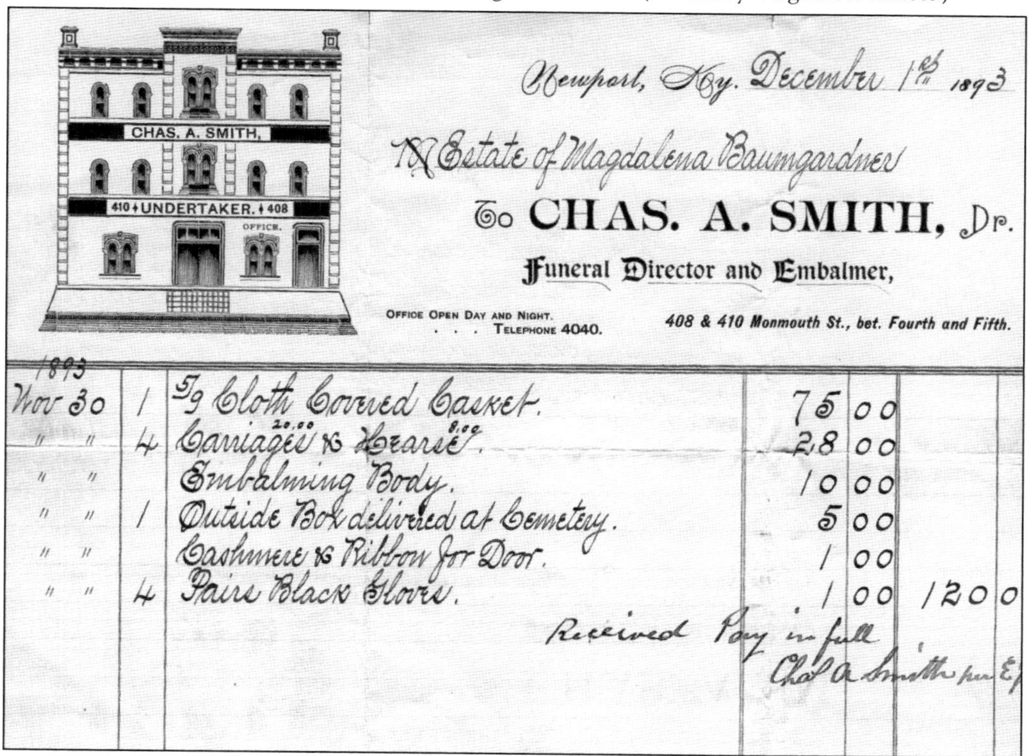
CHAS. A. SMITH,
410 UNDERTAKER. 408
OFFICE.

Newport, Ky. December 1st 1893

M Estate of Magdalena Baumgardner

To CHAS. A. SMITH, Dr.

Funeral Director and Embalmer,

Office Open Day and Night. . . . Telephone 4040.

408 & 410 Monmouth St., bet. Fourth and Fifth.

1893					
Nov 30	1	5/9 Cloth Covered Casket.	75	00	
" "	4	Carriages 20.00 & Hearse 8.00.	28	00	
" "		Embalming Body.	10	00	
" "	1	Outside Box delivered at Cemetery.	5	00	
" "		Cashmere & Ribbon for Door.	1	00	
" "	4	Pairs Black Gloves.	1	00	120 00

Received Pay in full
Chas A. Smith per E.

In 1893, $120 covered an elaborate funeral, which included embalming, a casket, and hearse and carriage service, as well as some other optional items. (Courtesy Virginia Bennett.)

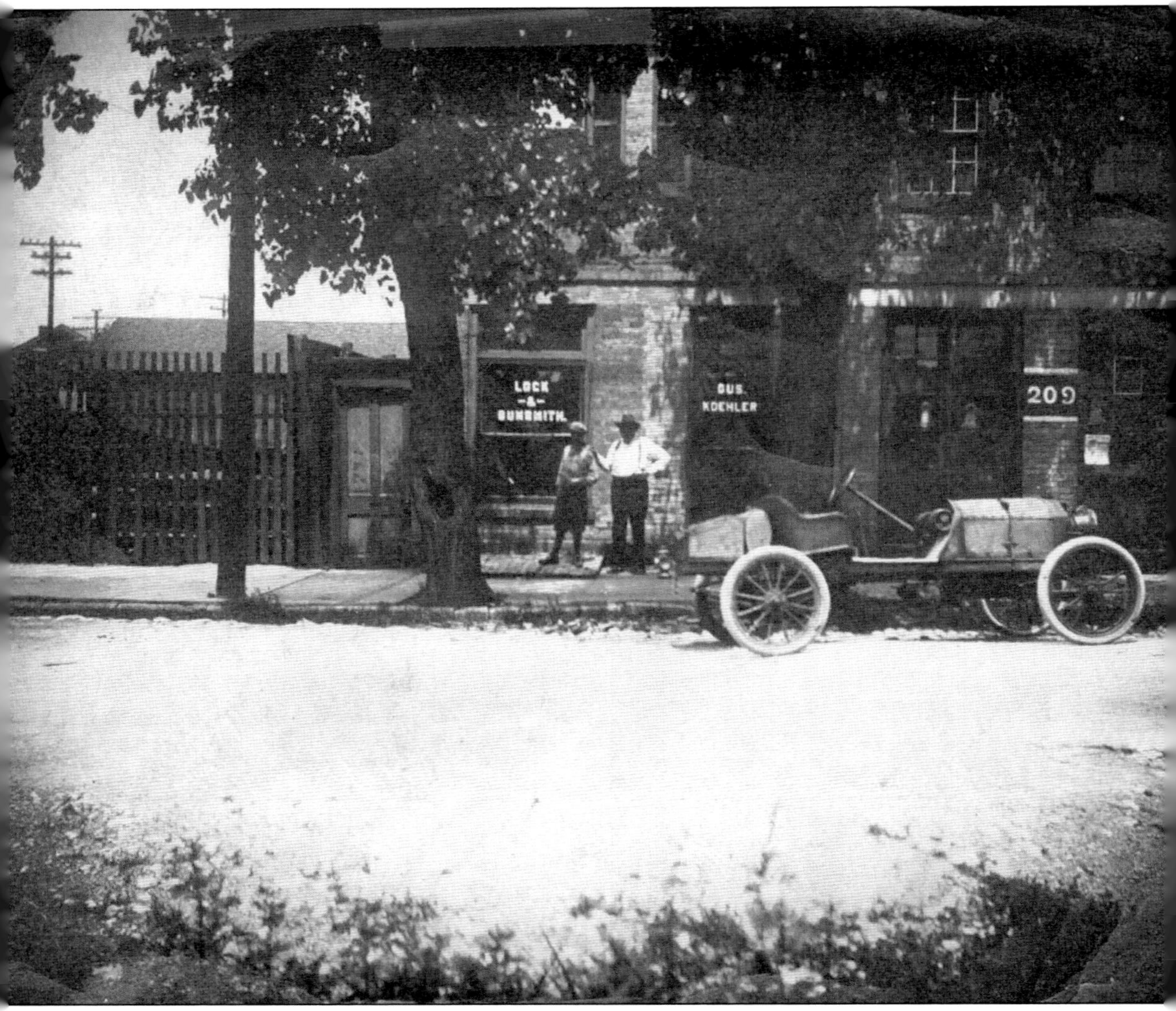

Gustave Koehler operated a lock and gunsmith shop at 207 York Street. So skilled was Koehler that the United States government frequently sent understudies to train with him. (Courtesy Peter Garrett.)

Gunsmith Gustave Koehler was also a musician. Besides the instrument shown at right, *The Kentucky Post* reported in 1908 that he also owned a genuine Antonius Stradivarius Cremonensis, a rare violin. The violin was reportedly given to Gus Koehler's grandfather in 1813 by a soldier musician in Napoleon's army "for samaritan services rendered in the march of the French army through Dresden, Germany, to the Battle of Waterloo." (Courtesy Peter Garrett.)

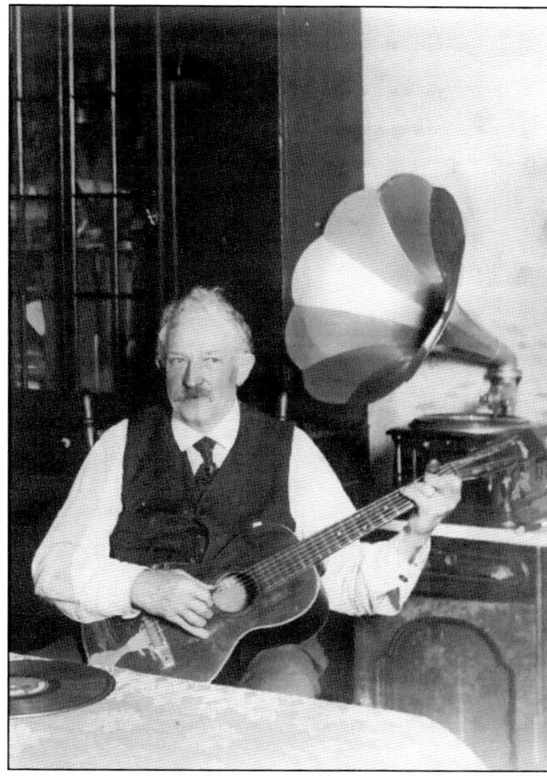

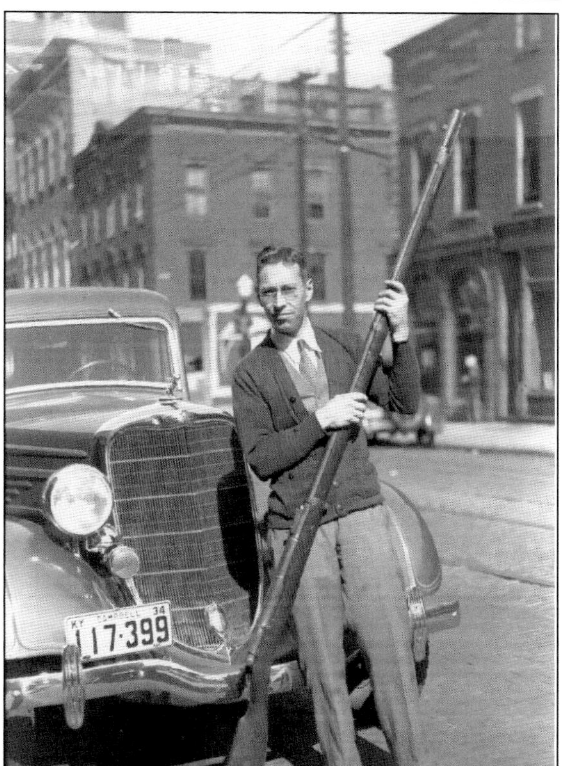

Billy Anderson, shown here in 1934 with a Chinese wall gun, took over retiring Gustave Koehler's gunsmith business. As with many businesses, recurrent flooding eventually necessitated movement further from the riverfront, and the shop was moved to 510 York Street. The business was acquired by current owner Peter Garrett in 1974, now operating at 838 Monmouth Street. (Courtesy Peter Garrett.)

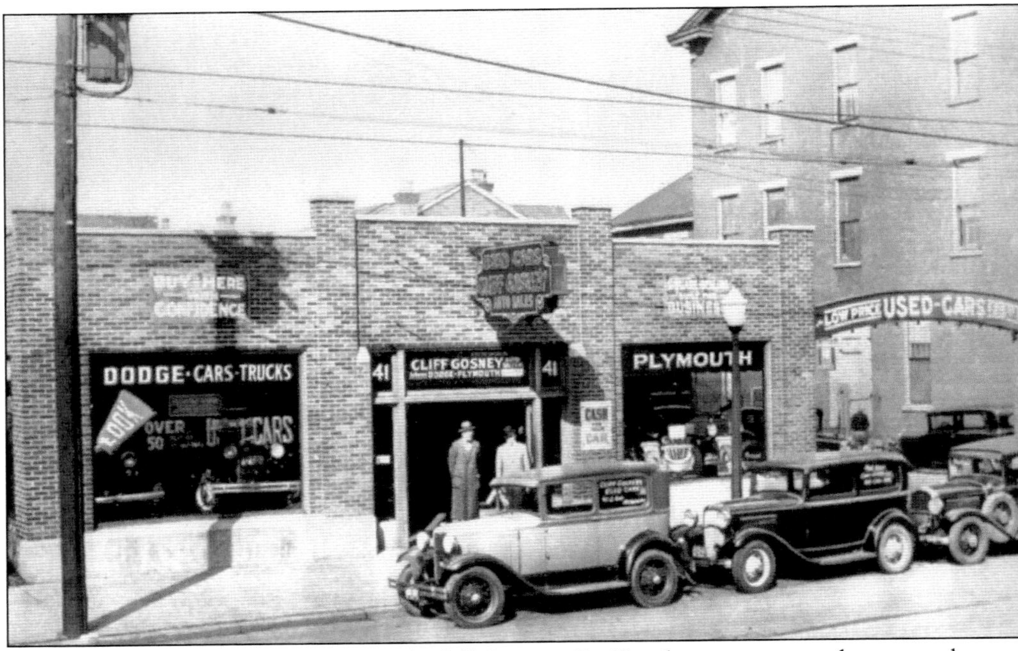

Automobile sales was the business of Cliff Gosney Sr. His showroom, seen here, was located at 41 East Third Street. Before opening this business in Newport, he operated an automobile service shop in Alexandria. (Courtesy Cliff B. Gosney Jr.)

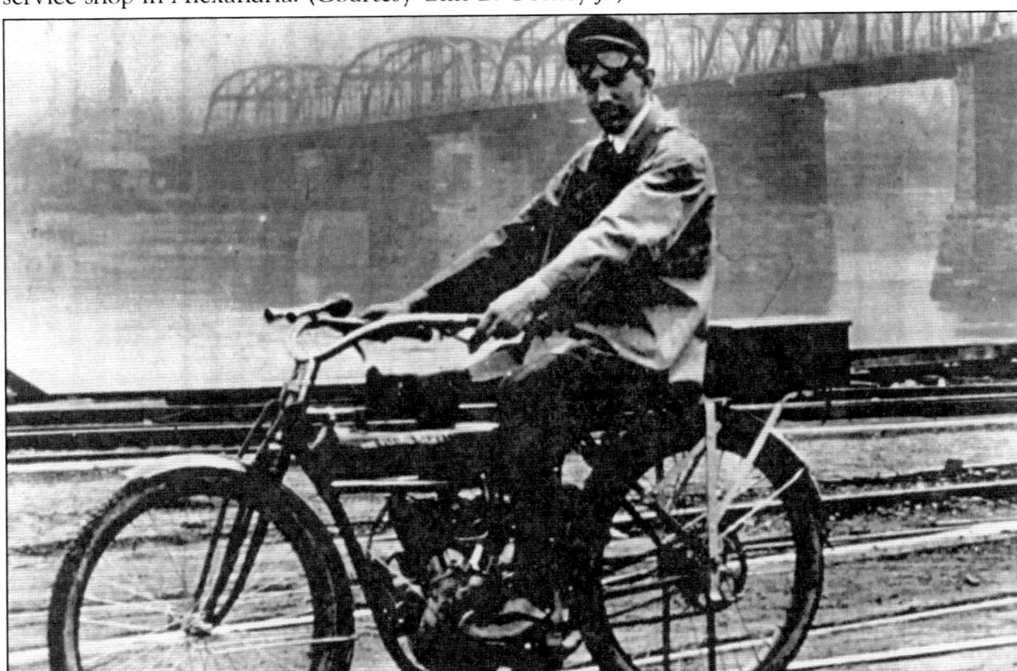

Cliff Gosney Sr. is shown here on his six-horsepower Flying Merkel. In a letter, he describes his first adventuresome eight months of ownership of this vehicle: "During this eight months running I covered 5350 miles on 88 gallons of gasoline and 9 gallons of oil. Had 7 punctures, 1 blow out, 6 spills, ran over 1 man, 3 dogs, 4 chickens, and 1 rabbit . . . Never had a scratch from riding and weigh 10 lb. more now than when I started riding." (Courtesy Cliff B. Gosney Jr.)

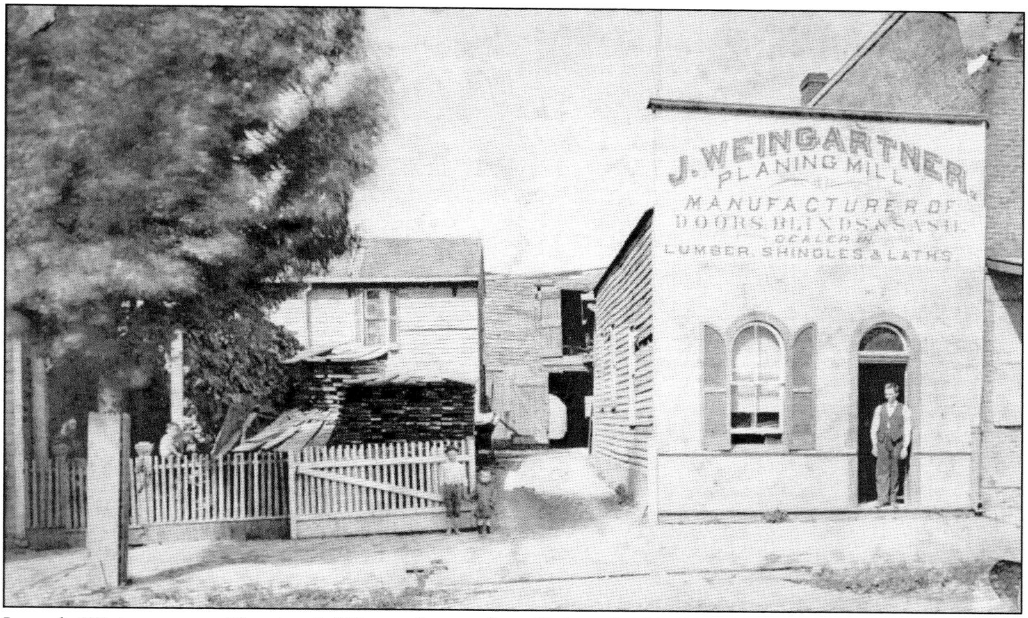

Joseph Weingartner Planing Mill was located at 296 and 298 Saratoga Street between Tibatts (later Tenth) and Williams, with offices at 303 and 305 Monmouth Street. (Courtesy Campbell County Historical Society.)

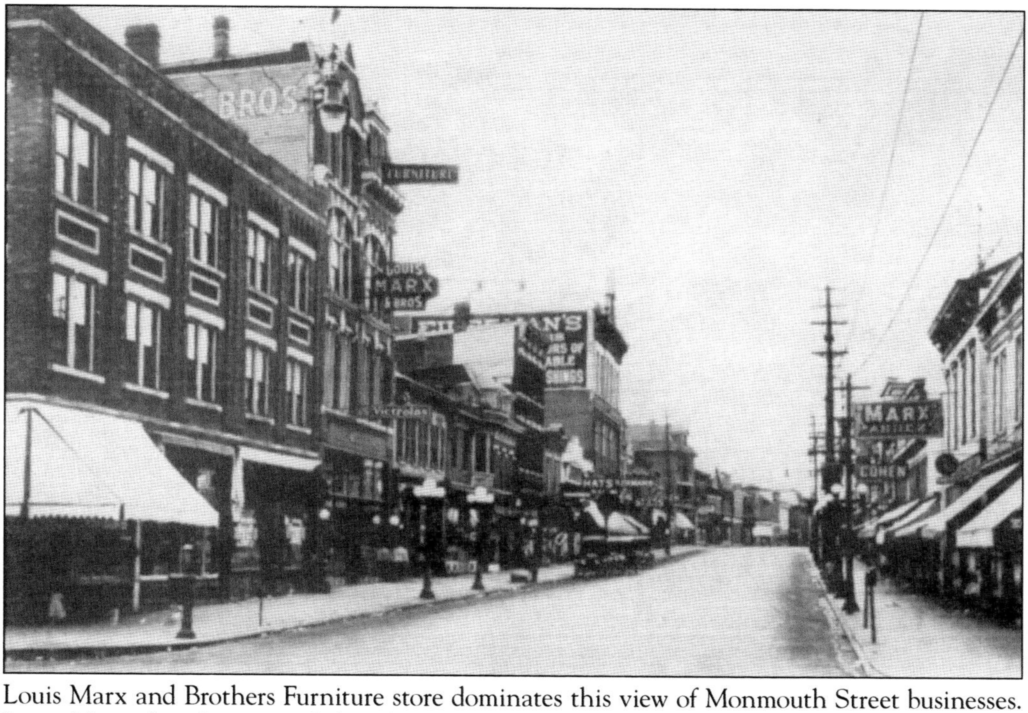

Louis Marx and Brothers Furniture store dominates this view of Monmouth Street businesses. Louis Marx, founder, opened the Newport store in 1888, with another store later established on Madison Avenue in Covington. Victrolas were one of their specialties. The Newport store closed in 1974, with the Covington business following suit in 1987. (Courtesy Special Collections and Archives, Northern Kentucky University.)

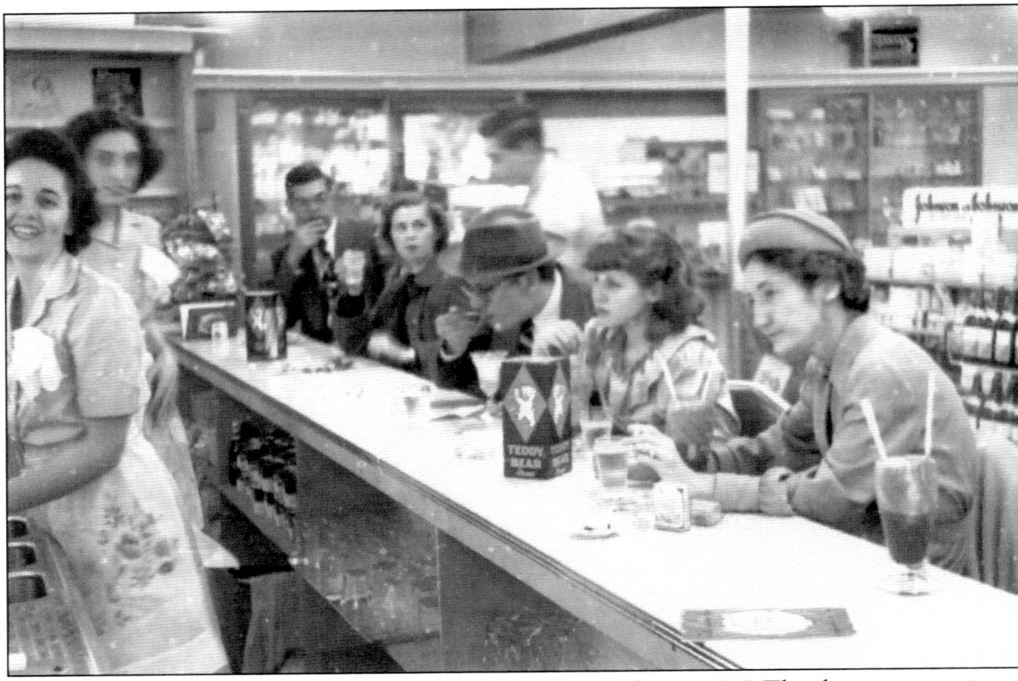

Opening day was a success at Klaserner Drug Store on September 24, 1949. The pharmacy continued at Eighteenth and Monmouth Streets until 1962. (Courtesy Olive Klaserner and family.)

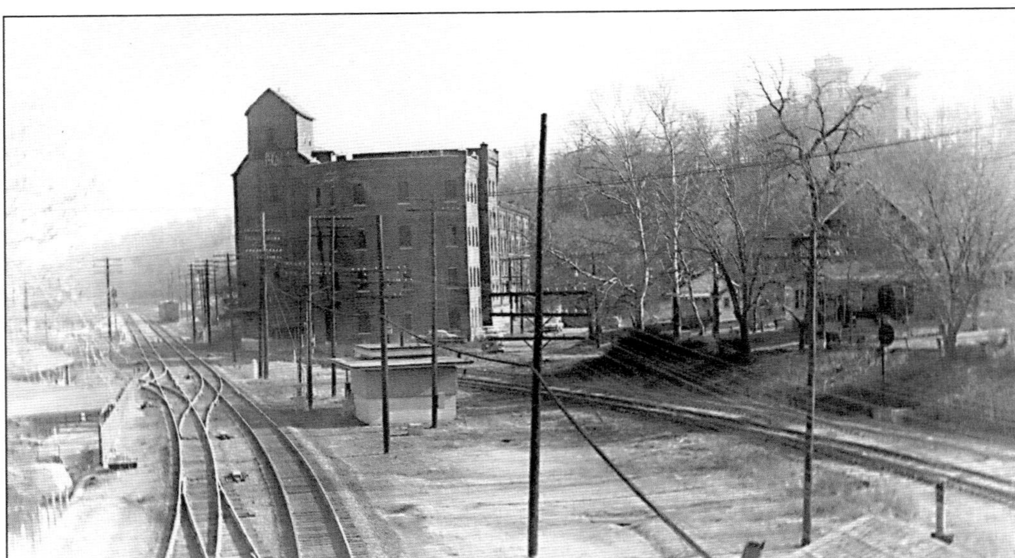

The George Wiedemann Brewery had humble beginnings when Wiedemann became partners with John Butcher in the Jefferson Street Brewery in 1870. He would later buy out Butcher for a sum of $28,000, and the business would experience marked expansion over the years. Wiedemann Brewery relinquished local ownership in 1967 when it was sold to the G. Heileman Brewing Company of Wisconsin. The plant closed in 1983, and this structure, the malt house, was subsequently demolished. In this view, Mount Saint Martin can be seen in the upper right corner. (Courtesy Mr. and Mrs. Richard Thompson.)

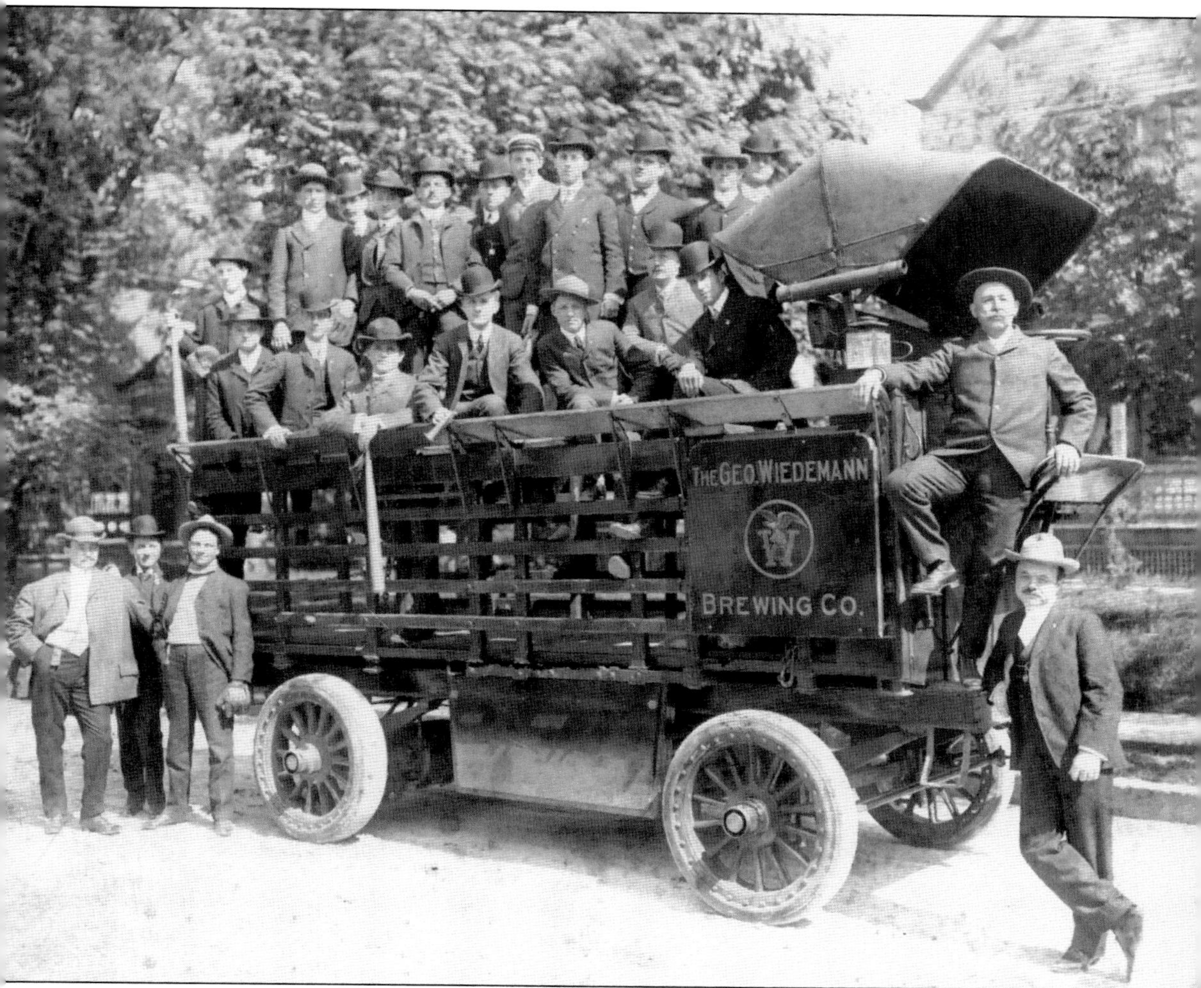

This is believed to be one of the earliest Wiedemann Beer delivery trucks. The employees appear to be on their way to a baseball game. (Courtesy Campbell County Historical Society.)

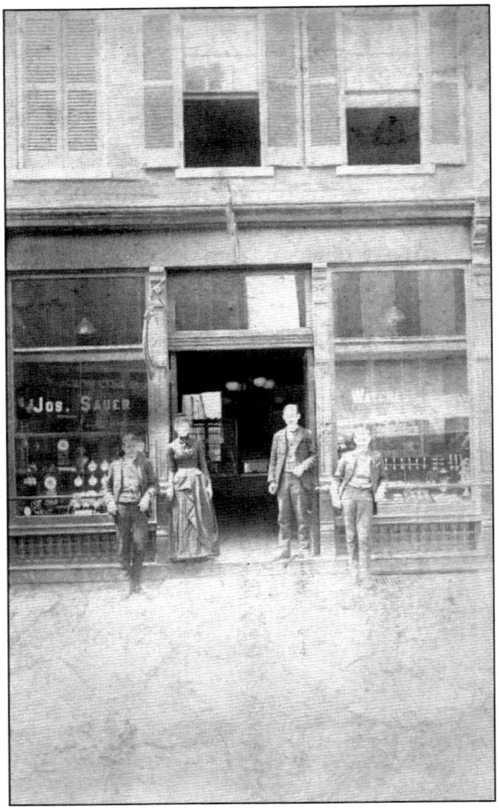

Joseph Sauer's Jewelry Store on Monmouth Street dates back to 1888. Brothers Joseph and Albert both owned jewelry businesses in Newport. (Courtesy Al Sauer.)

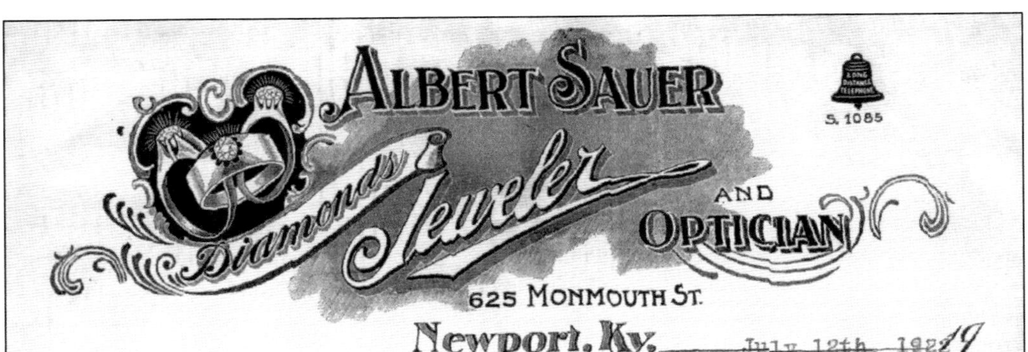

This letterhead from Albert Sauer's jewelry business at 625 Monmouth demonstrates that it was not uncommon for jewelers to also function as opticians. (Courtesy Al Sauer.)

Monmouth Street appears deserted outside Albert Sauer's Jewelry Store. His signature clock was a landmark on this street for many years. (Courtesy Al Sauer.)

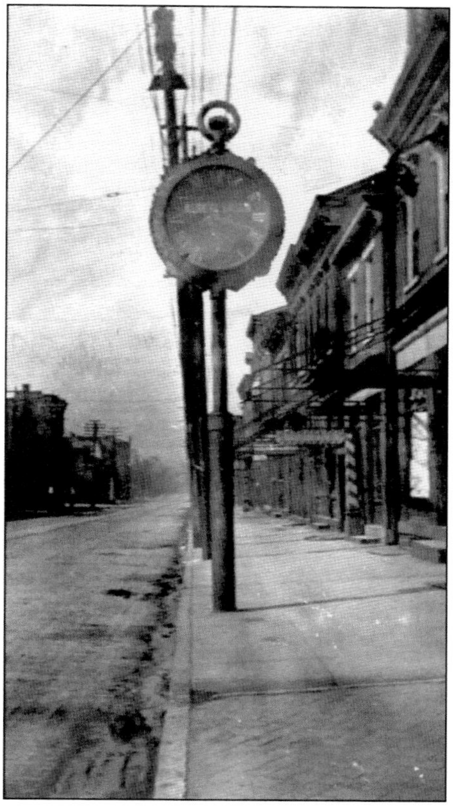

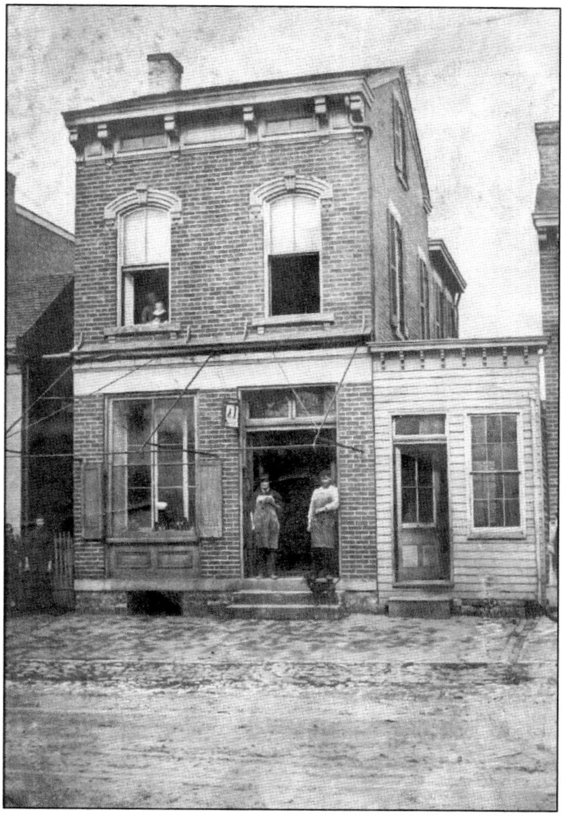

Yet another Sauer family business in Newport was a cobbler shop at 293 Washington Avenue, owned by John Sauer. This business is found in the city directory as far back as 1878. (Courtesy Al Sauer.)

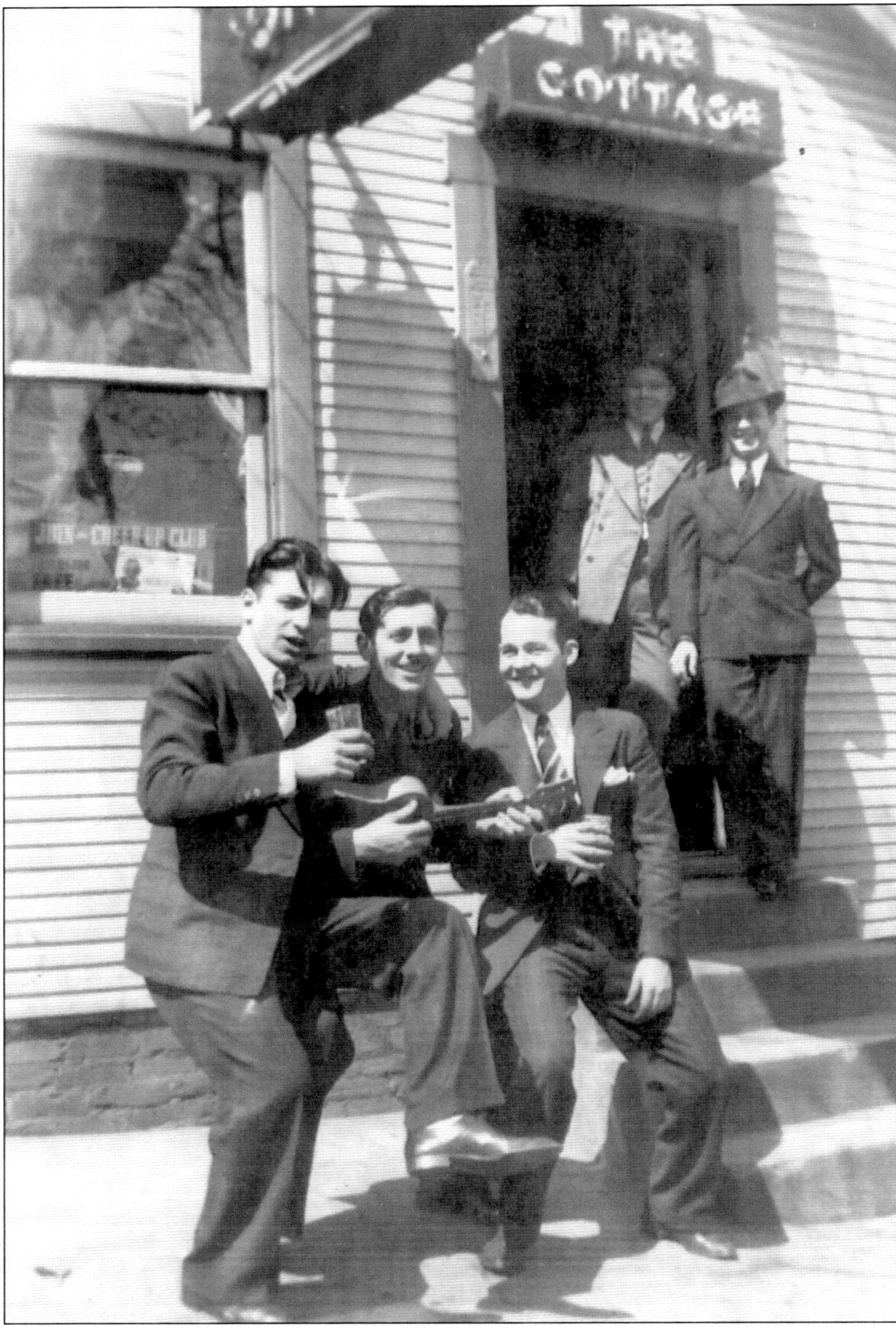

Frank Miller peers out the window at a group of friends gathered outside The Cottage on Main Street. The establishment is now known as Pic's Café. Pictured from left to right are Pat Ciafardini, Bill Greco, Roy Schweitzer, Bobby Evans, and John Piccirillo. (Courtesy Ciafardini family.)

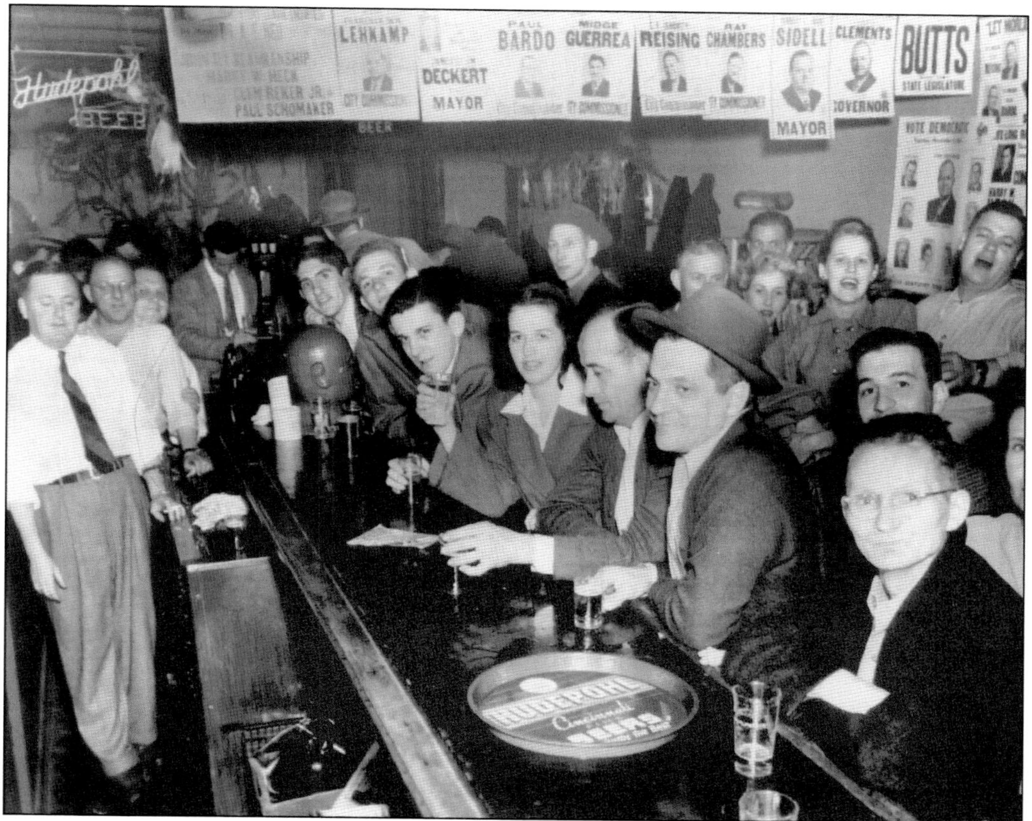

Patrons enjoy a good time inside The Cottage, well-populated with political announcements. (Courtesy Ciafardini family.)

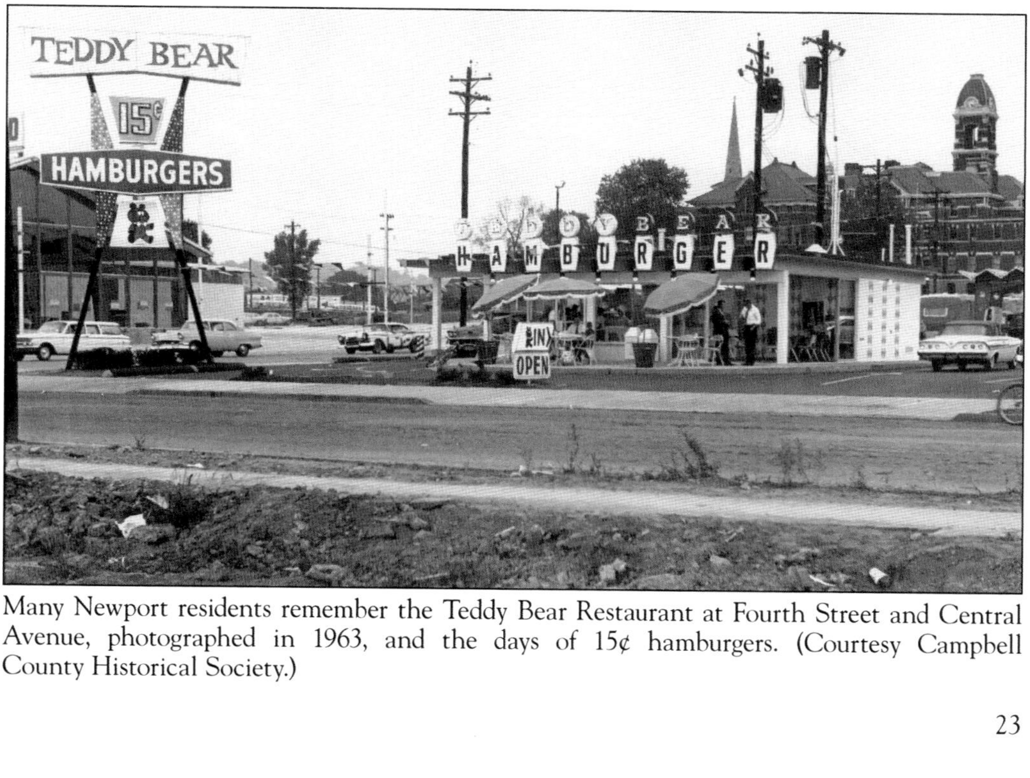

Many Newport residents remember the Teddy Bear Restaurant at Fourth Street and Central Avenue, photographed in 1963, and the days of 15¢ hamburgers. (Courtesy Campbell County Historical Society.)

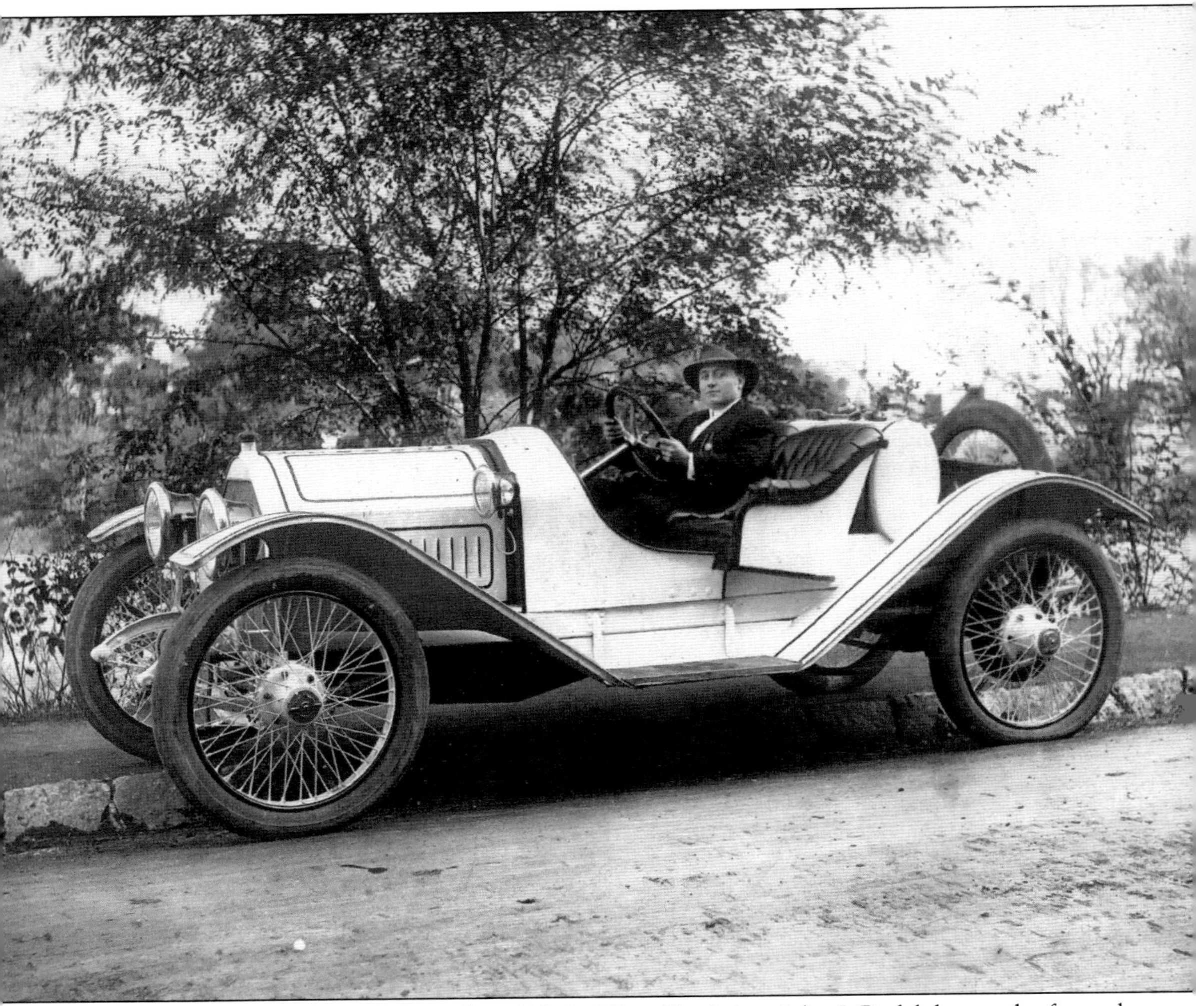

Henry J. Radel Sr. is seen here in his 1912 Cadillac. His father, John J. Radel, began the funeral business in 1856. The third generation of the Radel family continues to serve the families of Newport. (Courtesy Fares J. Radel.)

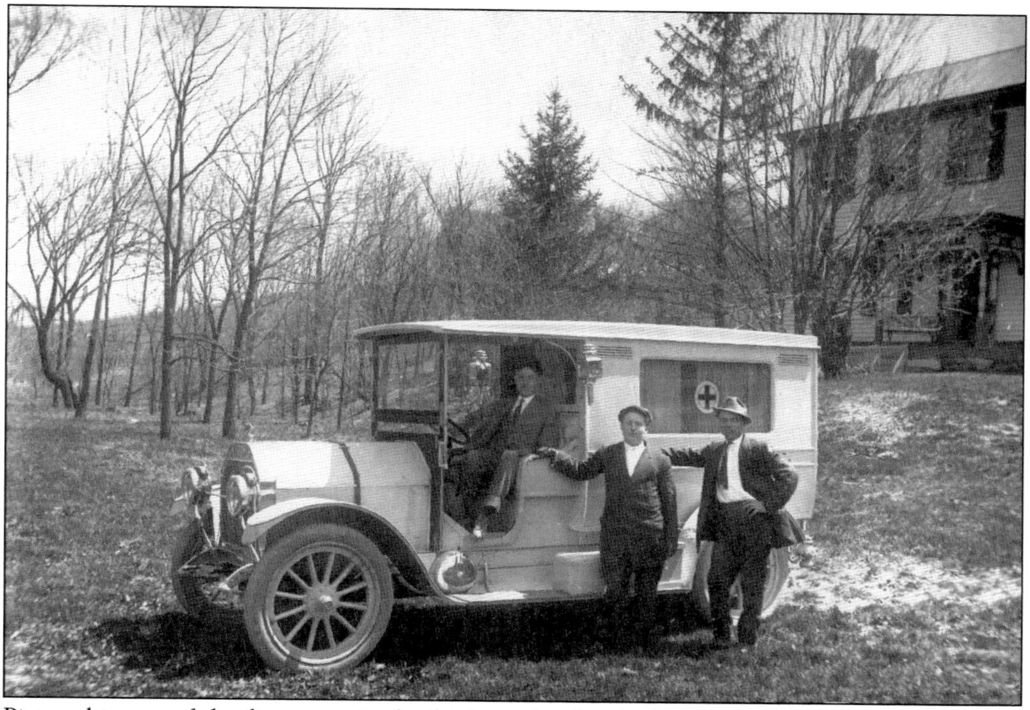

Pictured is one of the first motorized vehicles utilized as both ambulance and hearse by Radel Funeral Home. Hearses were drawn by horses until then. The make of the very early vehicle is unknown. Its self-generating headlights used carbide and water to make a gas to burn for light. From left to right are Edward Griefenkamp (driver), Henry Radel Sr., and Nicholas Radel. (Courtesy Fares J. Radel.)

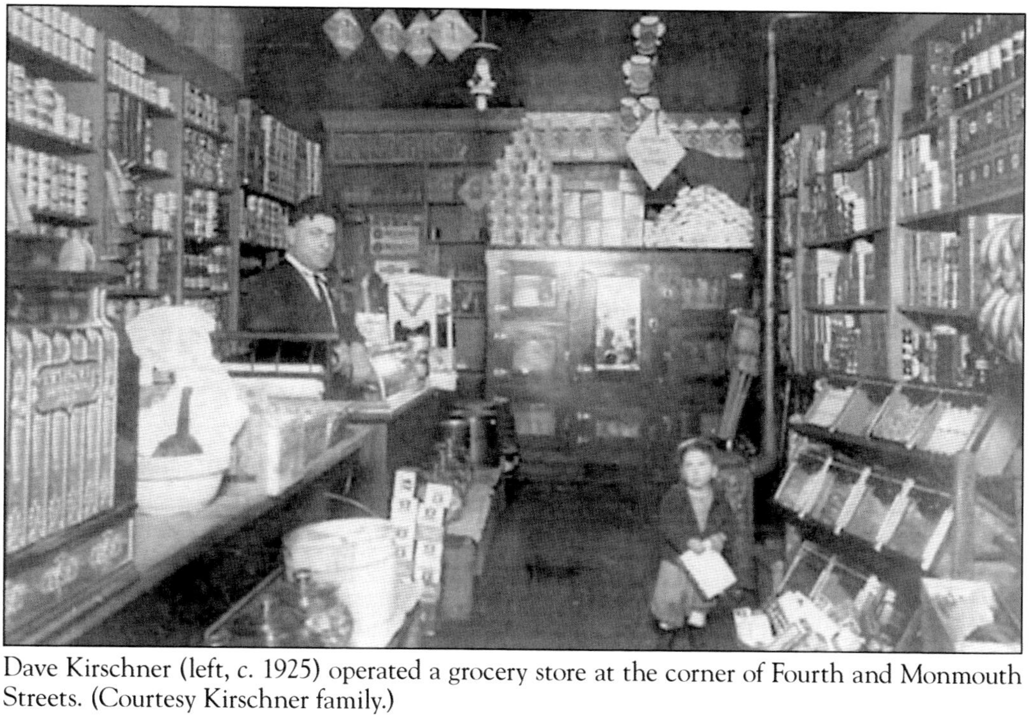

Dave Kirschner (left, c. 1925) operated a grocery store at the corner of Fourth and Monmouth Streets. (Courtesy Kirschner family.)

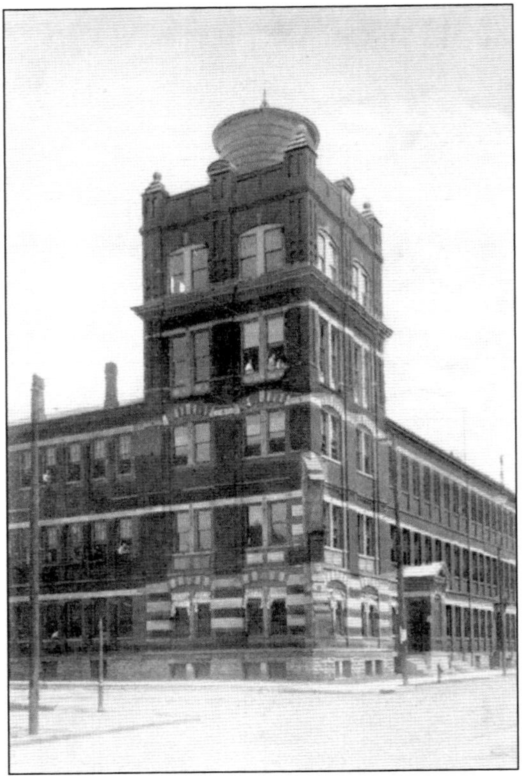

The Higgins Manufacturing Company, manufacturer of carriage trimmings and metal screens, was located at the southeast corner of Fifth Street and Washington Avenue. J.B. Tangeman was the company president; vice president was Henry Higgin. (Courtesy Campbell County Historical Society.)

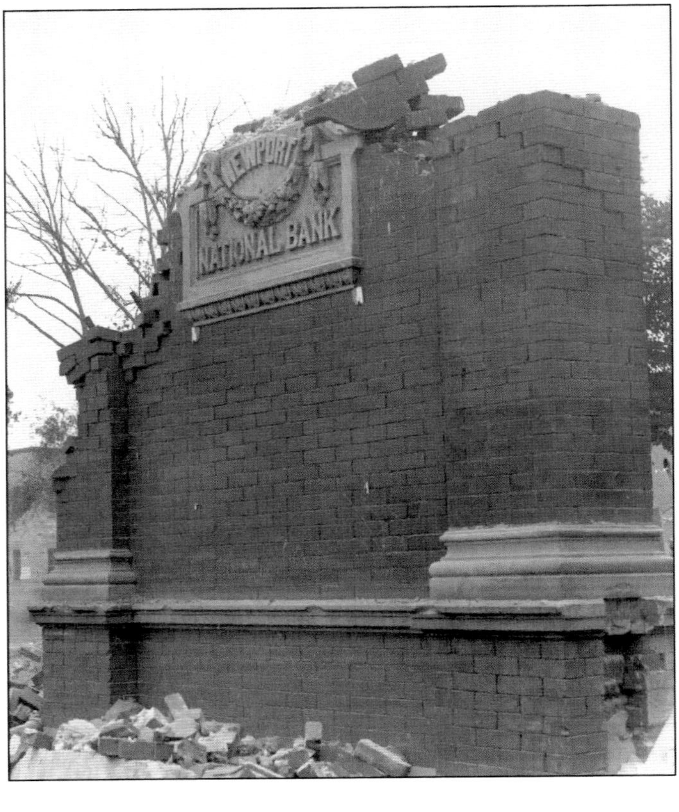

Before becoming the Newport National Bank, the building at the northwest corner of York Street and Madison (later Fifth) Street housed the First National Bank of Newport. First National sold the structure to the competing bank in 1897 after an embezzlement scandal proved fatal. The building was razed in 1966; a White Castle now occupies the lot. (Courtesy Campbell County Historical Society.)

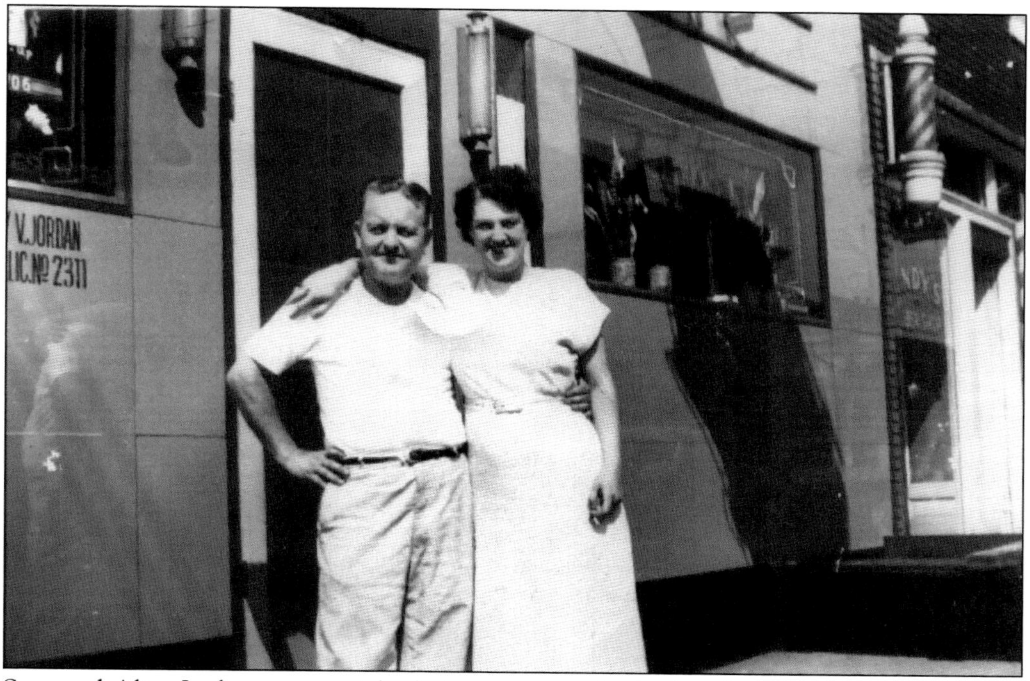

Stan and Alice Jordan pose outside their restaurant, the Jordan Grill & Café. The business, founded by Stan's mother Sophie Jordan in 1938, operated on Monmouth Street for nearly 40 years. (Courtesy Jordan family.)

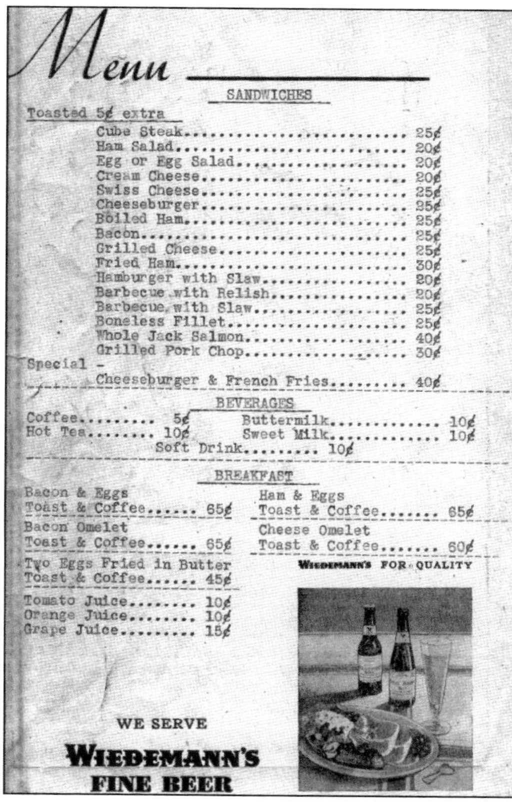

Menu

SANDWICHES

Toasted 5¢ extra

Cube Steak	25¢
Ham Salad	20¢
Egg or Egg Salad	20¢
Cream Cheese	20¢
Swiss Cheese	25¢
Cheeseburger	25¢
Boiled Ham	25¢
Bacon	25¢
Grilled Cheese	25¢
Fried Ham	30¢
Hamburger with Slaw	20¢
Barbecue with Relish	20¢
Barbecue with Slaw	25¢
Boneless Fillet	25¢
Whole Jack Salmon	40¢
Grilled Pork Chop	30¢

Special -
Cheeseburger & French Fries 40¢

BEVERAGES

Coffee	5¢	Buttermilk	10¢
Hot Tea	10¢	Sweet Milk	10¢
Soft Drink	10¢		

BREAKFAST

Bacon & Eggs Toast & Coffee	65¢	Ham & Eggs Toast & Coffee	65¢
Bacon Omelet Toast & Coffee	65¢	Cheese Omelet Toast & Coffee	60¢
Two Eggs Fried in Butter Toast & Coffee	45¢		
Tomato Juice	10¢		
Orange Juice	10¢		
Grape Juice	15¢		

WIEDEMANN'S FOR QUALITY

WE SERVE
WIEDEMANN'S
FINE BEER

The menu from the Jordan Grill & Café offers coffee for 5¢. (Courtesy Jordan family.)

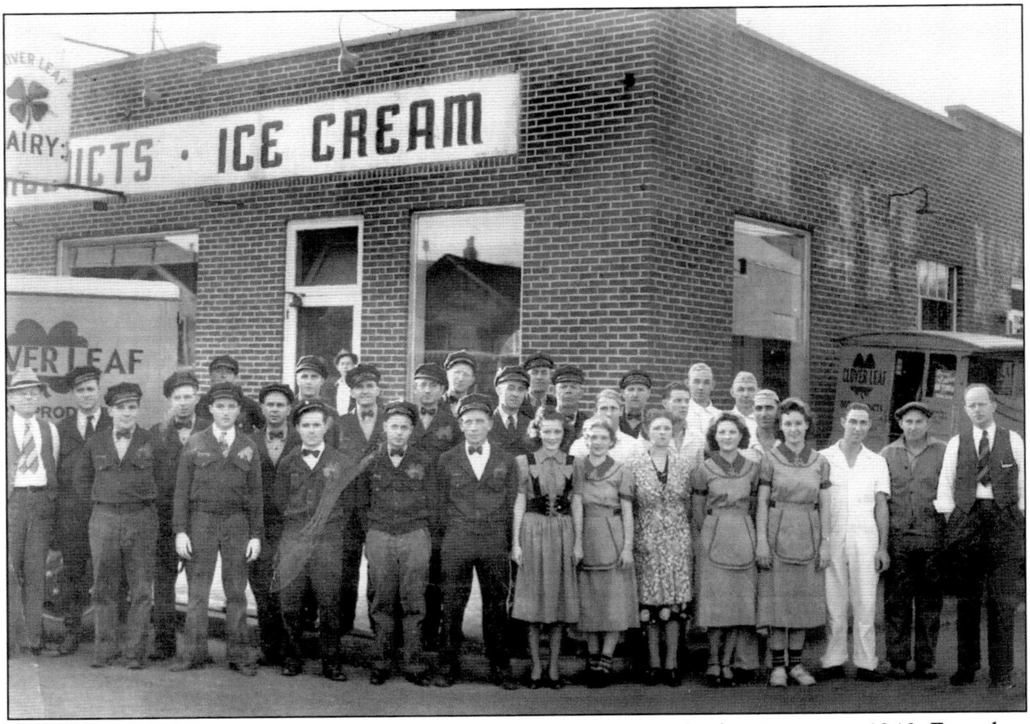

Clover Leaf Dairy employees are ready for work at Eleventh and John Streets, *c.* 1940. Founders were Anton Foellger and Emert Marschman. The Newport business was sold to Meyer Dairy in the 1970s. (Courtesy Paul Schuerman.)

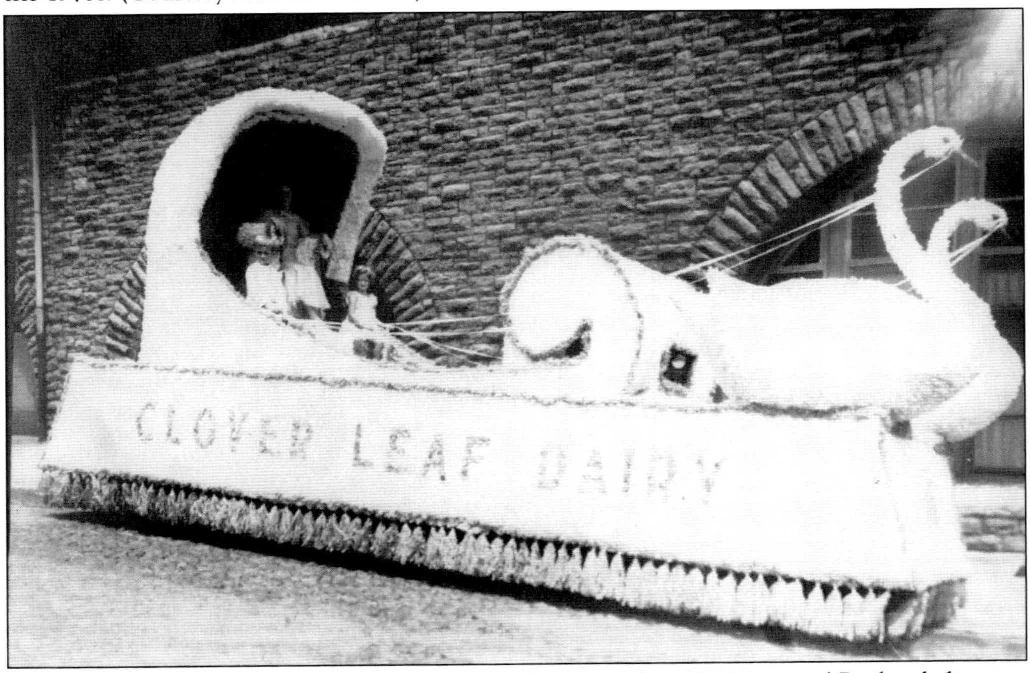

This prize winning float belonged to Clover Leaf Dairy in the 1935 Memorial Bridge dedication parade. Enjoying the ride are Albert Bathiany III, Nancy McDermott, and Jean Foellger. (Courtesy Bathiany family.)

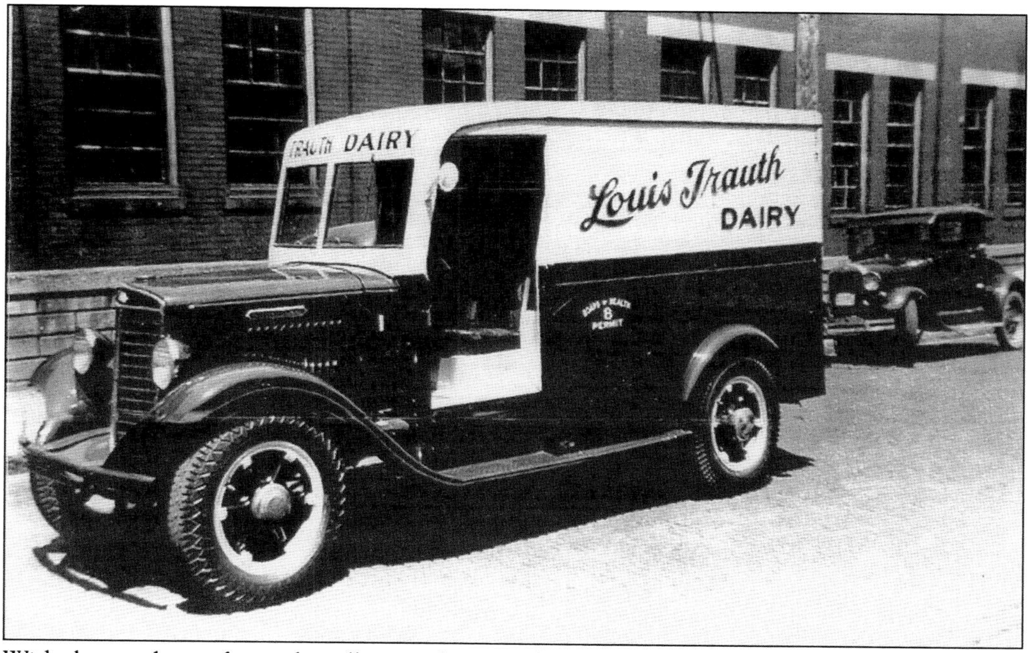

With the purchase of a single milk route from employer Fred Schuerman's Dairy in 1920, Louis J. and Clara Trauth founded Trauth Dairy. It was a family operation, run subsequently by their sons Louis Jr. and Albert, and then by the third generation grandsons David, Steve, and Andy. Although Trauth Dairy was sold to Dean Foods in 1998, some Trauth family members still help manage the day-to-day operations. (Courtesy Andy and Marilyn Trauth.)

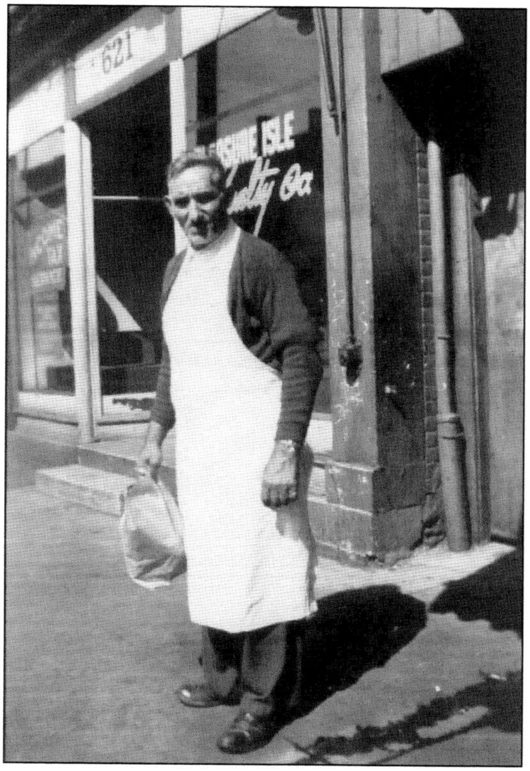

John Peluso Sr. conducted business at his grocery store at 623 Monmouth. Seen here in the 1930s, he did not speak any English. The business continues to be run by the Peluso family today. (Courtesy Peluso family.)

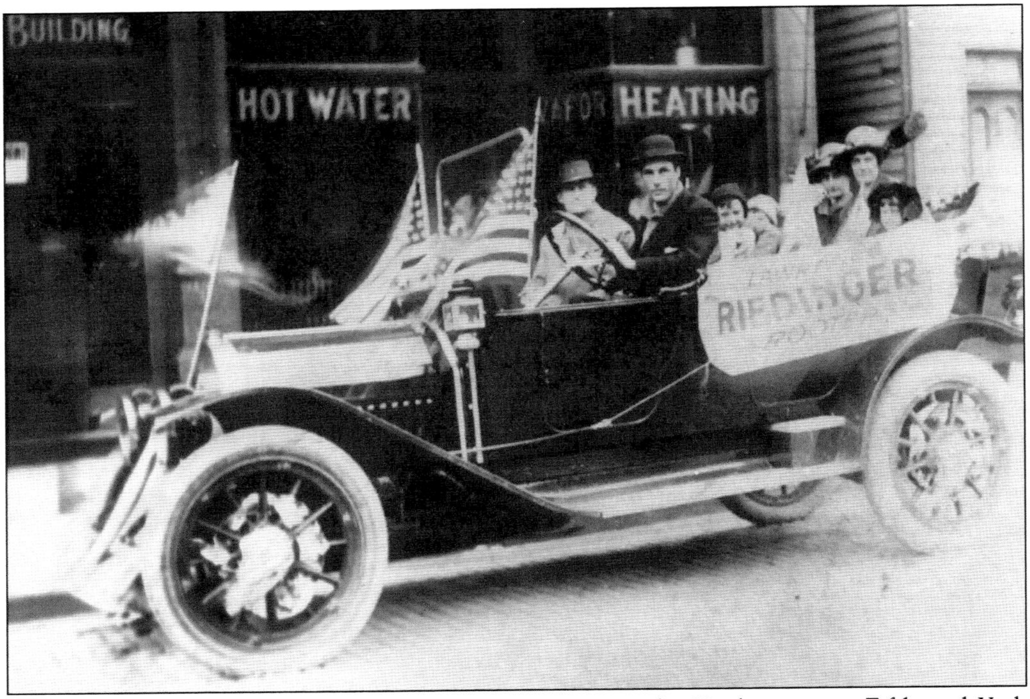

Lawrence Riedinger (driver) and friends partake in a parade. His business at Fifth and York Streets was that of real estate and insurance broker. In the background is the Fennell Building at 408 York Street. (Courtesy Campbell County Historical Society.)

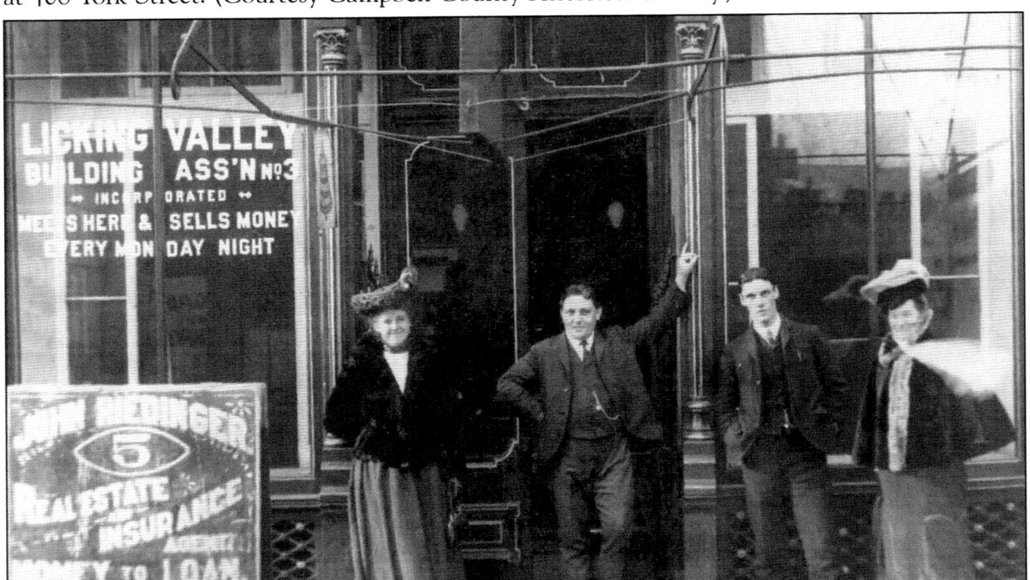

Outside the Licking Valley Building Association on East Fifth Street are John Riedinger (left) and Lawrence Riedinger (right). The women are unidentified. (Courtesy Campbell County Historical Society.)

Two

CITIZENS

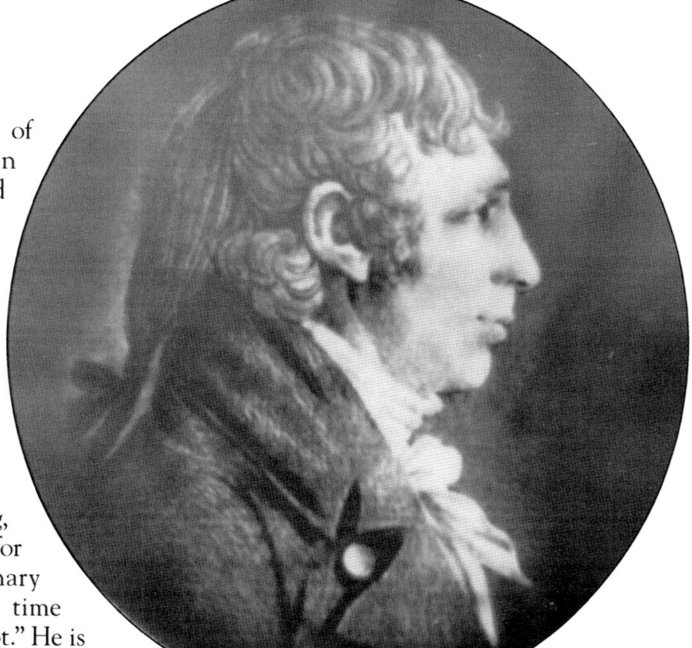

Gen. James Taylor, founder of Newport, settled here in 1793 and inherited the land granted to his father by the Commonwealth of Virginia. He would become a significant landowner and held a variety of positions, including paymaster of the Newport Barracks, bank director, and founder of the Newport Manufacturing Company. On his deathbed, only hours before his passing, he reportedly cast his vote for presidential candidate Zachary Taylor, his cousin, at that time stating "I have fired my last shot." He is buried at Evergreen Cemetery. (Courtesy Kenton County Public Library.)

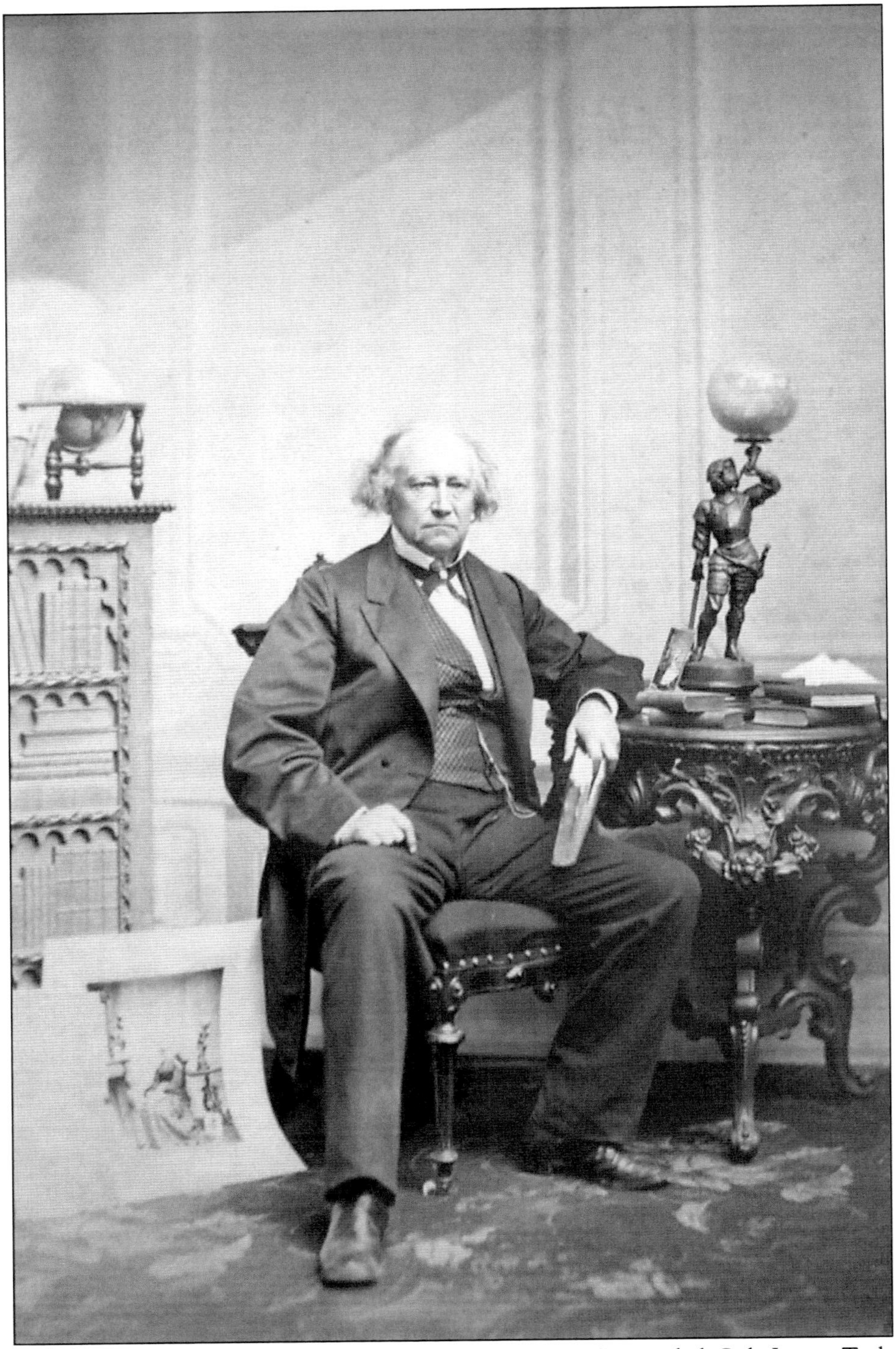

A land grant from the Commonwealth of Virginia in 1787 awarded Col. James Taylor of Caroline County 1,500 acres in the area that would later become Kentucky. His son Hubbard initially explored the area, but only his son James settled here. Although the elder Taylor was reported to have visited this area, he opted to return to Virginia where he resided until his death in 1814. (Courtesy Campbell County Historical Society.)

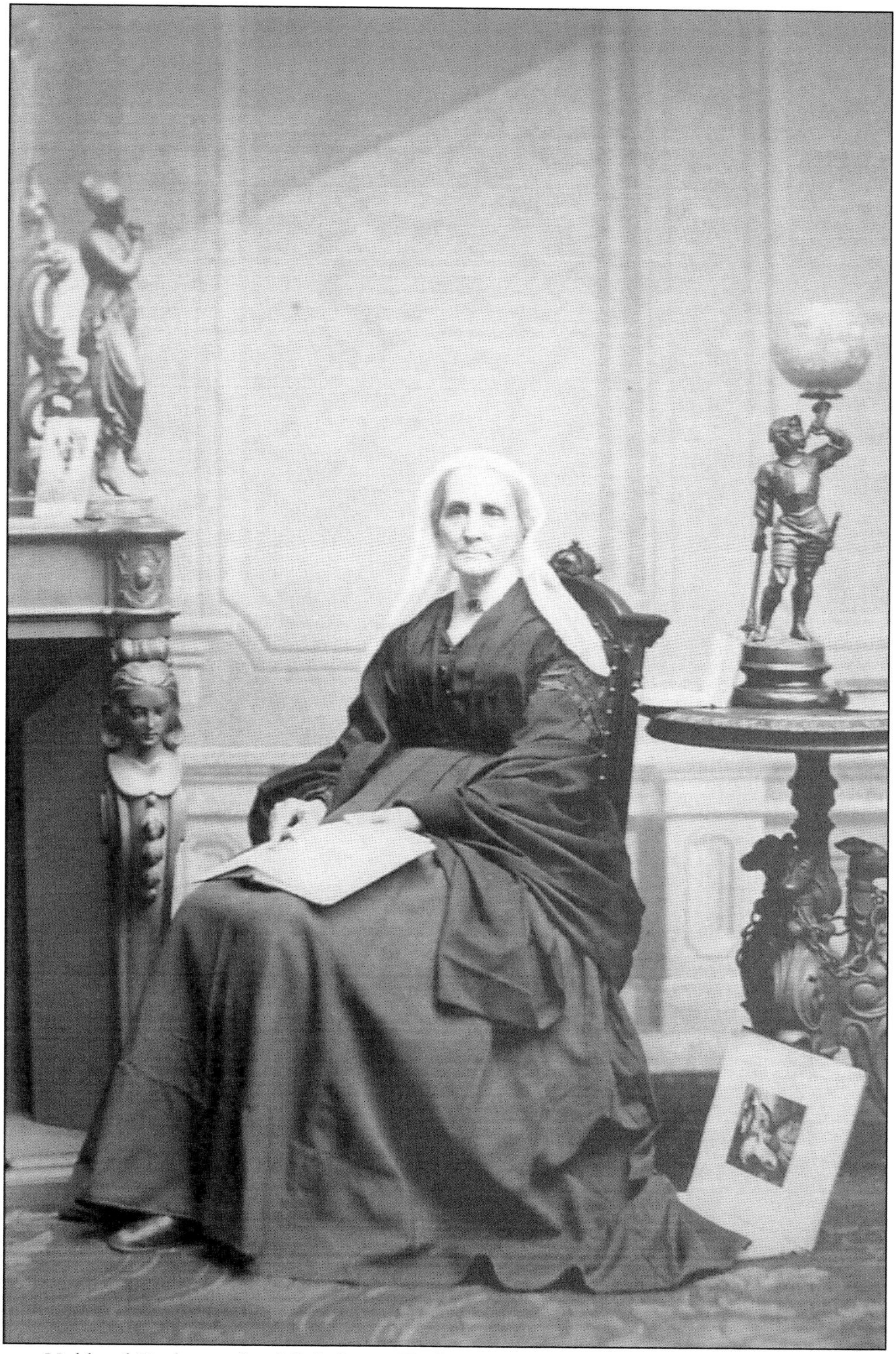

Anne Hubbard Taylor, wife of Col. James Taylor, is pictured here. They married in 1758. Ten children would subsequently come from their union, the fifth later becoming the founder of Newport. (Courtesy Campbell County Historical Society.)

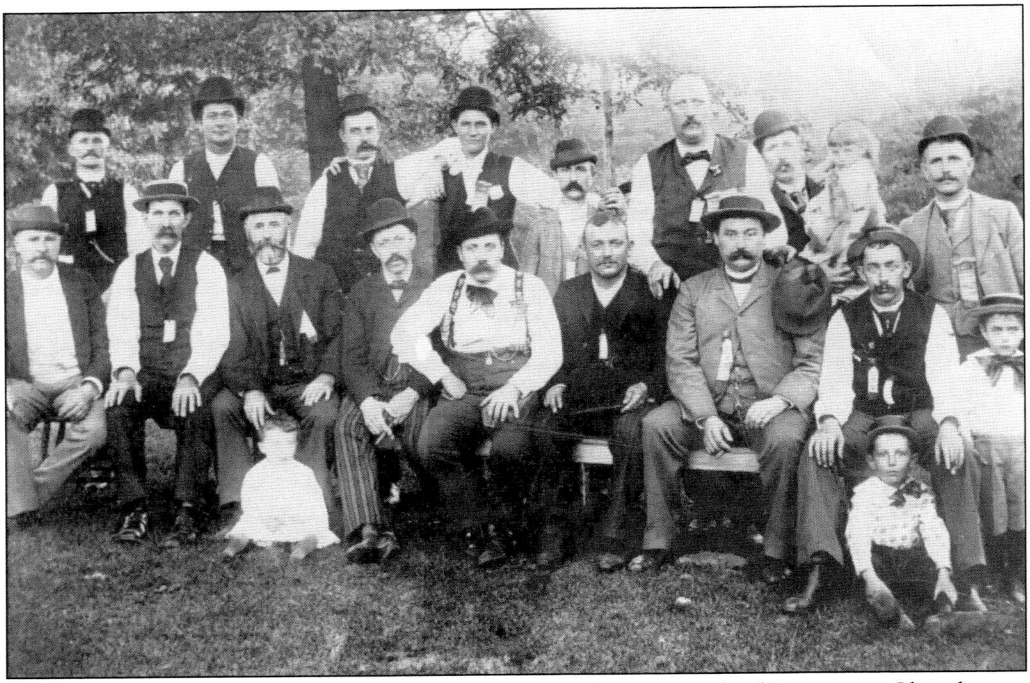

Members of an early Brotherhood Group from Saint John's Evangelical Protestant Church pose for a photograph. The only identified individuals are Peter Gruenholtz, seated on the far right, and Jacob Kohrmann, standing at the far right in the back row. (Courtesy Saint John's United Church of Christ.)

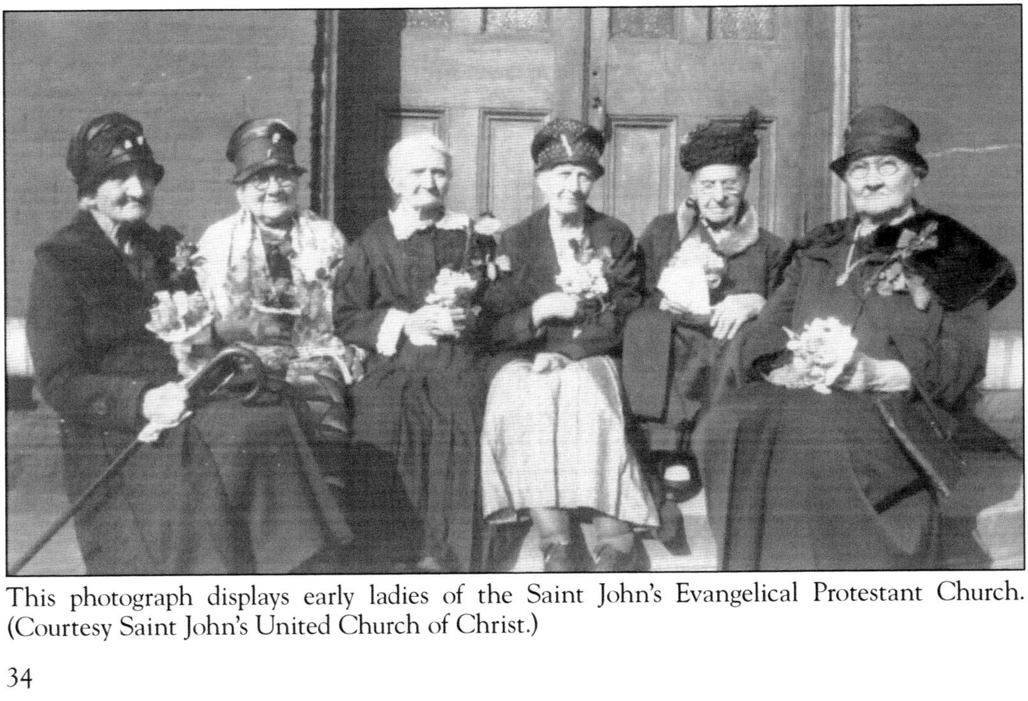

This photograph displays early ladies of the Saint John's Evangelical Protestant Church. (Courtesy Saint John's United Church of Christ.)

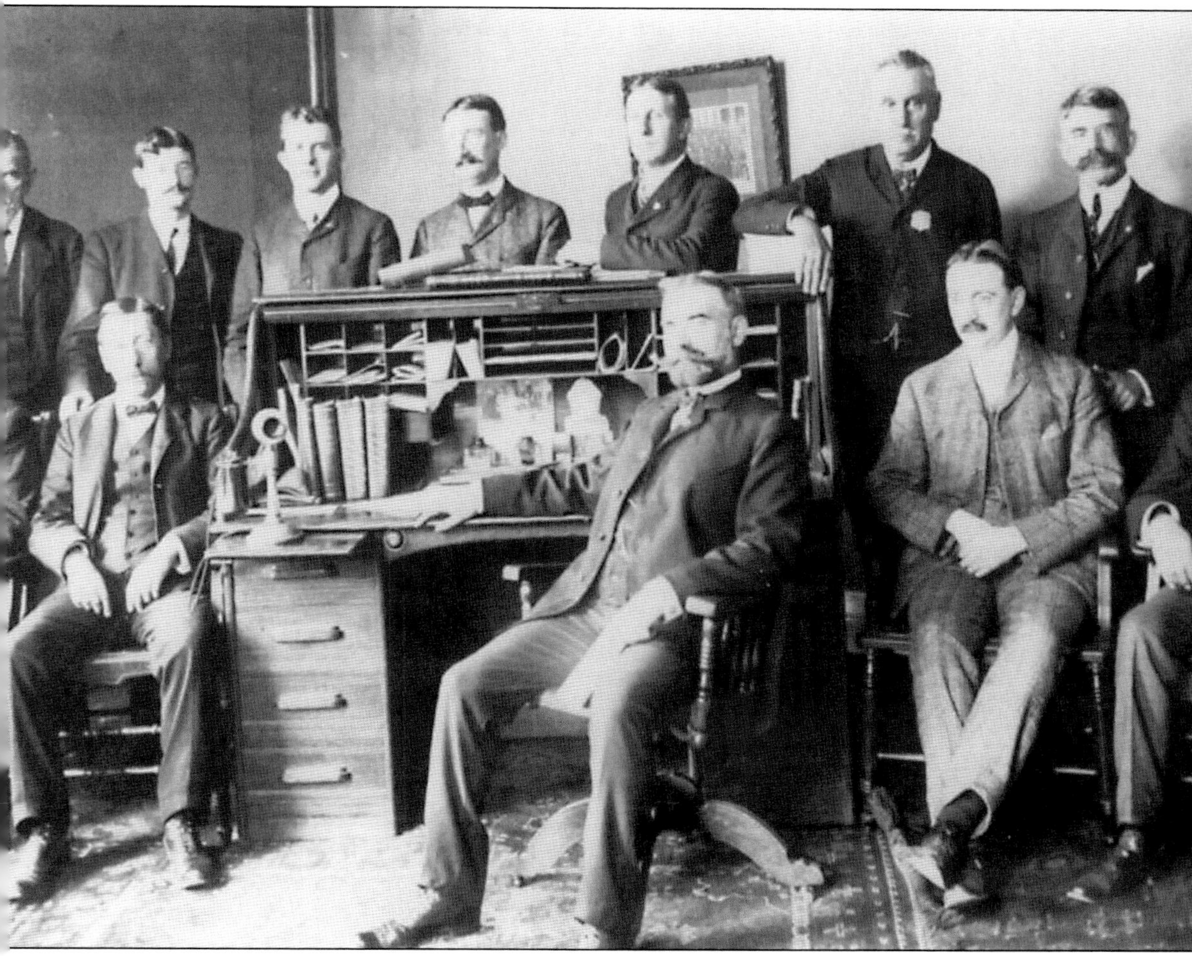

Mayor of Newport August Helmbold is pictured with his cabinet in 1904. He served in this capacity from 1904 to 1908 and then again from 1912 to 1916. (Courtesy Campbell County Historical Society.)

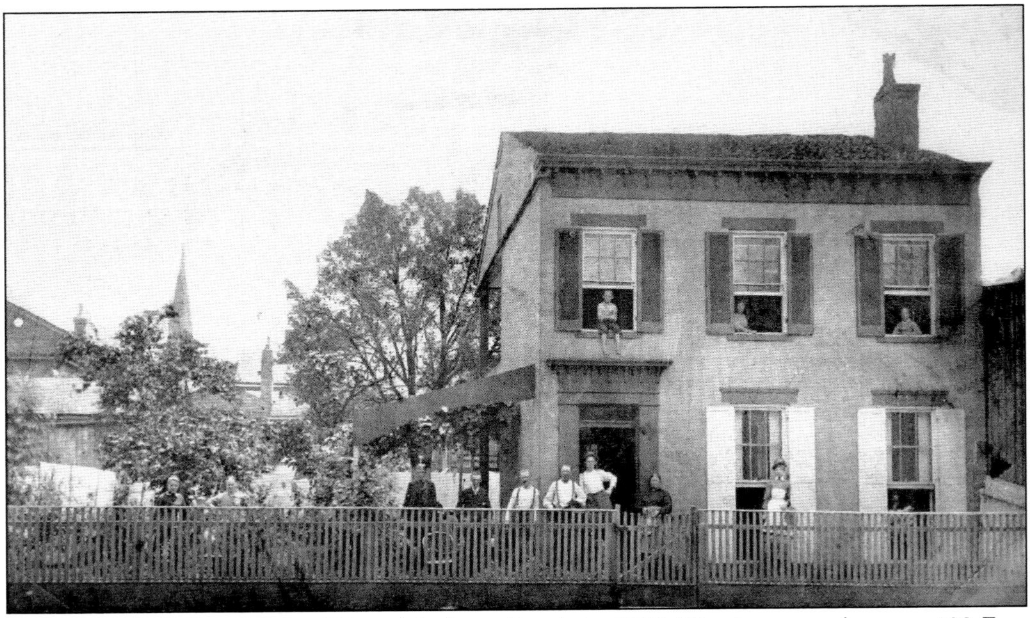

Above is the home of Capt. Edward Jackson Smith in 1882. The homestead was at 108 East Fourth Street. If still standing, the house would be next to the old library, facing north. Captain Smith was a steamboat pilot during the Civil War whose boat was commandeered by the Union Army and used to transport soldiers to Vicksburg. (Courtesy Virginia Bennett.)

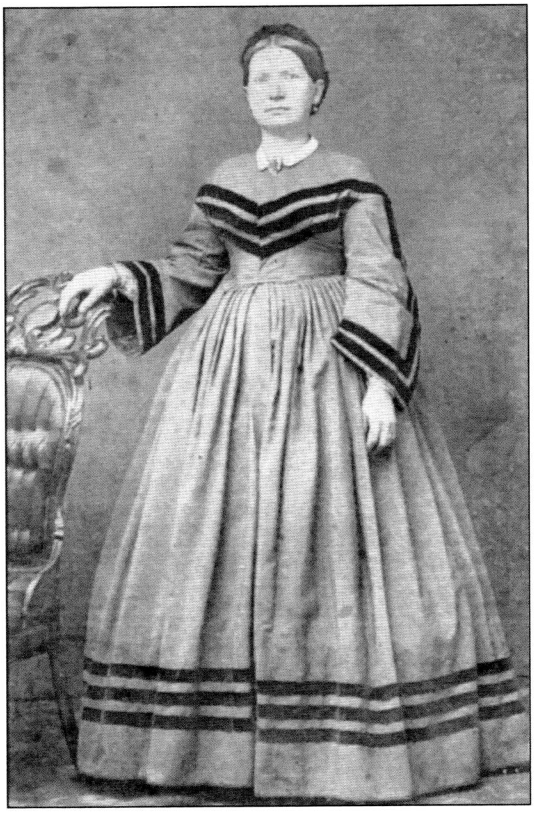

Mary "Molly" Smith was the wife of riverboat Capt. Edward Smith. The captain was more elusive; no photos of him are known to exist. (Courtesy Virginia Bennett.)

Graduating from the Cincinnati Law School in 1858, Albert S. Berry was one of Newport's most politically active citizens. City attorney and circuit judge were only two of his many positions. During the Civil War, he was an officer for the Confederate Army. He was subsequently held as a prisoner of war after the surrender at Sailor's Creek in 1865 until pardoned by President Johnson. Newport welcomed him home, and he went on to serve as mayor from 1876 to 1877 and again from 1888 to 1891. The year 1892 would see him elected to the United States House of Representatives, where he would eventually serve four terms. He died on January 6, 1908, and is interred at Evergreen Cemetery. (Courtesy Kenton County Public Library.)

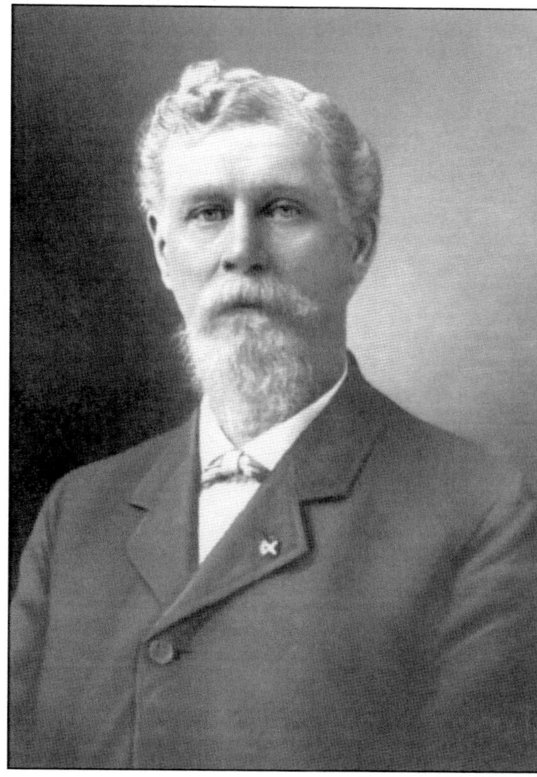

Albert Sauer, below left, shares in a game of dominoes with his father Johann Sauer at their home at 1005 Washington Avenue in 1870. (Courtesy Al Sauer.)

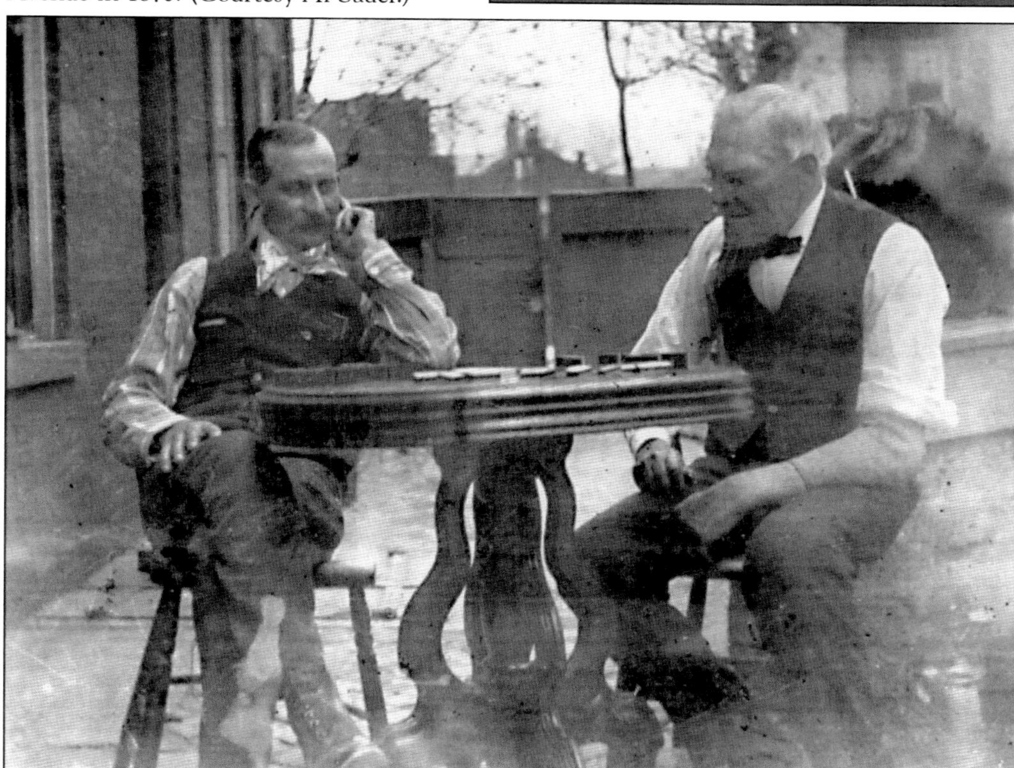

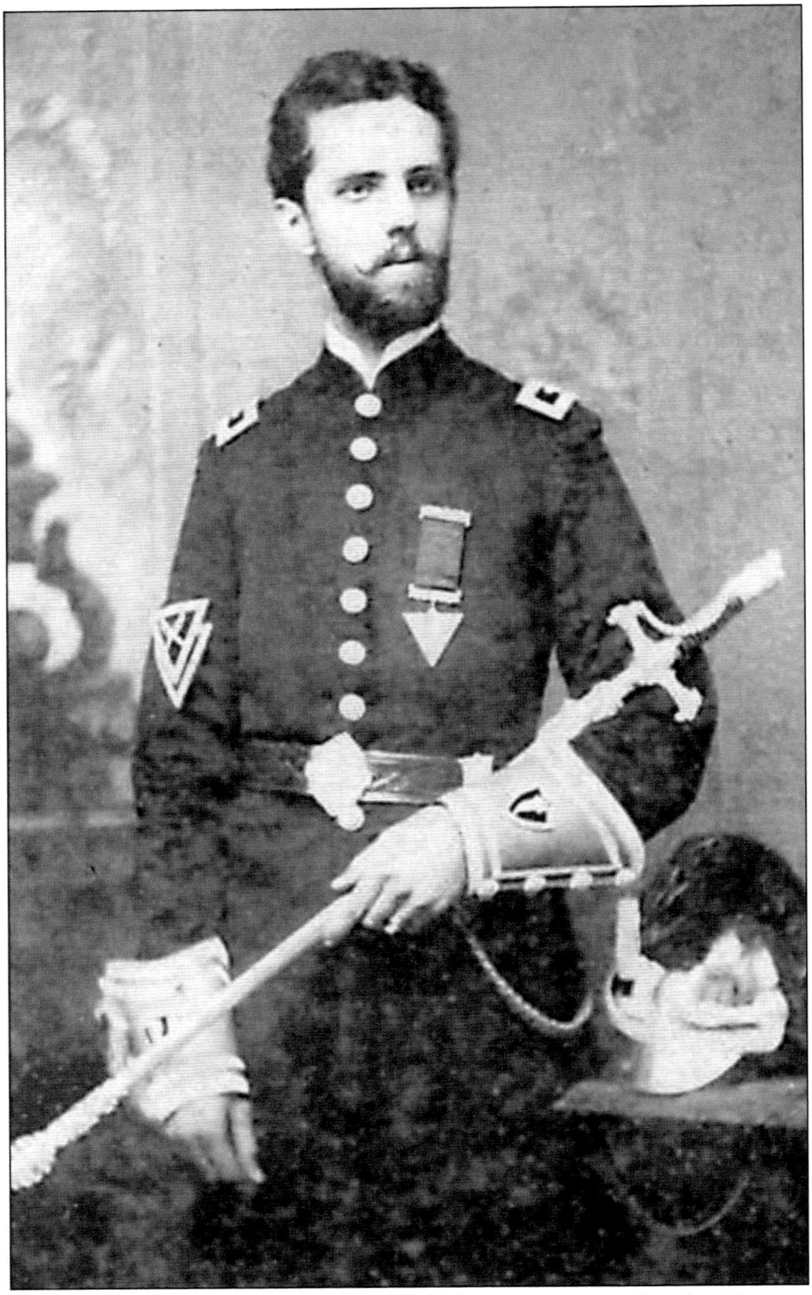

William K. West, pictured here at age 26 in 1886, was a printer for the Newport Printing and Newspaper Company at the southwest corner of York and Bellevue Streets. His uniform enlightens us to the fact that he was a member of the Knights of Pythias, a nationwide organization founded in 1864. The group was founded on three cardinal principles: friendship, charity, and benevolence. They were one of numerous "benevolent organizations" active at that time; others included the Ancient Order of Druids, the Improved Order of Red Men, and the Independent Order of Odd Fellows. The Knights of Pythias continue to be an active group nationally to this day, although there is no longer a local chapter. (Courtesy Campbell County Historical Society.)

Aquilla A. Simms is seen in his World War I uniform on the porch of 841 Washington Avenue, later known as the Vendome. He was a Newport native who worked in the watch trade. (Courtesy Donna and Roger Weddle.)

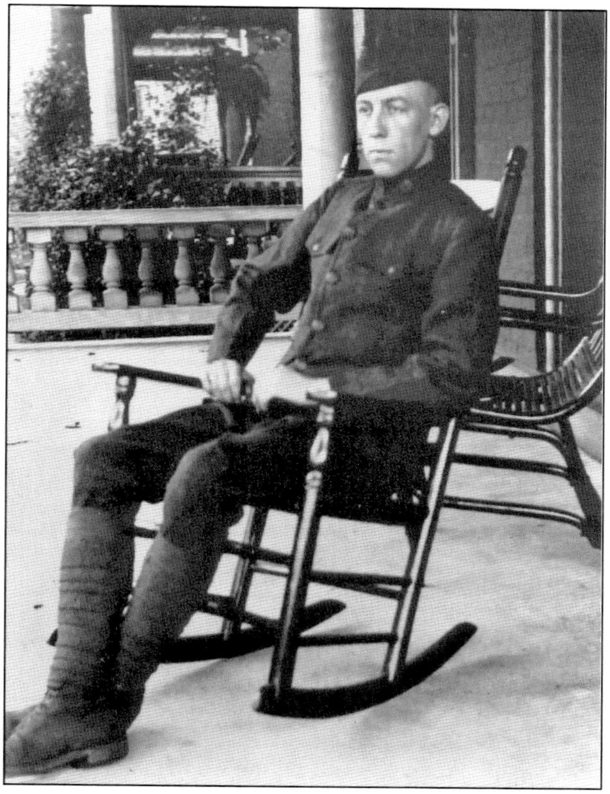

This photograph illustrates the clerks of the Newport Post Office on October 1, 1904. From left to right are (front row) John J. Davies, John H. Meyer (postmaster), and William Hamilton (assistant postmaster); (back row) Harrison Weigele, Edward Halloran, Fred Bary, and William Wiebe. (Courtesy Campbell County Historical Society.)

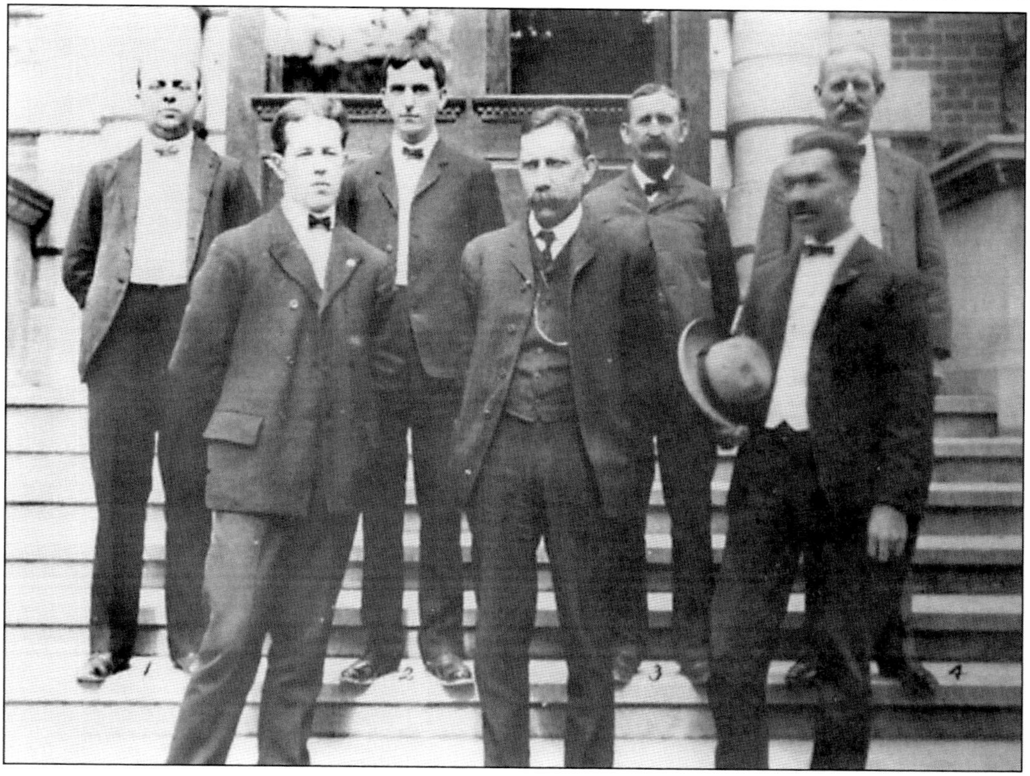

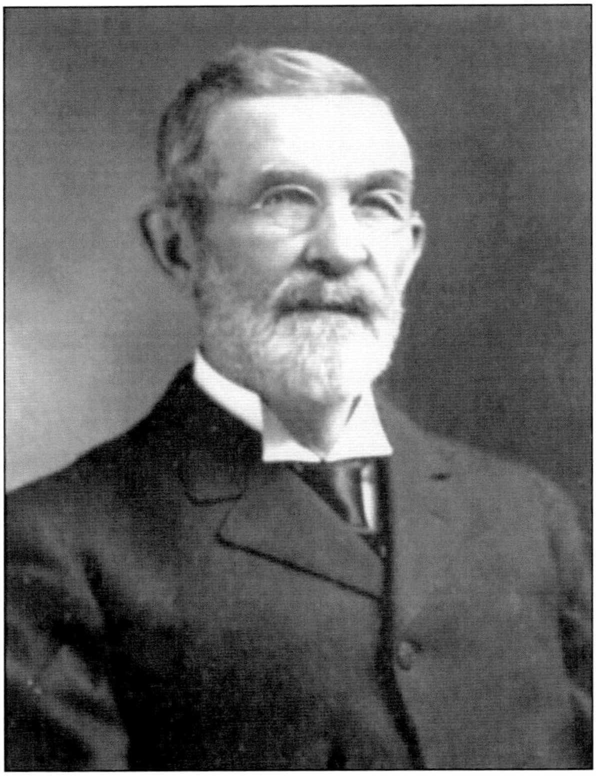

John Brown Lindsey served as Newport's mayor from 1838 to 1839, and then again from 1845 to 1849. His home at the corner of Front and Columbia Streets was the first brick house in Newport. (Courtesy Special Collections and Archives, Northern Kentucky University.)

The members of the Newport Board of Education take time out for a photo in 1904. (Courtesy Campbell County Historical Society.)

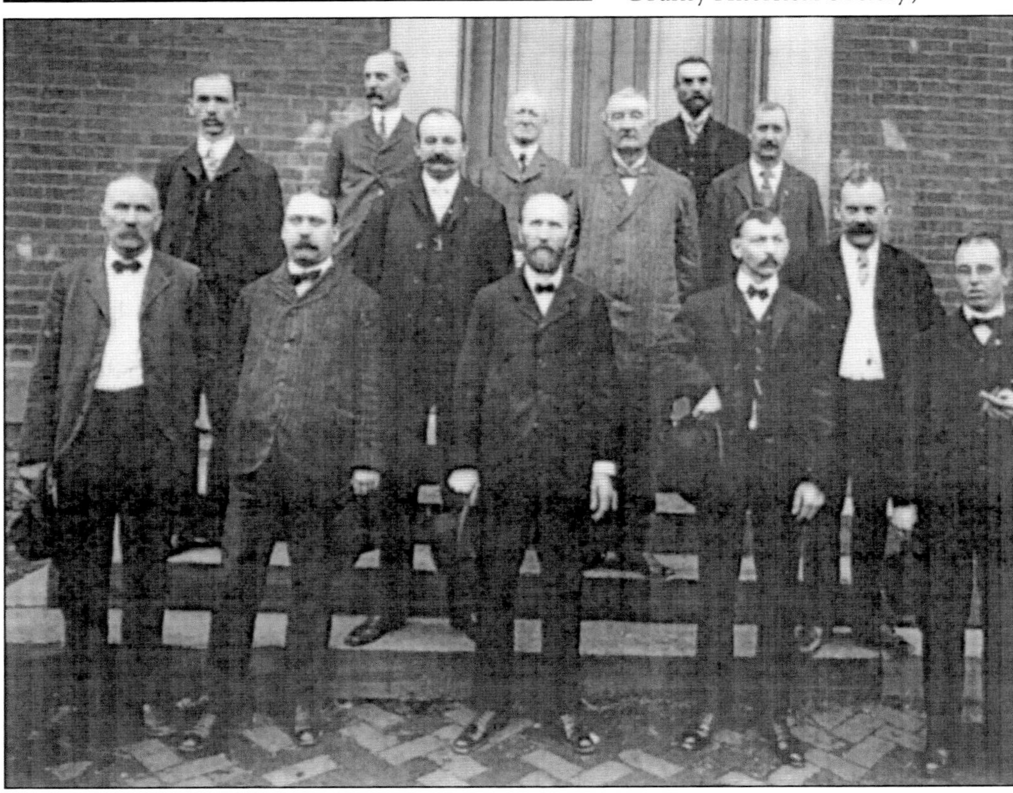

Harry J. Braun of Newport is seen in his CCC uniform. The Civilian Conservation Corps was initiated in 1935 during President Roosevelt's New Deal era and provided jobs for men during a time when they were scarce. Men enlisted for six month terms and performed such duties as building roads, planting trees, digging erosion ditches, and erecting fences. The CCC existed for seven years until 1942. (Courtesy Dr. Douglas Braun.)

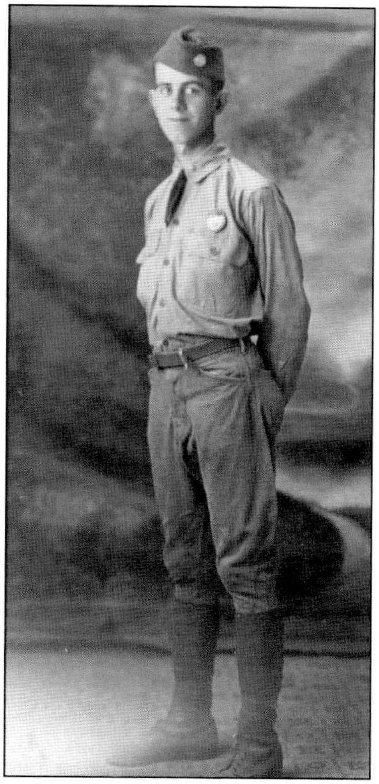

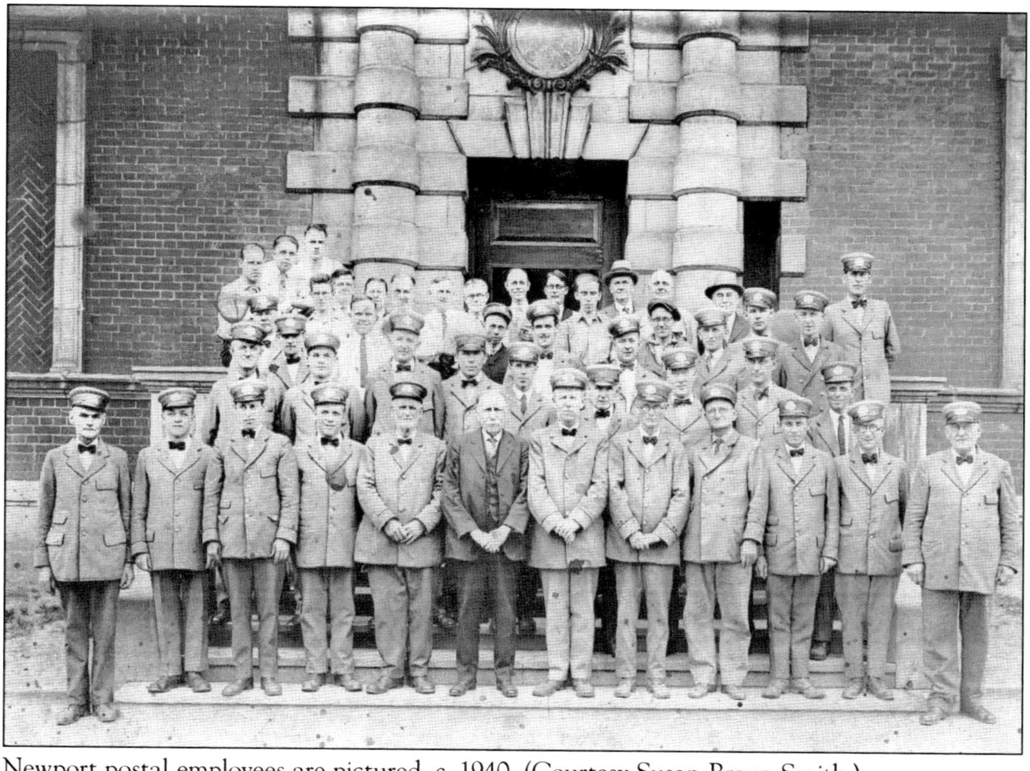

Newport postal employees are pictured, c. 1940. (Courtesy Susan Braun Smith.)

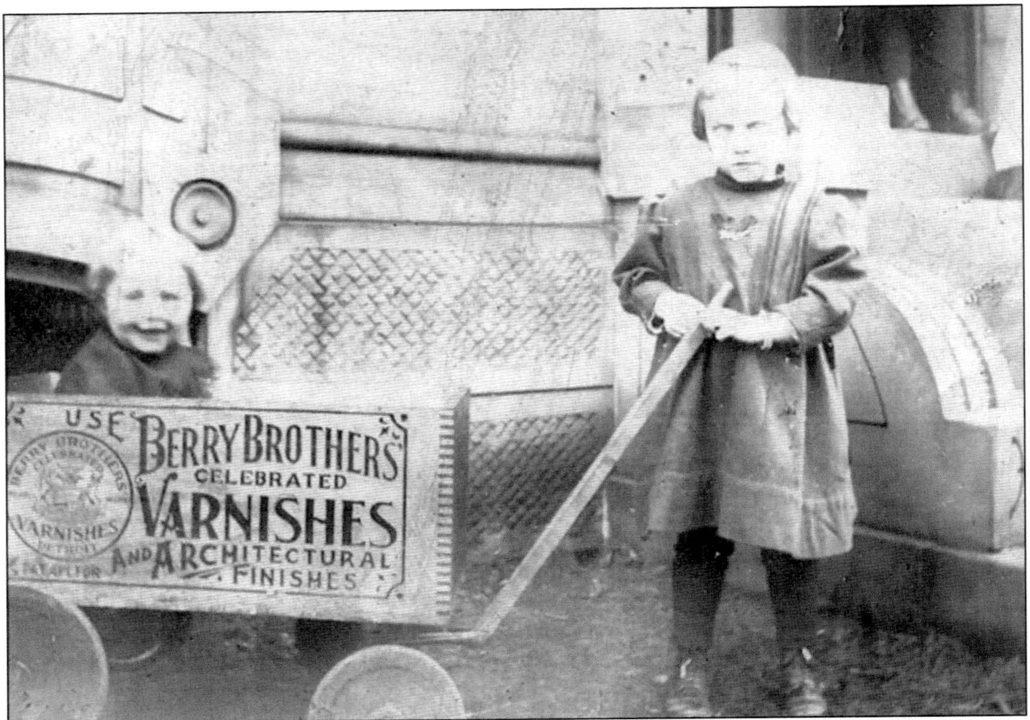

Two young unidentified girls play in front of the Harmeyer residence. The Harmeyer family once owned this home at 624 Monroe Street. Barney Kroger, founder of the Kroger Company, owned the Newport home previously. (Courtesy Michael and Tylene Cronin.)

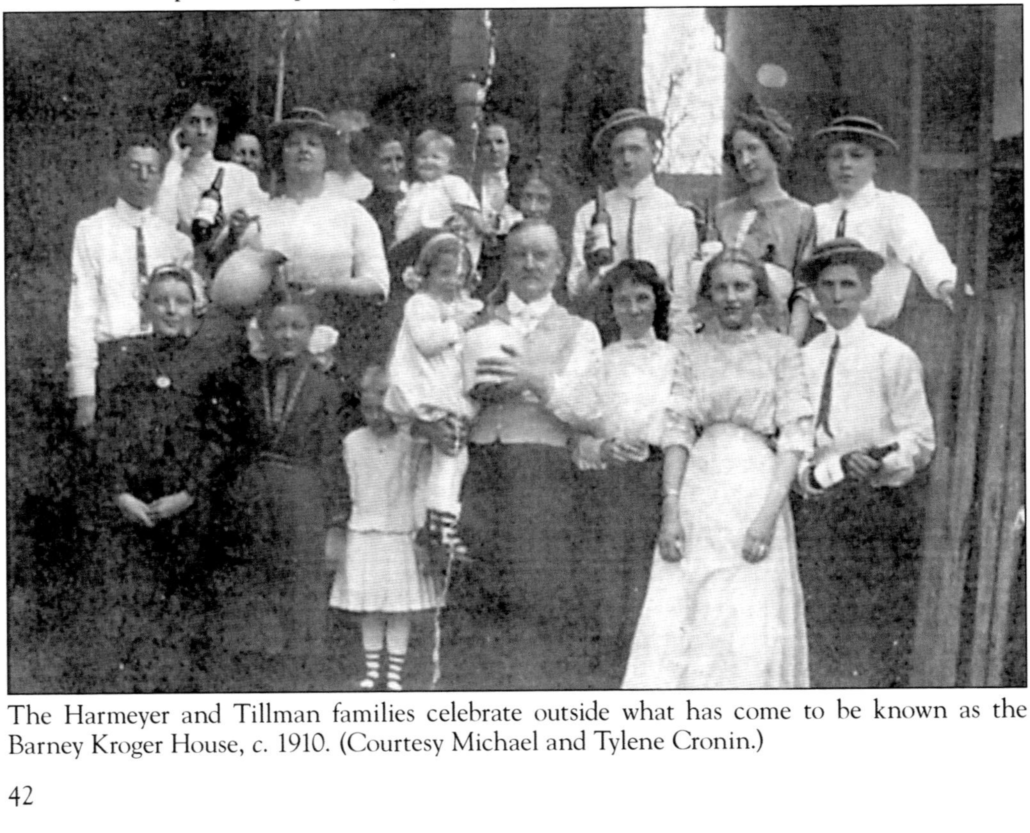

The Harmeyer and Tillman families celebrate outside what has come to be known as the Barney Kroger House, c. 1910. (Courtesy Michael and Tylene Cronin.)

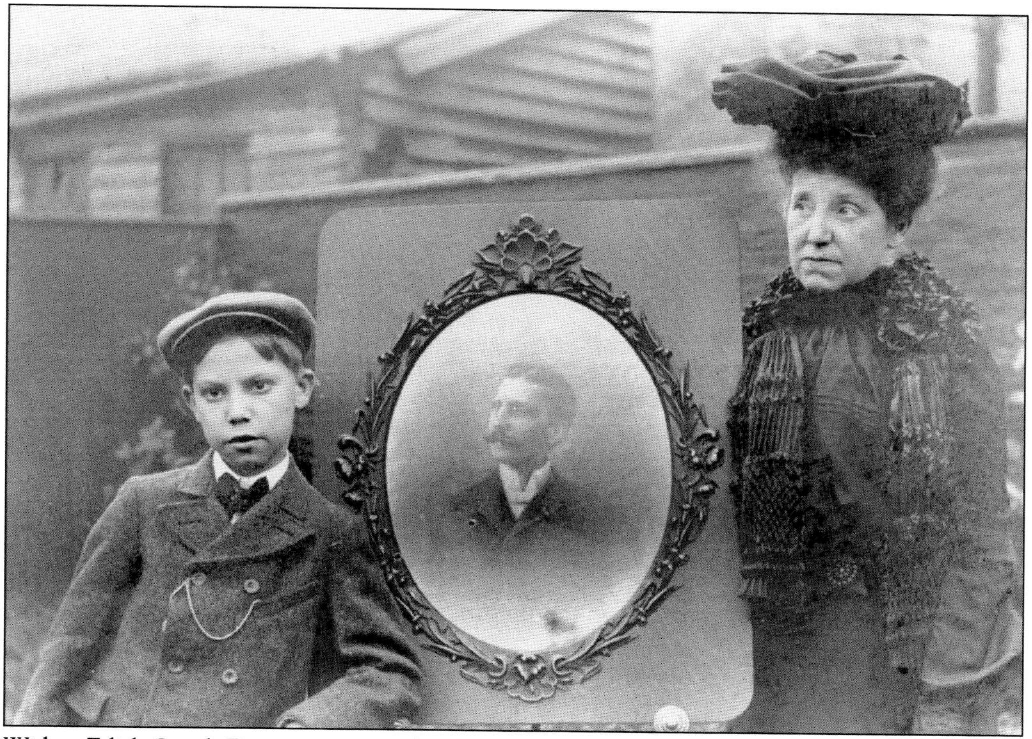

Widow Edith Smith Bennett mourns her husband Saunders Bennett in 1902. Their son Elmer Bennett is also pictured. (Courtesy Virginia Bennett.)

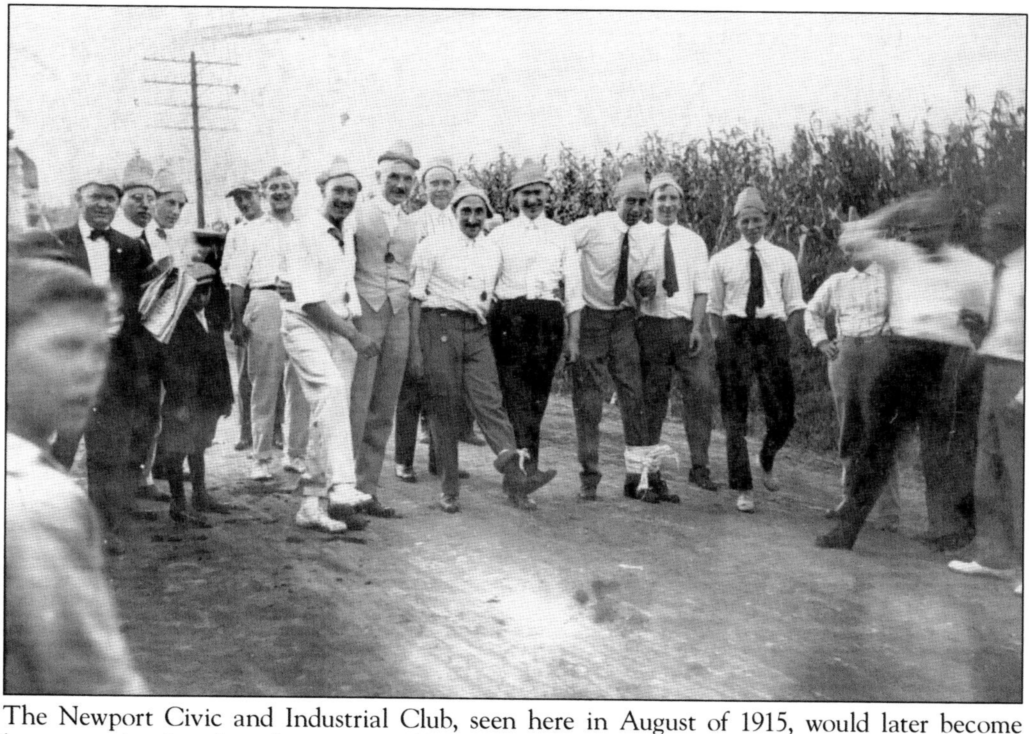

The Newport Civic and Industrial Club, seen here in August of 1915, would later become known as the chamber of commerce. (Courtesy Campbell County Historical Society.)

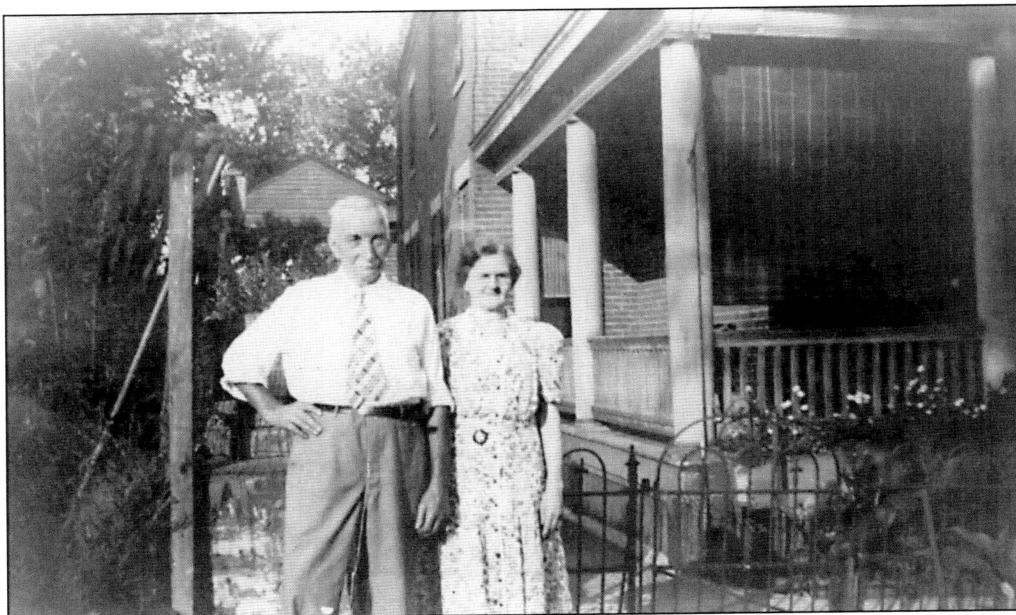

This home sat where the Newport Shopping Center is found today. Fred and Elizabeth Schuerman ran a dairy at that location. Construction on the shopping center began in 1954. (Courtesy Paul Schuerman.)

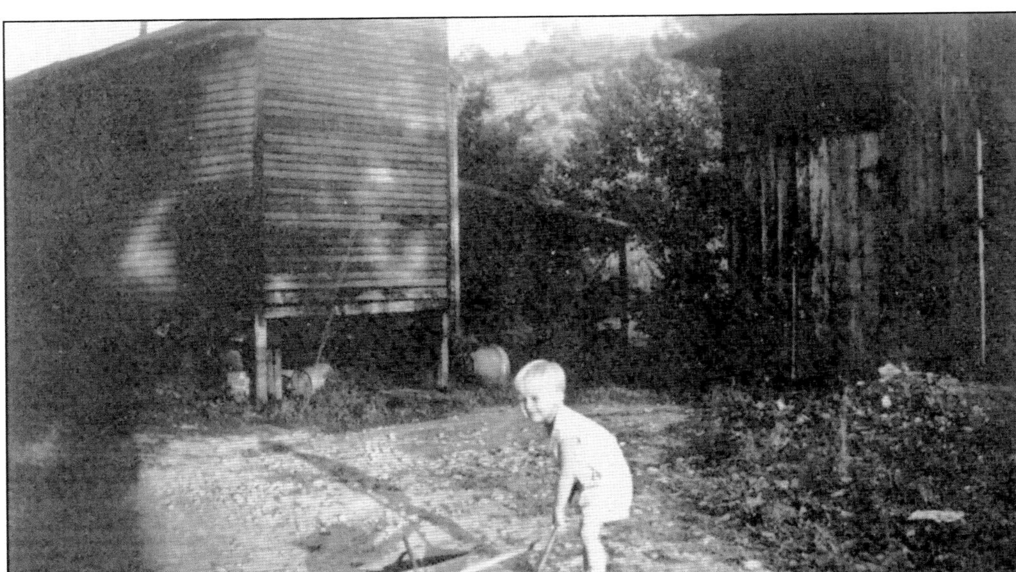

Paul Schuerman is playing outside the same family home in 1934. "The hill," still recognized by many Newport residents, can be seen in the background. (Courtesy Paul Schuerman.)

Newport resident Pvt. Clarence Sauer is pictured in his World War I uniform. (Courtesy Al Sauer.)

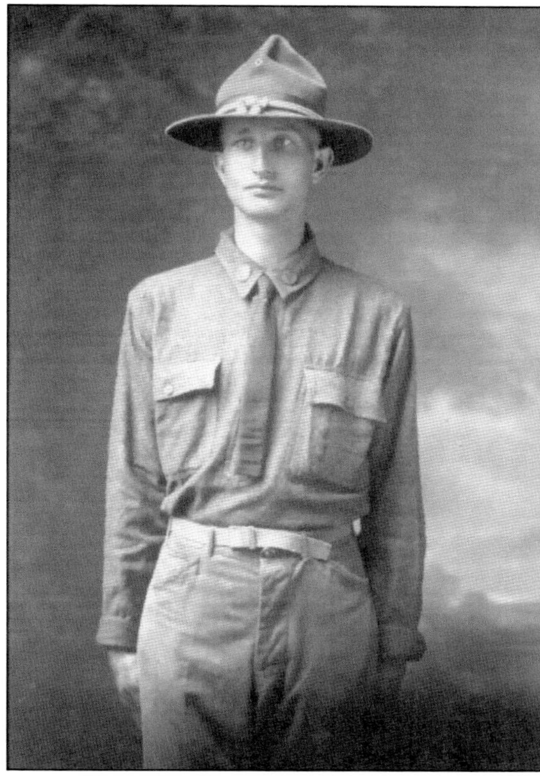

LeRoy Hoffman, in uniform, is welcomed home by his family at 502 Thornton Street on Easter Sunday, 1941. Mr. Hoffman was a combat infantryman in World War II, later served as a Newport policeman, and has become known as one of Newport's most valued historians. Pictured from left to right are Frank Fessler, Julie and John Schneider, LeRoy Hoffman (holding daughter Carol), Henry and Myrtle Hoffman, and Geneva Fessler. (Courtesy LeRoy Hoffman.)

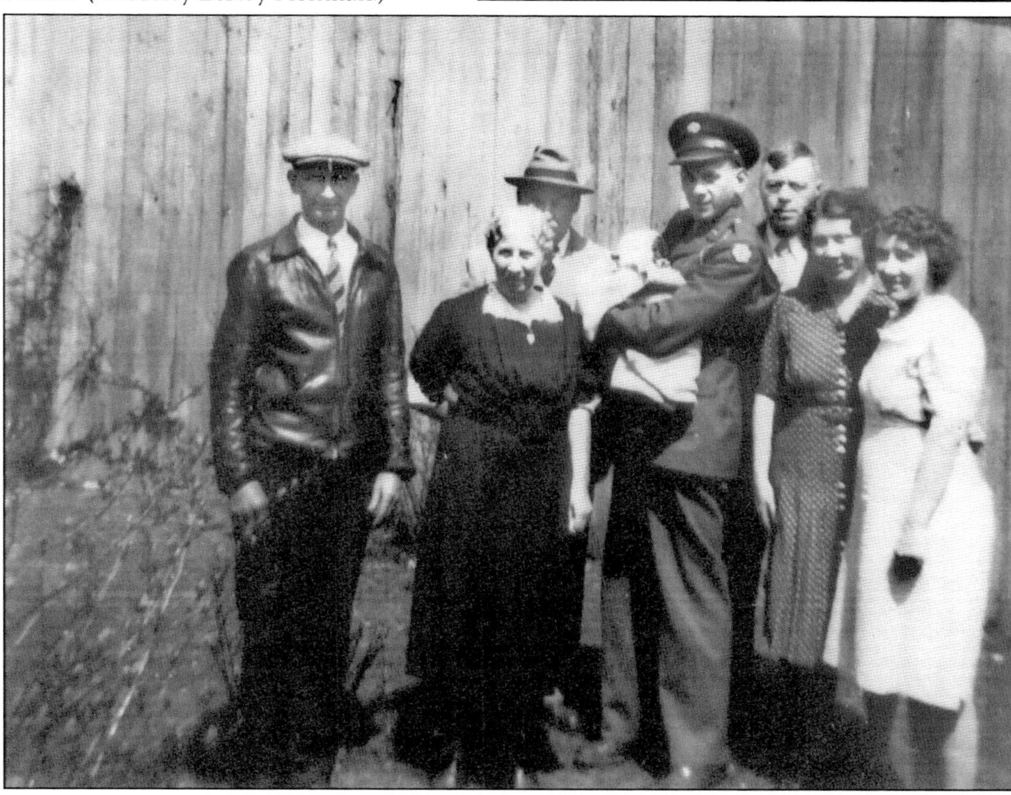

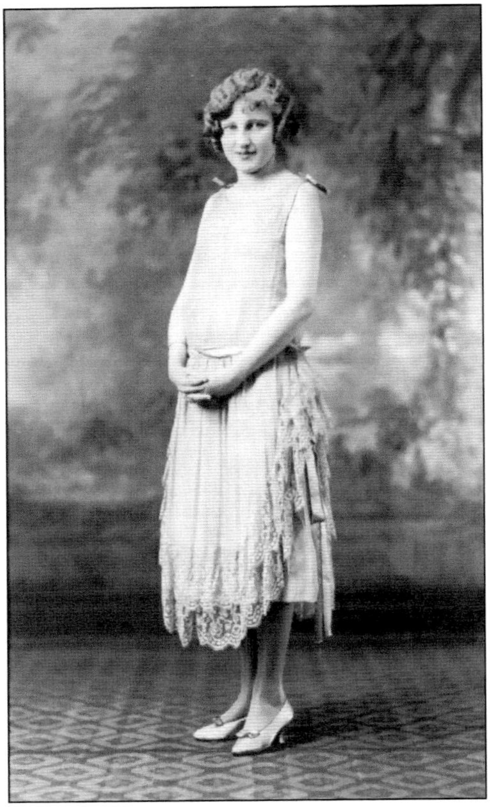

The voice of soprano Marguerite Kountz provided enjoyment for local residents over many years. She sang with the Dunbar Opera Company when they were in Cincinnati. (Courtesy Mr. and Mrs. Richard Thompson.)

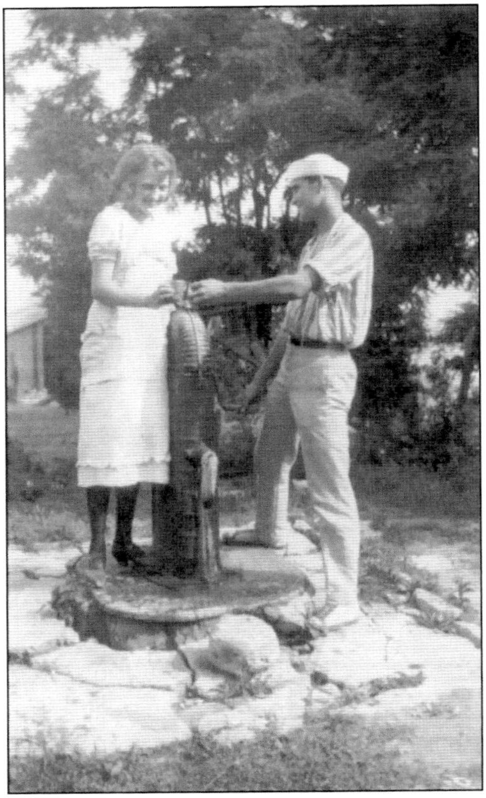

Accidentally shot by a friend while they were shooting rats at the Ninth Street dump, Harold Bogart of 718 Maple Street died tragically at the age of 18 in 1923. His parents were a vaudeville team performing under the name of Bogart and Nichols, and he was a skilled violinist. He and his sweetheart, Miss Marguerite Kountz, were a talented couple. They had planned to be married that summer and hoped to pursue a career in music together. (Courtesy Mr. and Mrs. Richard Thompson.)

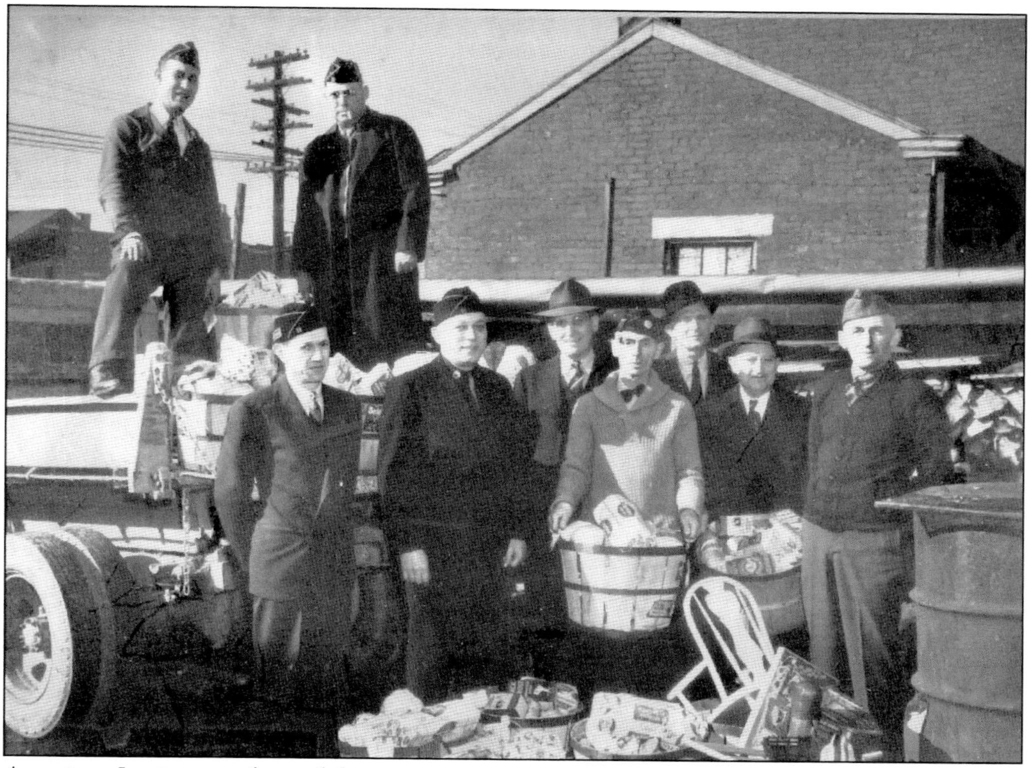

American Legion members of the James Wallace Costigan Post No. 11 pass out Christmas baskets in 1940. (Courtesy Connie Jett at James Wallace Costigan Post No. 11.)

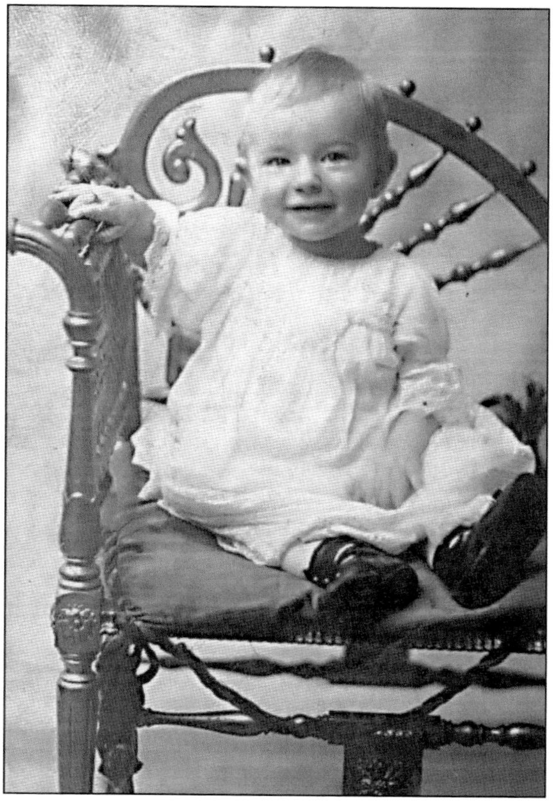

Joseph Ridimann, a lifelong Newport resident, was born on December 27, 1912. He has served on the Campbell County Police force as well as with the Newport Auxiliary Police Department. At the time of this writing, he was anticipating his 92nd birthday. (Courtesy Joseph Ridimann.)

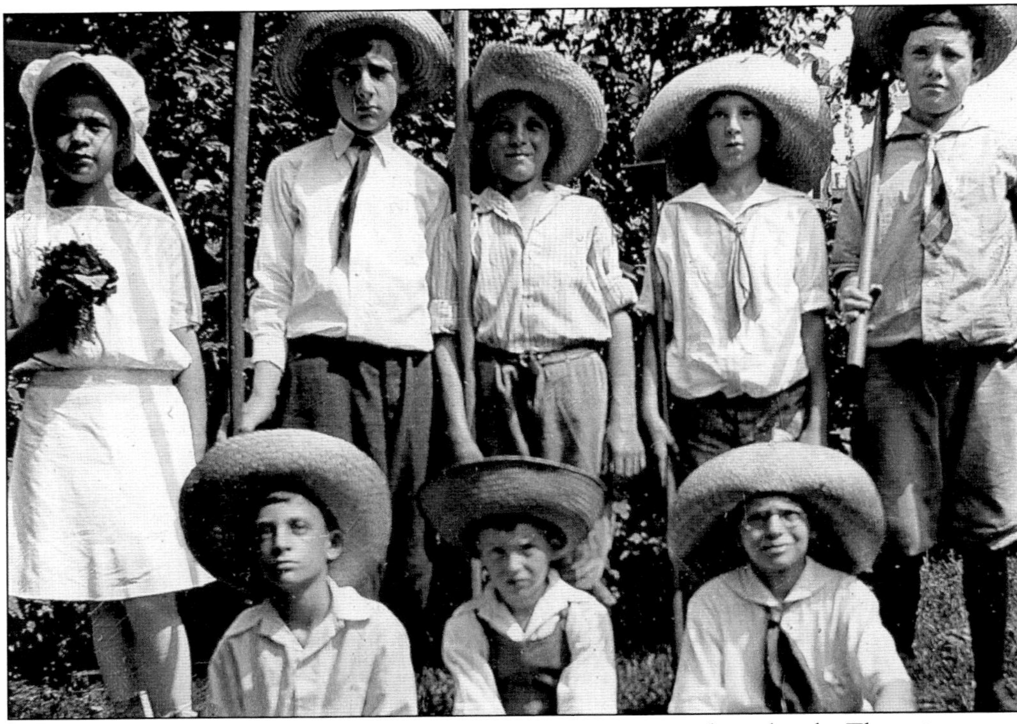

Garden prize winners from a 1916 competition in Newport take a break. These images of garden winners were reproduced from glass lantern slides, an early method of projecting images. (Courtesy Peter Garrett.)

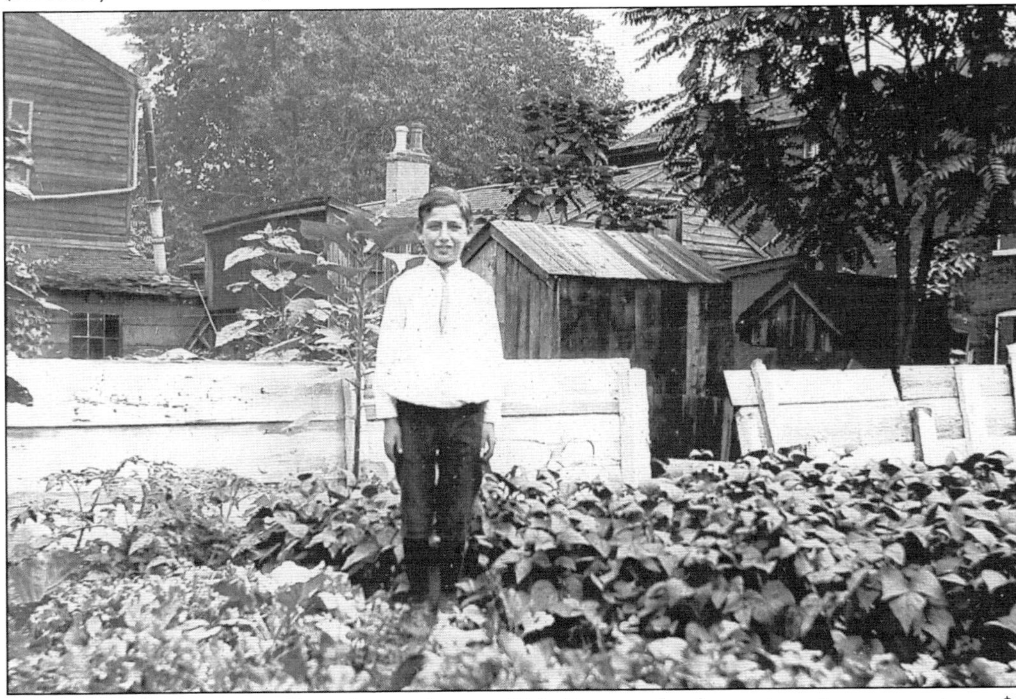

Charles Glick poses proudly in his garden in 1915. He was the first prize winner, earning a $5 award. (Courtesy Peter Garrett.)

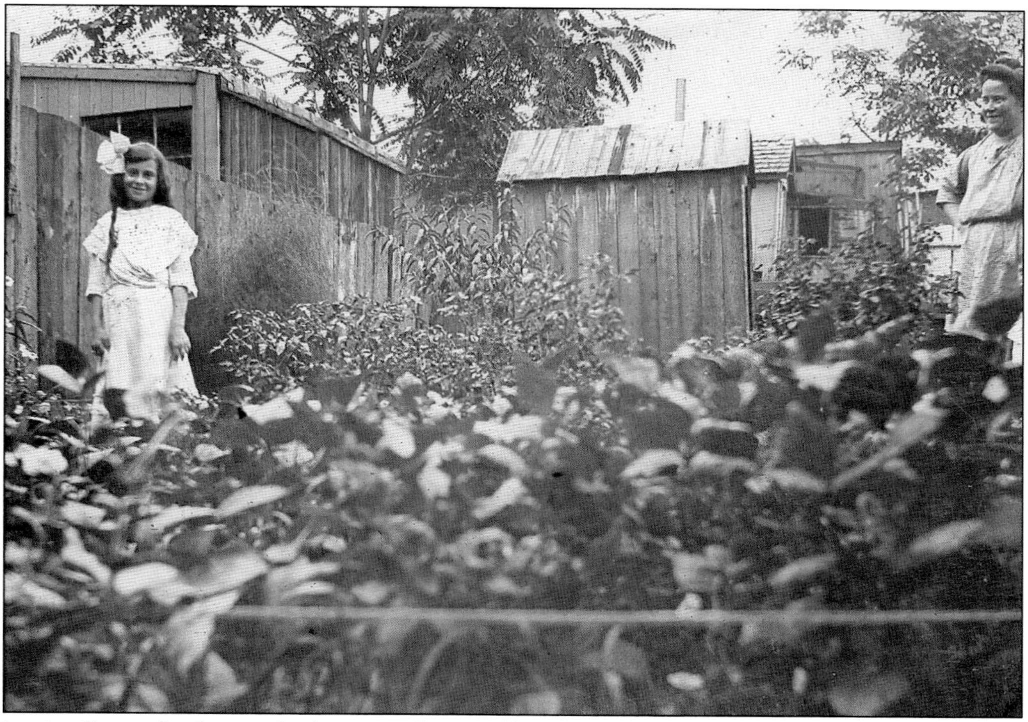

Louise Sanzenbacker took the second prize ($2.50) in the 1914 garden contest. Her family resided on East Seventh Street. (Courtesy Peter Garrett.)

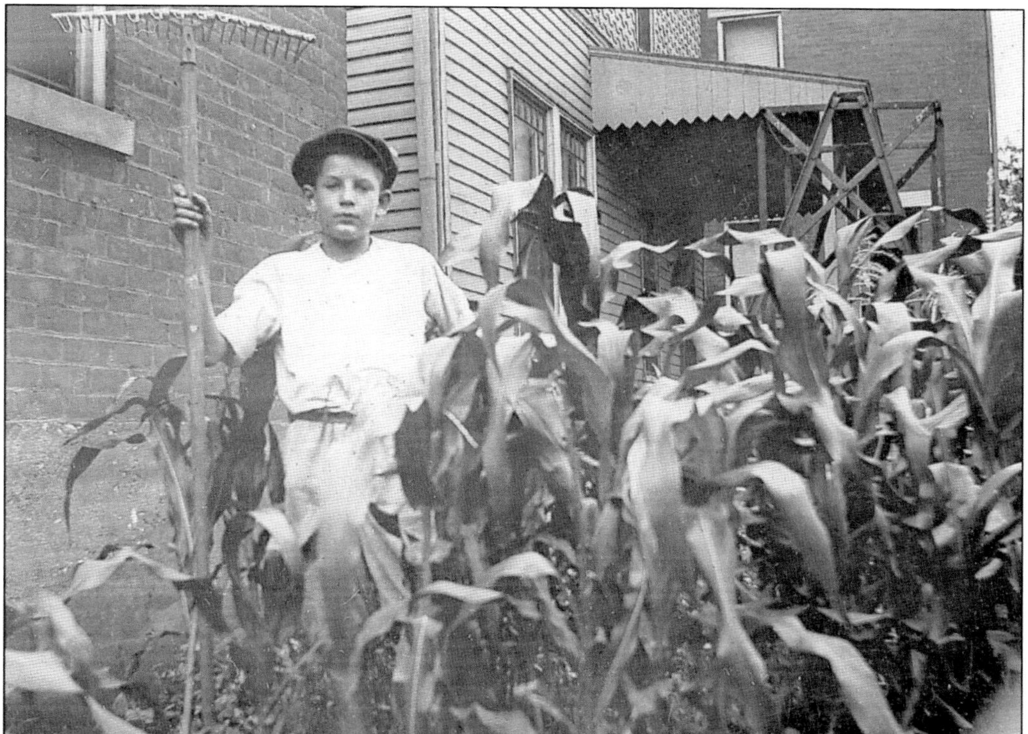

Edmund Berry was the $1 prize winner for his garden in 1915. (Courtesy Peter Garrett.)

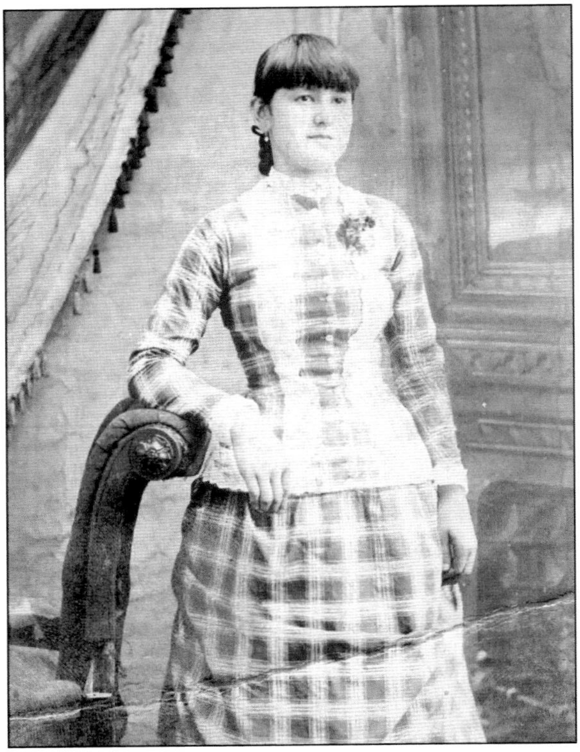

In early America, infectious diseases posed great risk. It was not uncommon for people to die from entities easily treatable in today's world. Such was the case with Emma Braun of Newport (left). She died in 1890 at the young age of 19, with her death attributed to typhoid. (Courtesy Susan Braun Smith.)

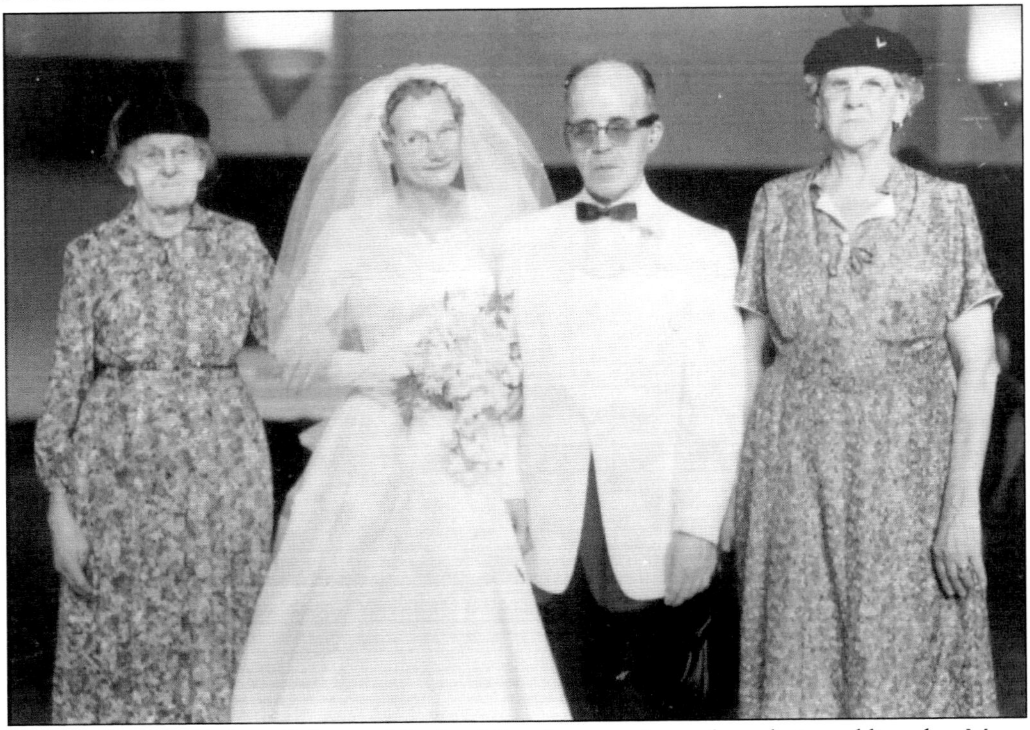

Bride and groom Delores Pelzer and Richard Pomfrey are pictured on their wedding day. Many Newport residents remember the blind Miss Pelzer working at her snack stand in the Campbell County Courthouse. The couple is seen with the bride's aunts. (Courtesy Paul Schuerman.)

Three

Fire and Police Departments

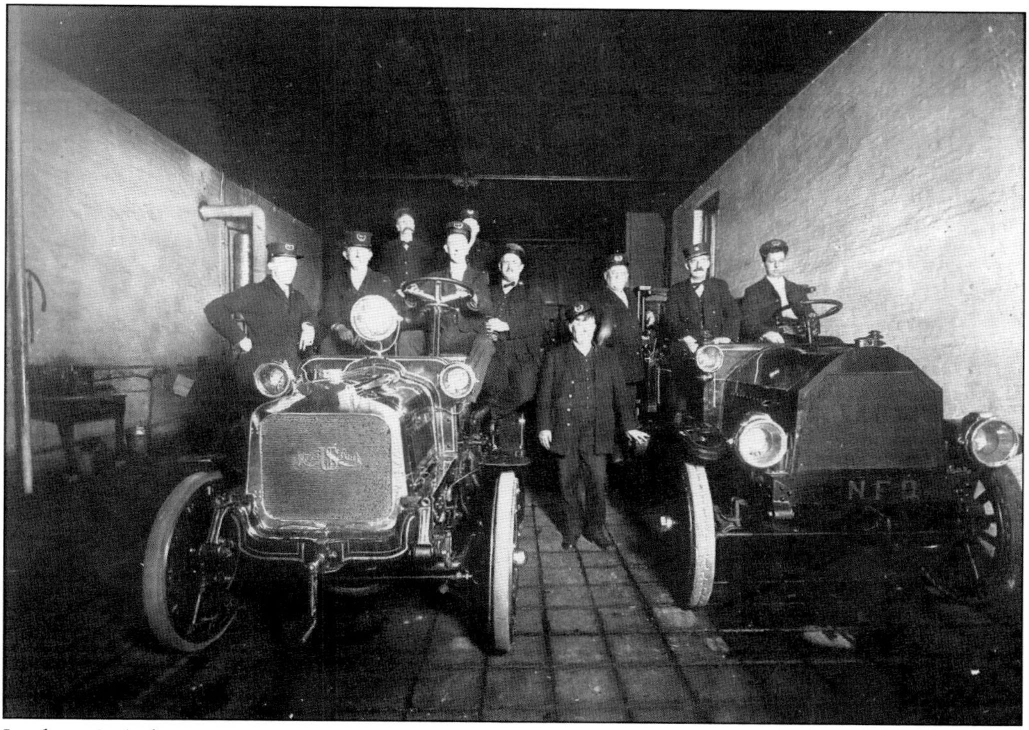

In this 1915 photo, Newport Fire Department members are seen with their first motorized hose wagon, which was obtained from Schacht Motor Car Company of Cincinnati. Horses were completely eliminated from the fire department several years later in 1918. (Courtesy Chief Larry Atwell, Newport Fire Department.)

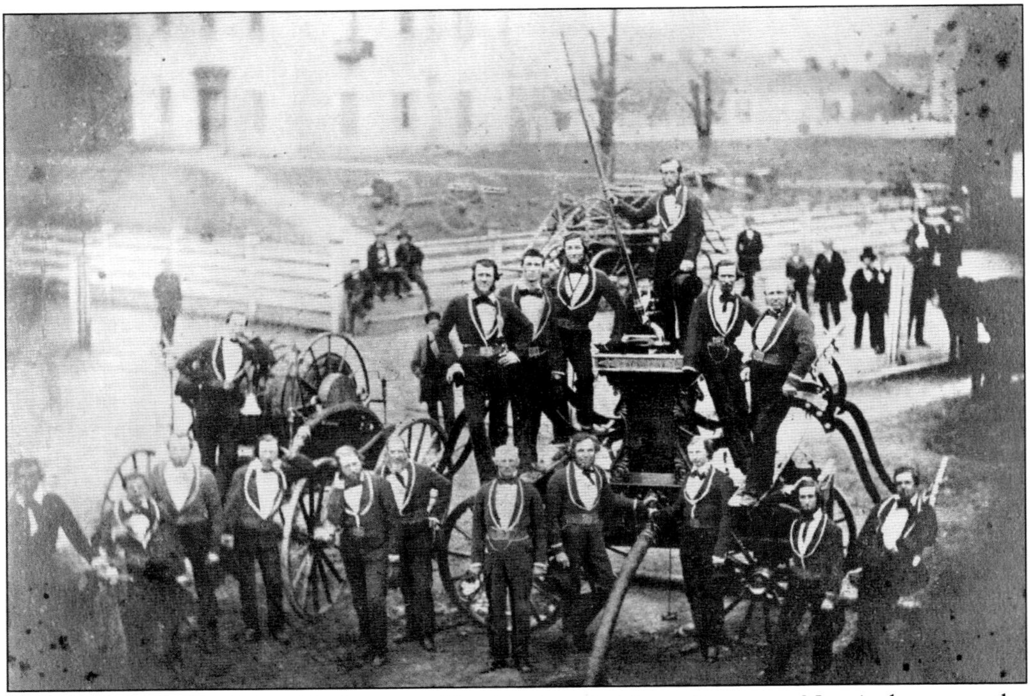

Two early photos of the Washington Fire Engine & Hose Company No. 1 showcase the volunteer organization, c. 1860. Although volunteers, the members took their responsibility seriously. Absentees at roll call after fires would be fined 10¢. A much more considerable fine of $3 was imposed for the offense of ringing the fire bell without a legitimate company purpose. The volunteer fire company disbanded in 1869 at which time it was replaced by a paid fire department. (Courtesy Special Collections and Archives, Northern Kentucky University.)

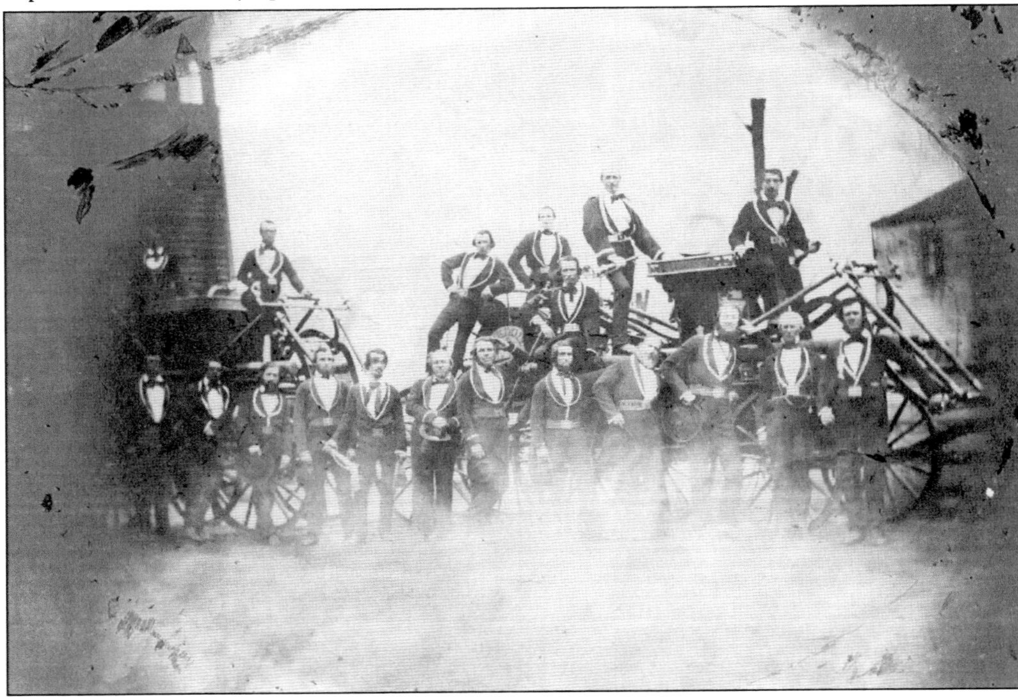

John Waters served as Newport Fire Department's third and fifth fire chief, first from 1890 to 1897 and again from 1902 to 1908. (Courtesy Chief Larry Atwell, Newport Fire Department.)

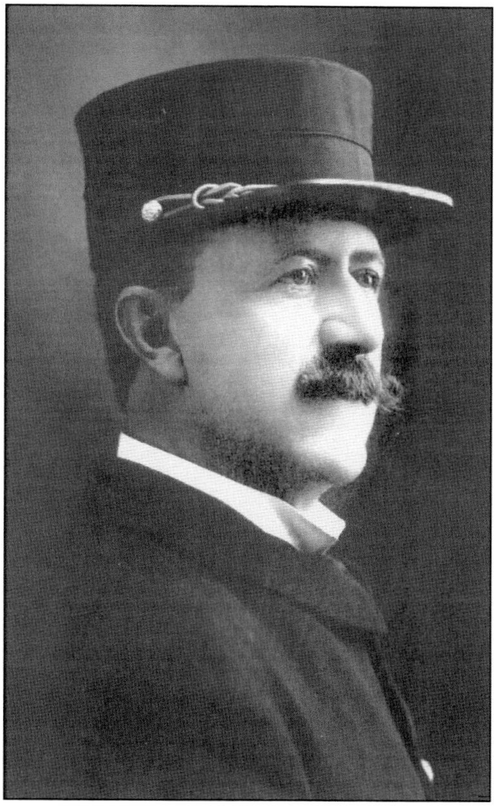

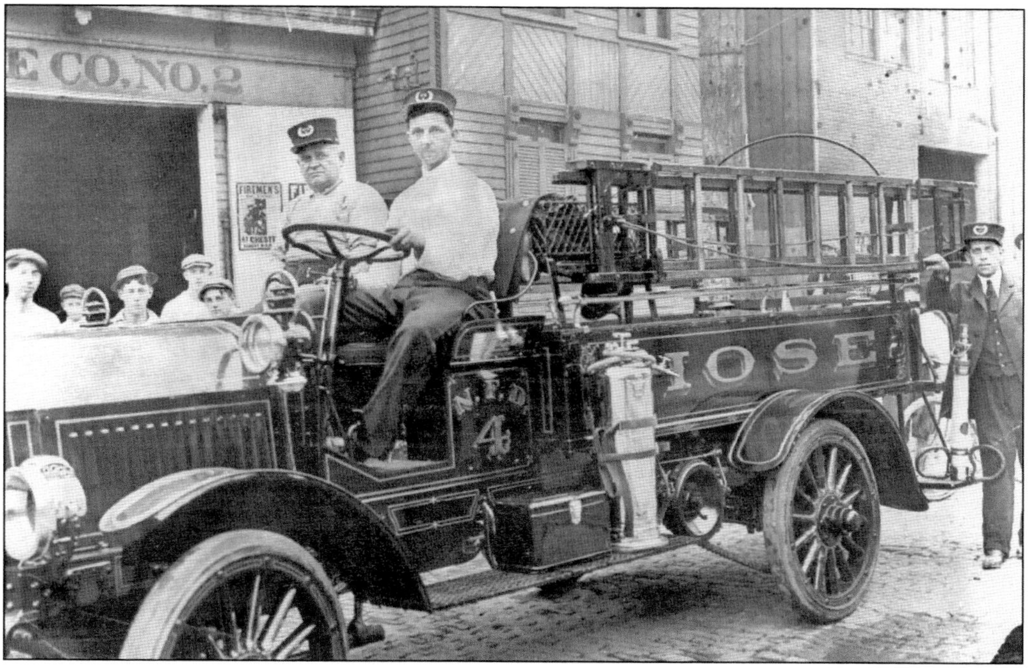

Newport Fire Company No. 2, also known as the Phoenix Fire Company, was located on Monmouth Street between Tenth and Eleventh Streets. (Courtesy Chief Larry Atwell, Newport Fire Department.)

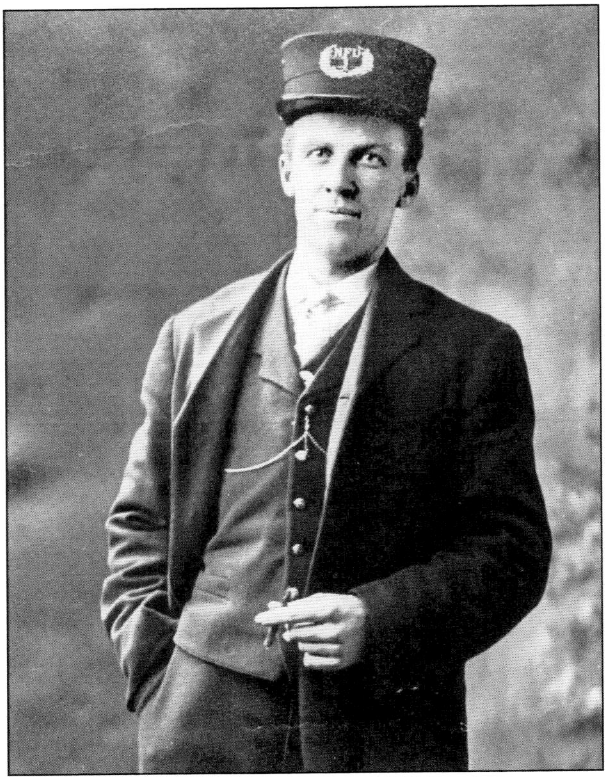

A distinguished-appearing member of the early Newport Fire Department is unidentified in this photograph. (Courtesy Chief Larry Atwell, Newport Fire Department.)

Labor organization for the fire department was initially established in 1918 with the creation of Local 45. Here, the fire company's Local 386 participate in a Newport parade. (Courtesy Chief Larry Atwell, Newport Fire Department.)

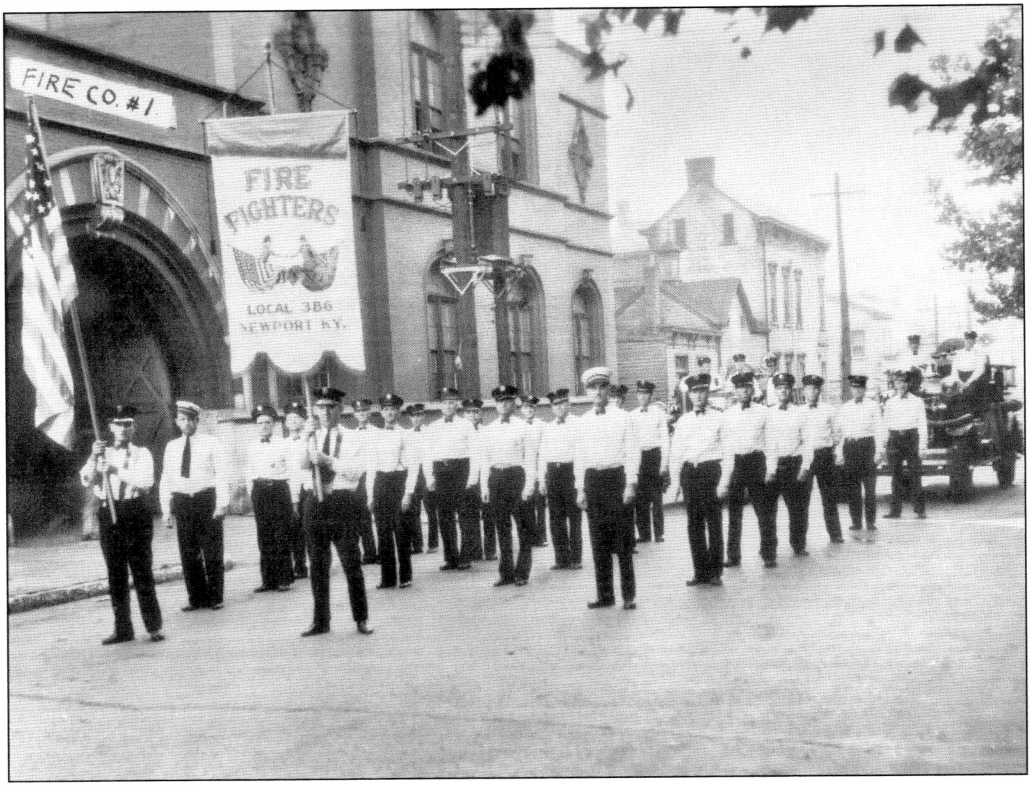

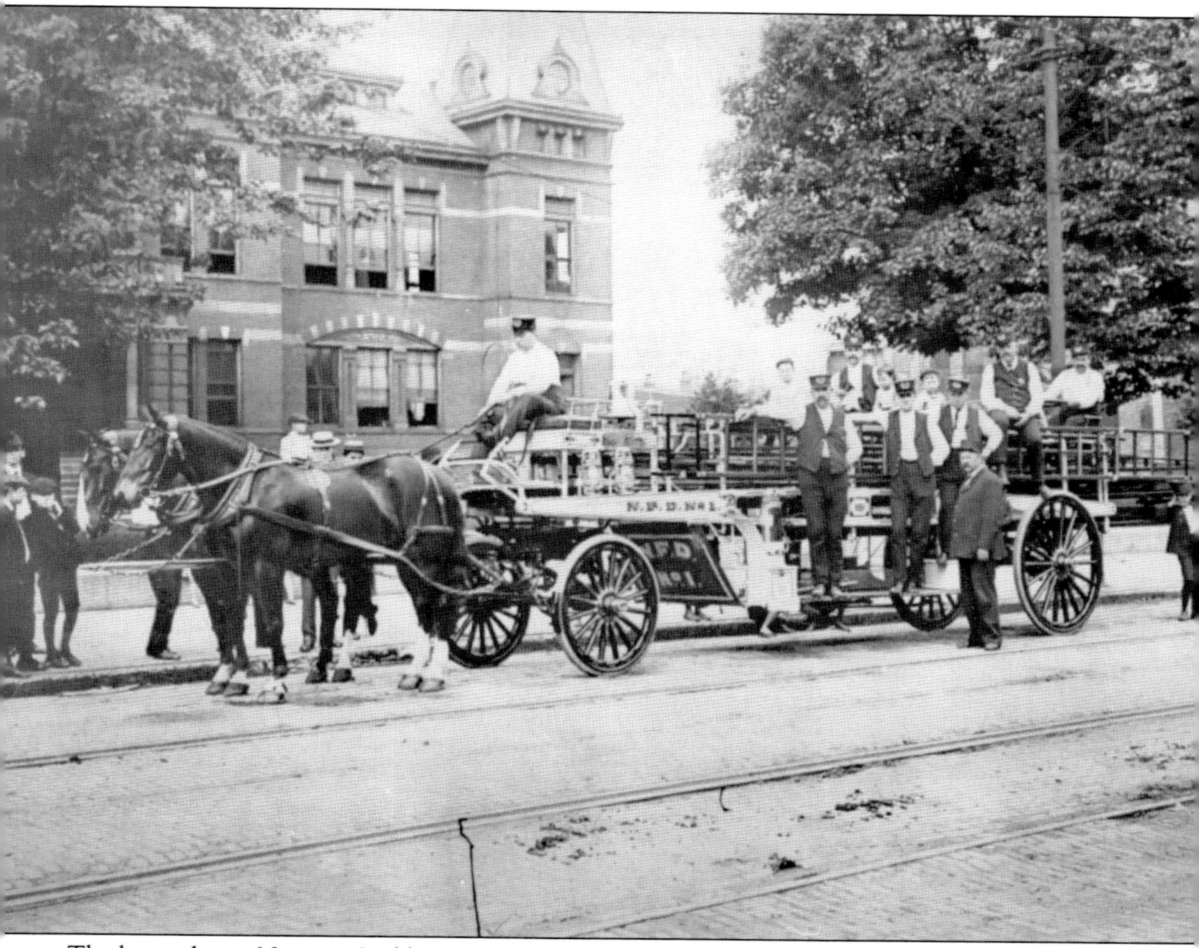

The horse-drawn Newport Ladder Truck is posed in front of the courthouse at Fourth and York Streets on June 18, 1904. Chief John Waters is seen standing in the street. The driver of the truck is identified as Joseph Maus. (Courtesy Chief Larry Atwell, Newport Fire Department.)

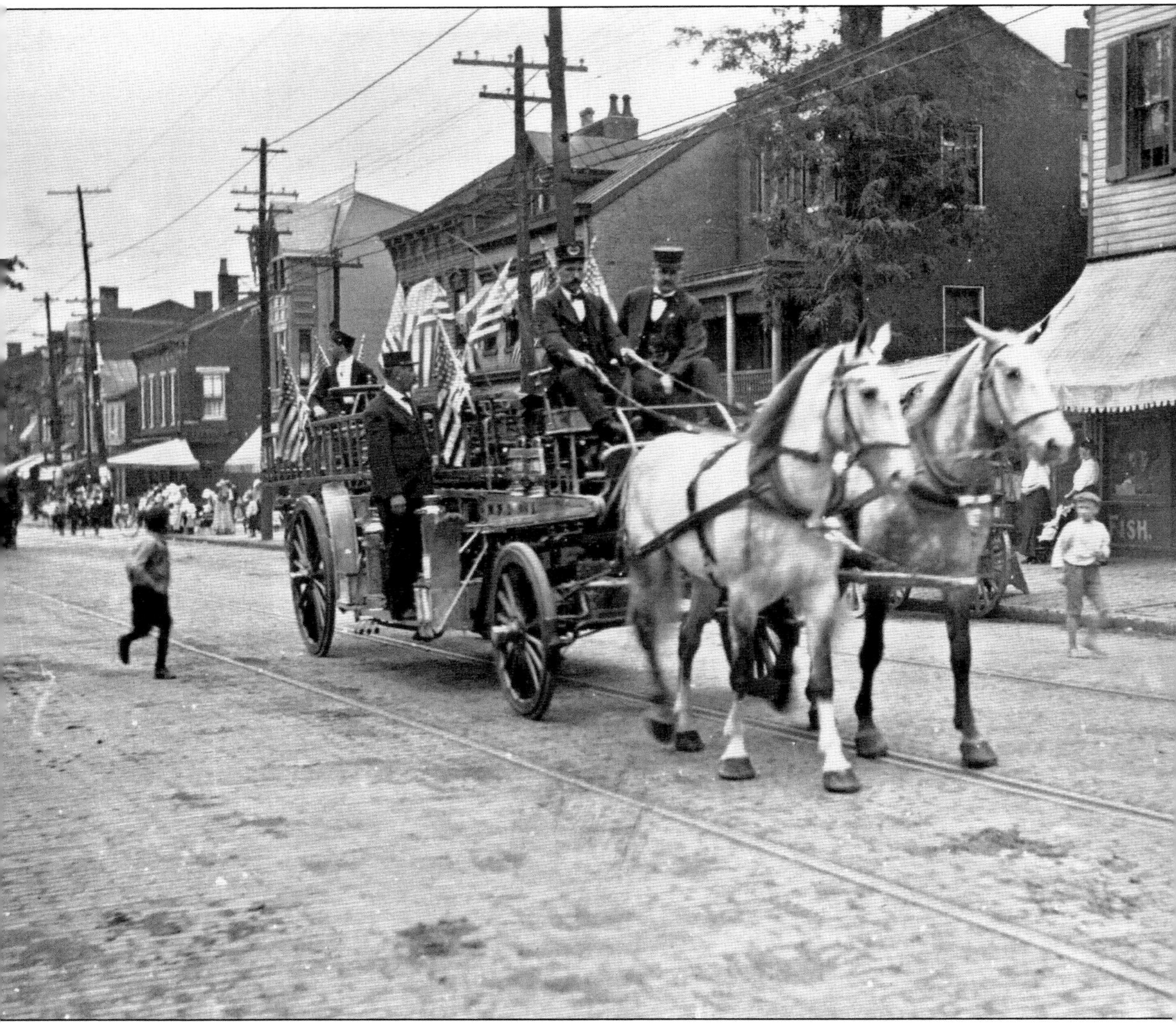

A youngster runs alongside the Newport Fire Truck in the 1907 Decoration Day Parade. (Courtesy Kenton County Public Library.)

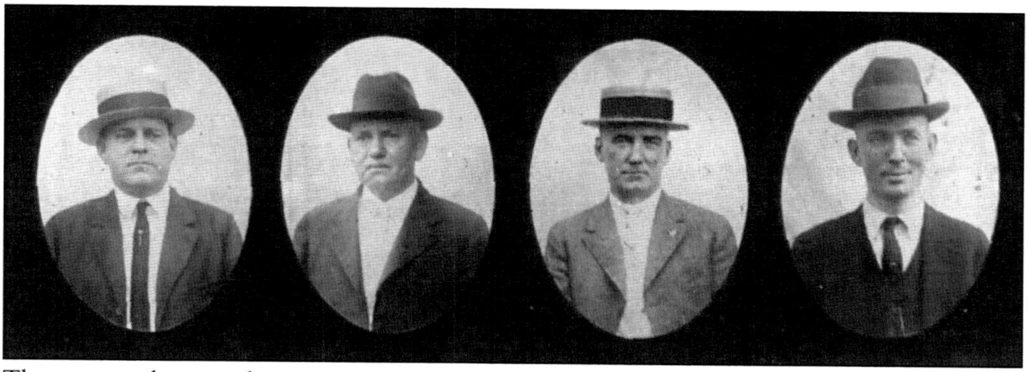

These two photographs portray very early unidentified members of the Newport Police Department. (Courtesy Chief Thomas Fromme, Newport Police Department.)

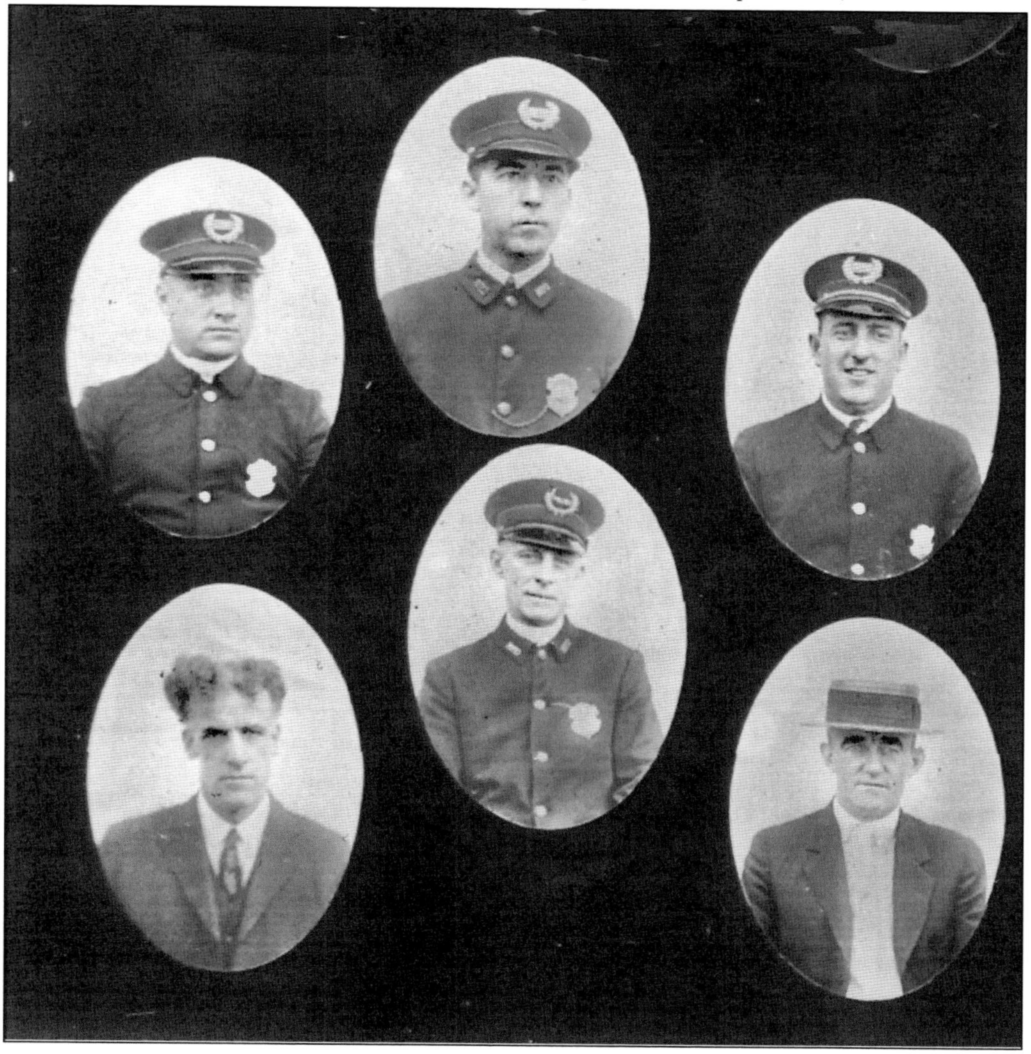

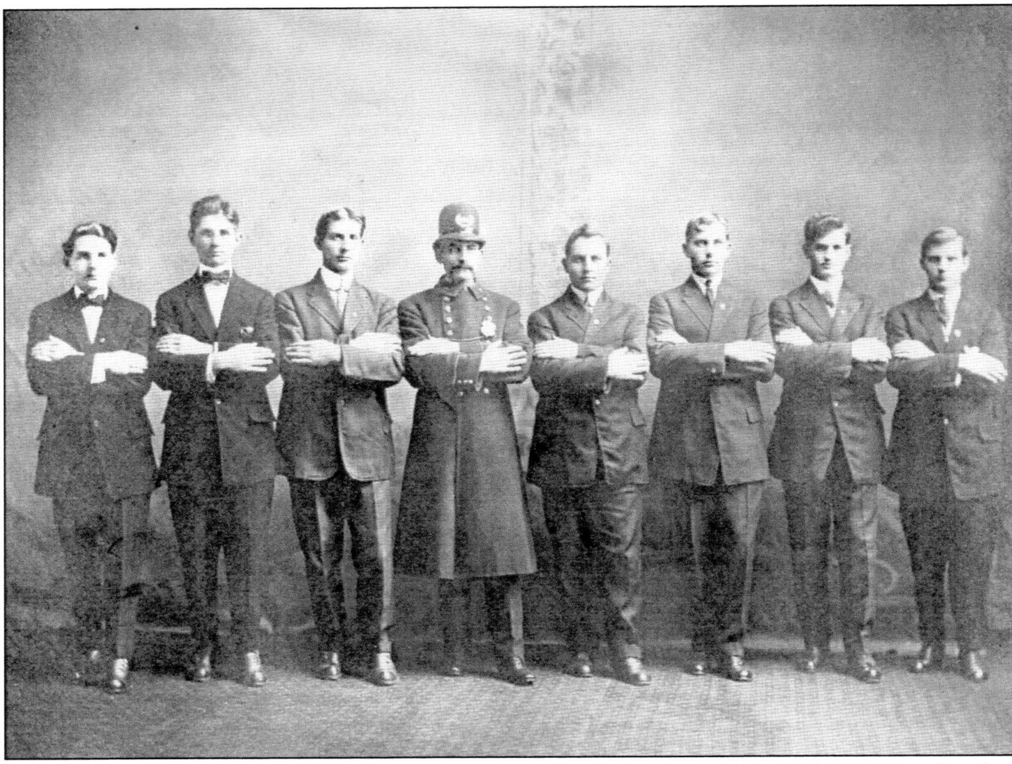

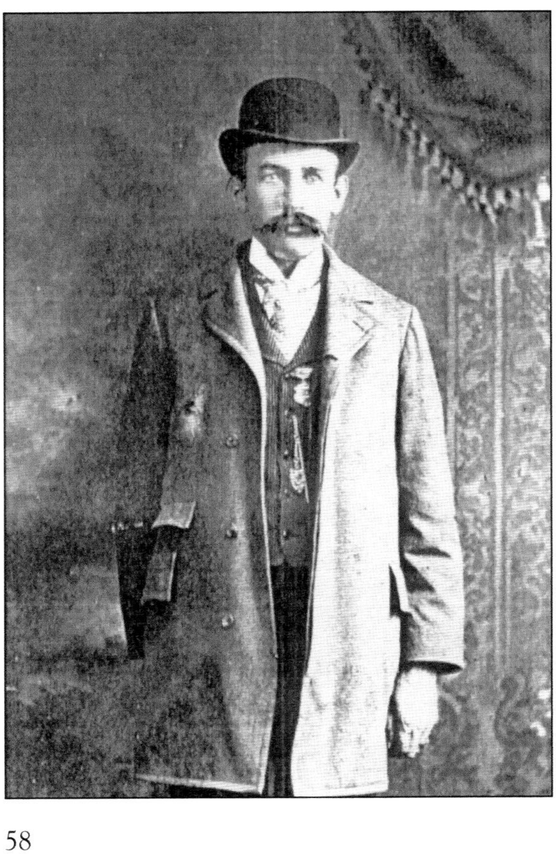

Pride is apparent in this photo of early Newport Police Department members. Newport had a town marshal until 1875 at which time the position of police chief was created. (Courtesy Campbell County Historical Society.)

Fred Miller was Campbell County sheriff at the turn of the century, from 1898 until 1902. (Courtesy Campbell County Historical Society.)

David Kirschner (right) appears in the uniform of the Newport Auxiliary Police. The auxiliary police provided support services during special events and assisted with traffic control. They were disbanded in 1992 because of changes in state regulations. Mr. Kirschner was decorated by the government of Italy after World War I for bravery. He was also commander of the Jane Wallace Costigan American Legion Post in Newport. The man on the left is unidentified. (Courtesy Kirschner family.)

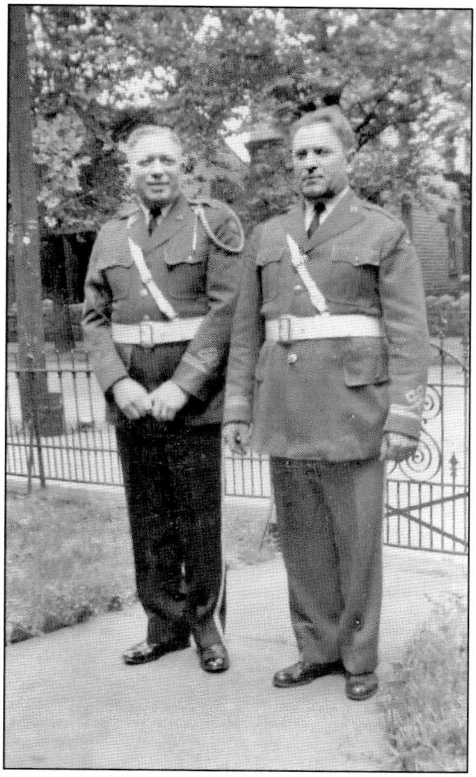

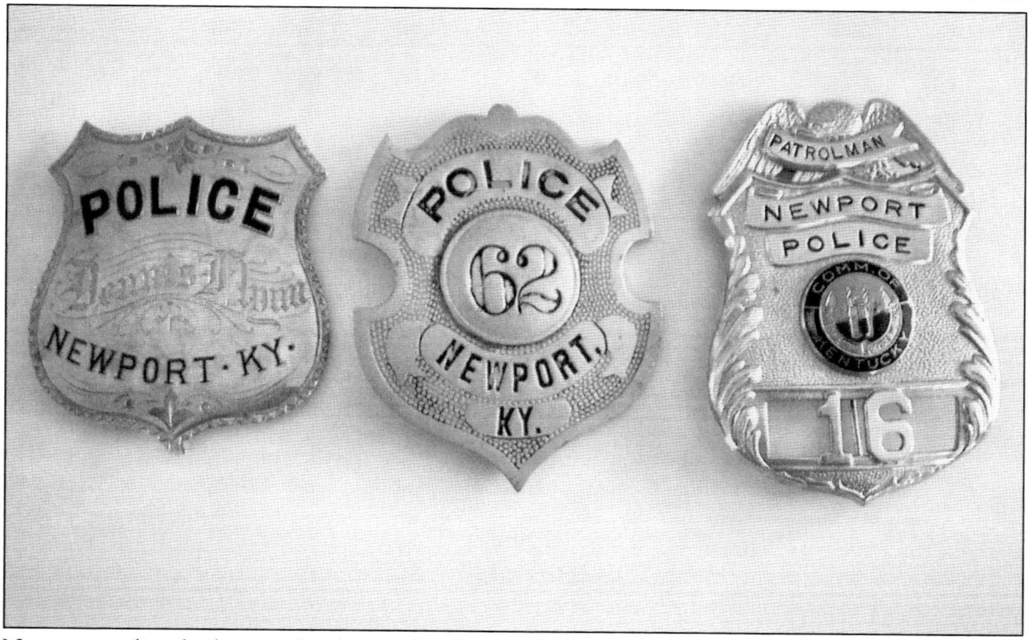

Newport police badges evolved in style. Originally, the name of the officer was engraved on the badge, later giving way to numbers. The badge on the left belonged to Dennis Flynn, c. 1900. The middle badge represents the badge style of the 1930s. On the right is the badge of Anthony Jansen who was killed in the line of duty in 1984. (Courtesy Chief Thomas Fromme, Newport Police Department.)

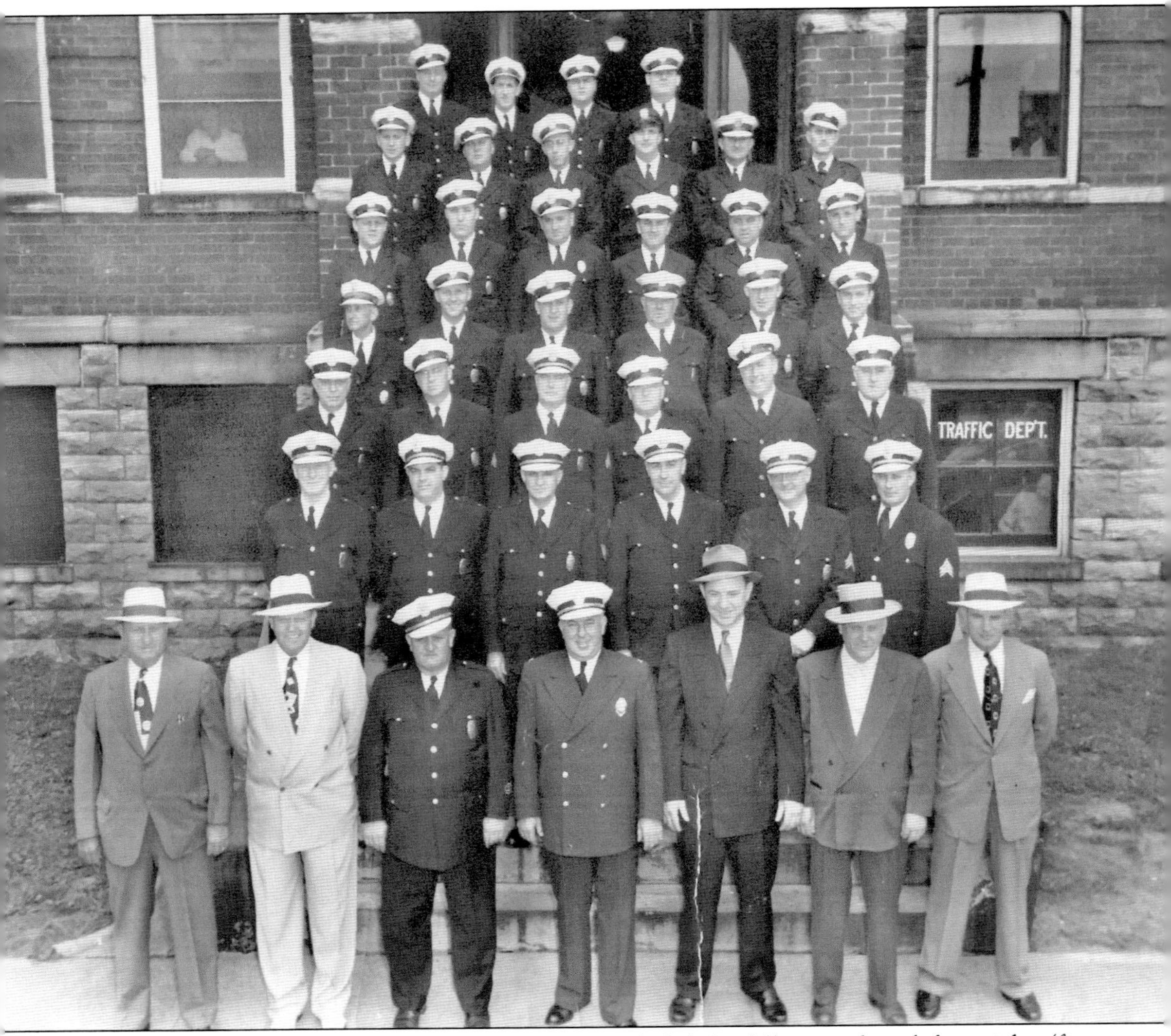

Newport Police Department members, *c.* 1960, included the following, from left to right: (first row) Ray Hawthorne, John Reed, Desmond Tehan, George Gugel, Leroy Fredericks, Kenneth Collins, and W. Malden; (second row) James Fuller, James Gallucci, William Henley, Al Bauermeister, Asa Damerson, and Jack Thiem; (third row) Walter Raabe, Cecil Cate, William Livingston, Dan Shea, Clyde Bishop, and Earl Hosier; (fourth row) Leo Huck, Kenneth Collins Jr., Robert Schindler, John Matz, Upshere White, and Pat Ciafardini; (fifth row) William Schoepf, Charles Pack, Walter Neises, Edward Gugel, Earl Huck, and William Grau; (sixth row) LeRoy Hoffman, Carl Austin, Joseph Quitter III, Neil Rothe, Ray Dullaghan, and Carl Lape; (seventh row) Fred Wessling, Nicholas Gross, Milton Morris, and Robert MacSorley. (Courtesy Chief Thomas Fromme, Newport Police Department.)

Four

LANDMARKS

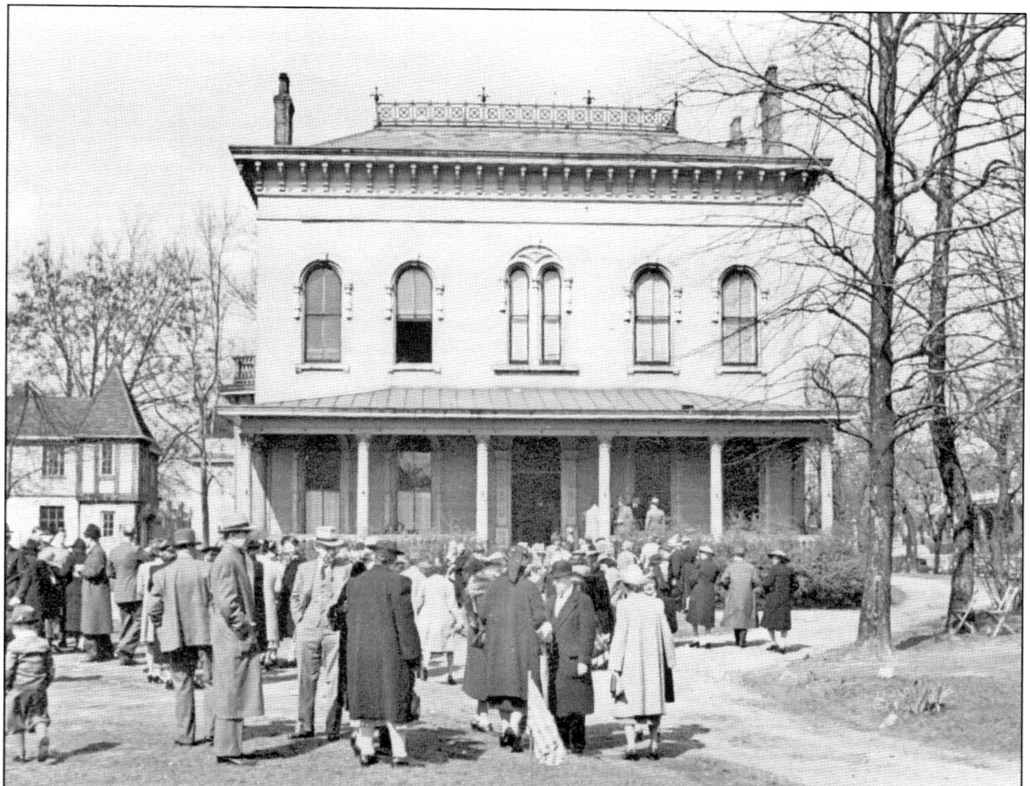

The Col. Henry Nelson homestead was located at Park Avenue and Nelson Place. It was sold by Colonel Nelson's heirs to Saint John's Evangelical Congregational Church in 1939 for $10,000. The church was built in the lot in front of the home, with the building utilized by the church for a time, but church expansion eventually led to the demise of the Nelson home. (Courtesy Saint John's United Church of Christ.)

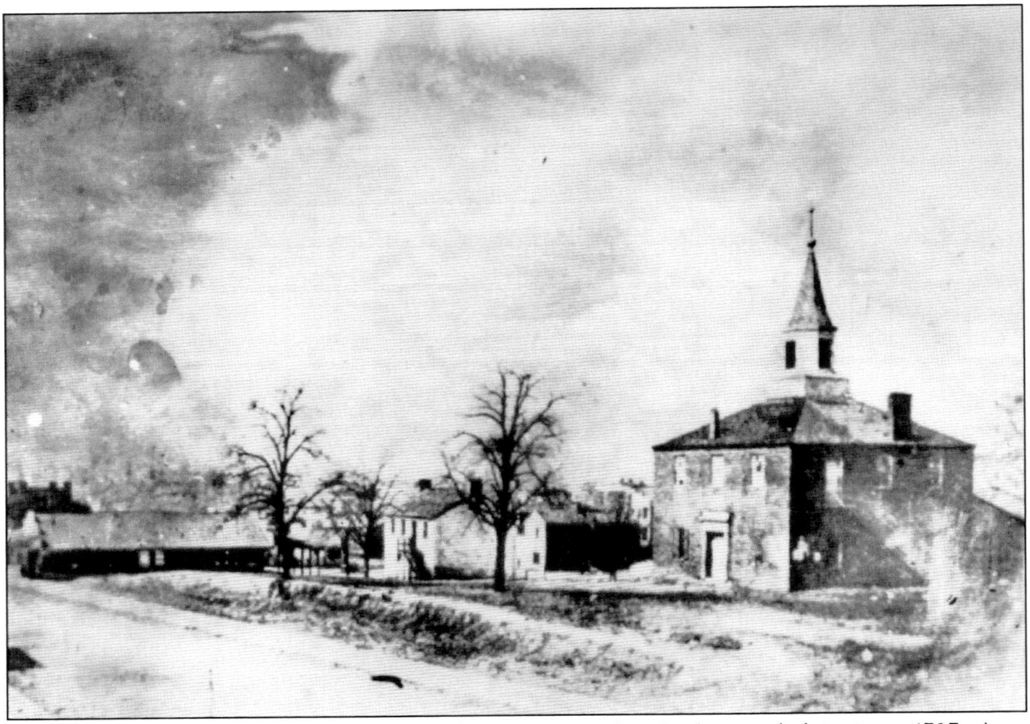

This two-story courthouse replaced the log structure that had preceded it since 1797. At a cost of just over $3,000, it was completed in 1815. The structure was razed in 1883 to build the current courthouse. (Courtesy Judge Lambert Hehl Jr.)

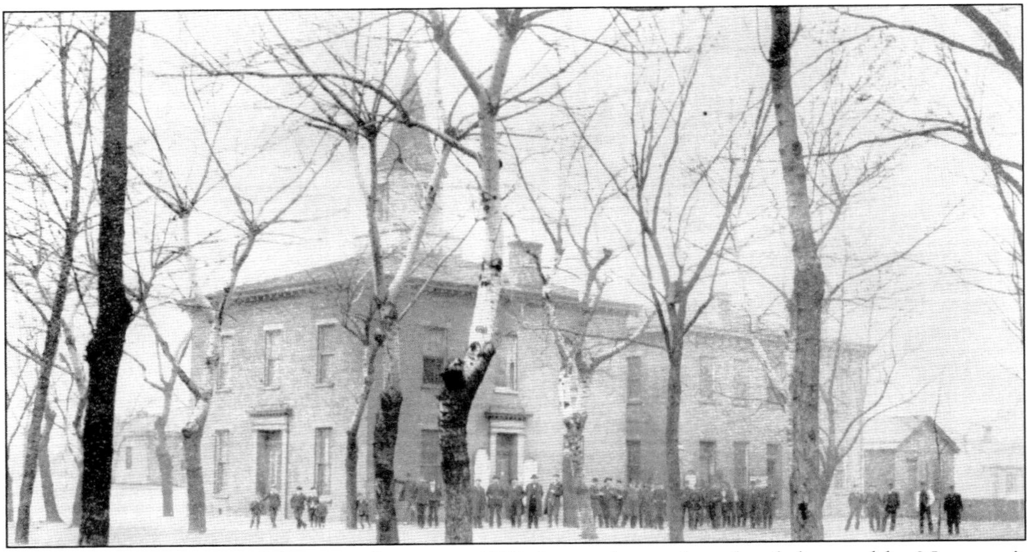

Here is another view of the courthouse, c. 1870. It was located on land donated by Newport's founder, James Taylor. He donated town lots number 79 through 84 to the county to be utilized as a public square. (Courtesy Judge Lambert Hehl Jr.)

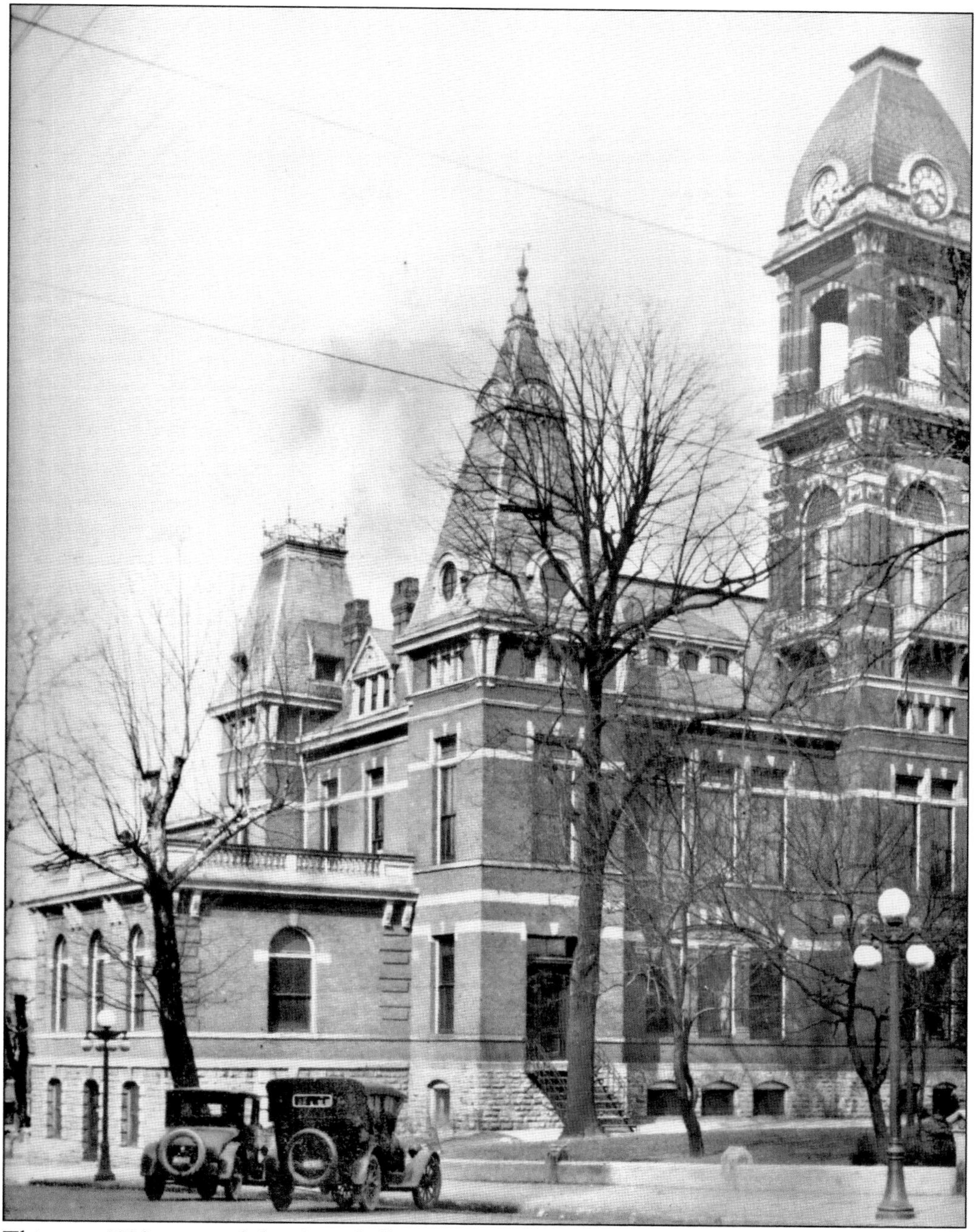

This is a 1920s view of the Campbell County Courthouse at Fourth and York Streets. After delays relating to the 1884 flood and a sawmill fire that limited lumber availability, business commenced within the courthouse in September of 1884. Designed by architect A.C. Nash of Cincinnati, this landmark was placed on the National Register of Historic Places in 1984. (Courtesy Judge Lambert Hehl Jr.)

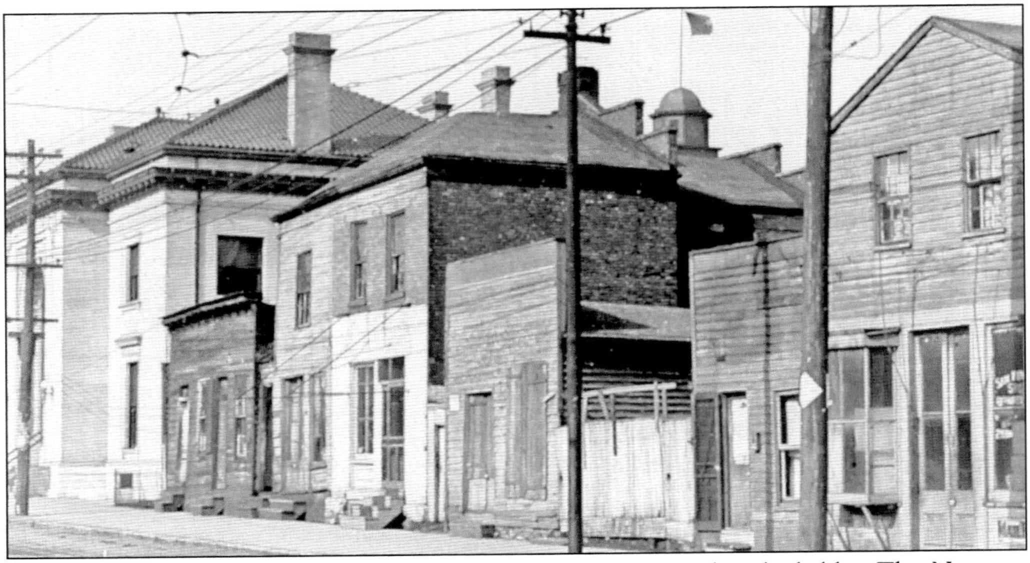

This view shows what the 400-block of Monmouth Street used to look like. The Newport Public Library (later the Campbell County Public Library) is seen on the left; Sam Fennell's is on the far right. Of the structures pictured, only the library building still stands. (Courtesy Peter Garrett.)

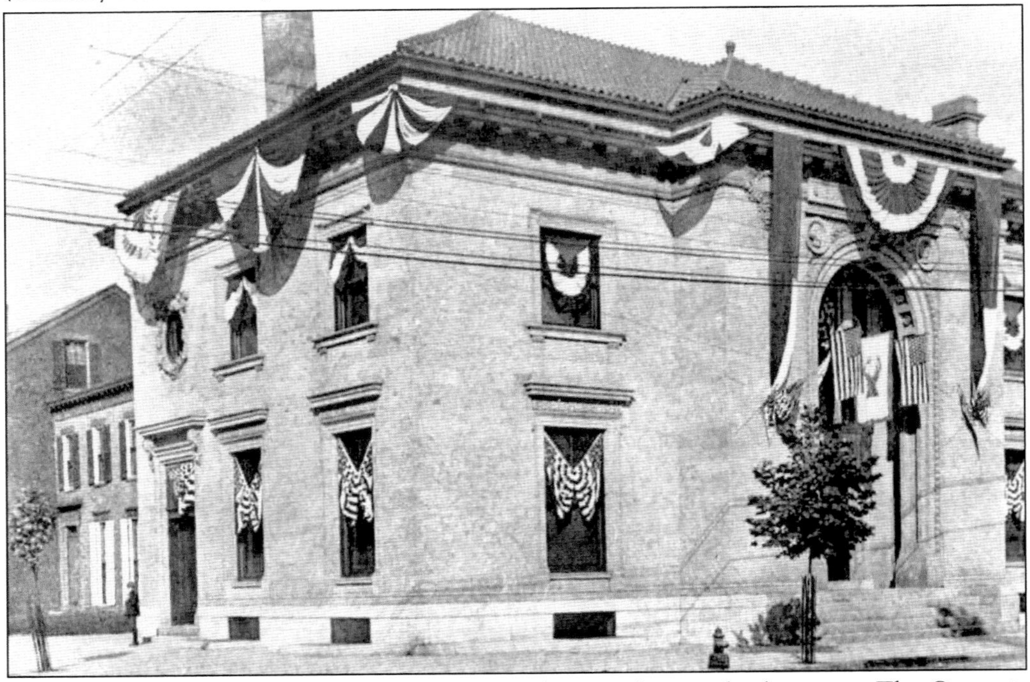

The Newport Public Library, seen in this 1904 photograph, was also known as The Carnegie Free Library. It was the product of donations totaling $26,500 from steel industry philanthropist Andrew Carnegie, who generously shared his fortune to fund over 1,600 public library buildings throughout the states. The library's grand opening took place on June 25, 1902. Prior to this building being erected, Newport housed a small public library within the Mutual Fire Insurance Building also at Fourth and York Streets, on the opposite corner. (Courtesy Campbell County Historical Society.)

The impressive Masonic Temple on the northeast corner of York and Mayo (later Seventh) Streets was built in 1886. The building still stands today. (From the Collection of the Public Library of Cincinnati and Hamilton County.)

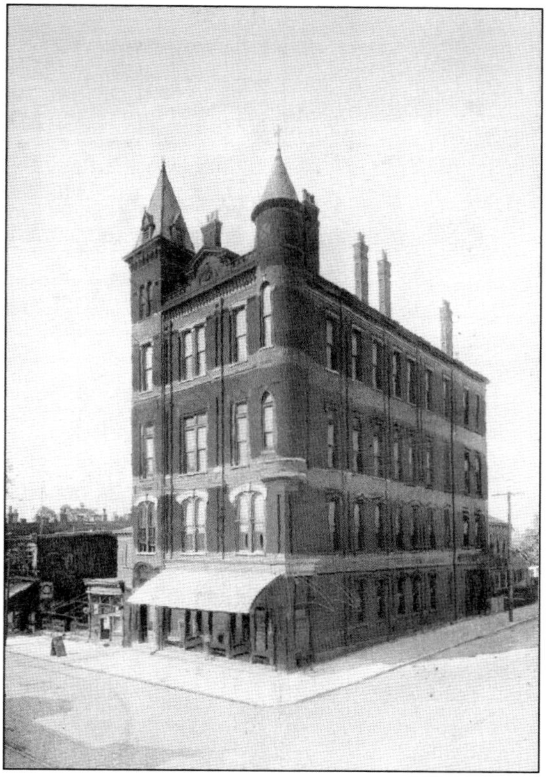

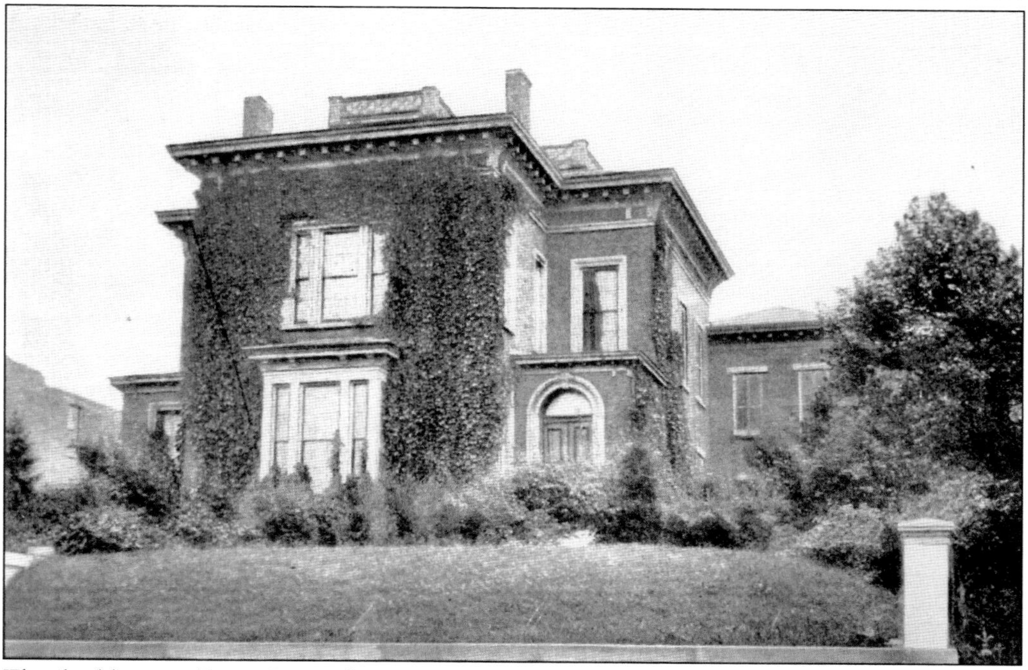

This building on Front Street (later First Street), constructed around 1845, was the home of Dr. Nathaniel B. Shaler, a graduate of Harvard. In 1861, his position as surgeon at the Newport Barracks earned him a salary of $100 per month! Born here was his son Nathaniel S. Shaler who would become a nationally recognized geologist. (Courtesy Kenton County Public Library.)

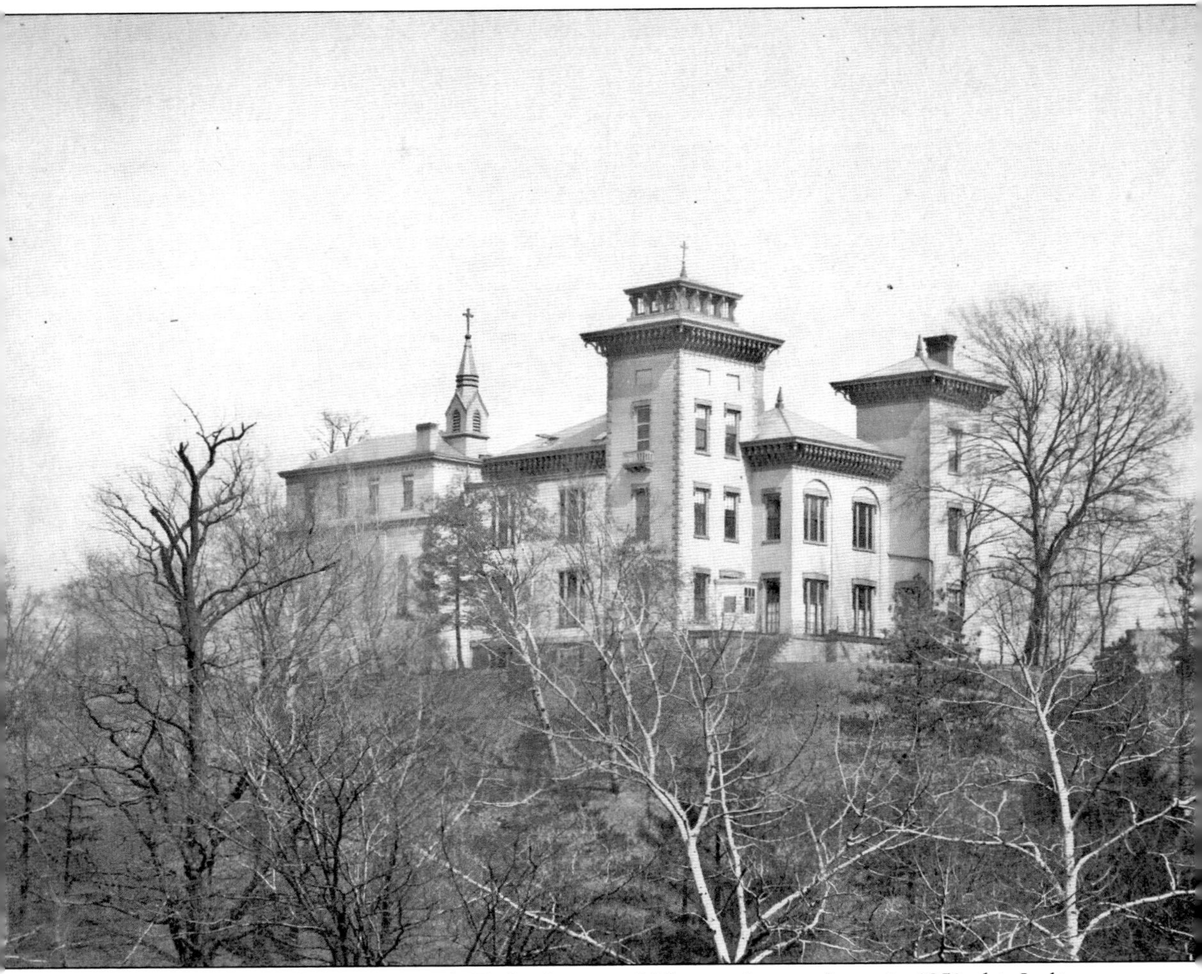

Built for newlyweds Mary Keturah Taylor Jones and Thomas Lauren Jones in 1851, this Italianate villa–style mansion, the Jones Mansion, was located in the vicinity of Monmouth and Fifteenth Streets. Mrs. Jones sold the home to the Diocese of Covington in 1889 after her husband's death. It then became the American mother home for the Sisters of Divine Providence, with the first three sisters arriving from France that same year: Sr. Mary Chantal, Sr. Mary Lucy, and Sr. Mary Camilla. Mount Saint Martin Academy, also known as the French Academy, opened in the fall of 1889 with the enrollment of three pupils. Eventually, the academy needed more space, and in 1903, a new building was constructed at Sixth Street and Linden Avenue for that purpose. Through the years, the mansion would also function as a home for working girls and a shelter for Vietnamese refugees. When the Sisters of Divine Providence moved to Saint Anne's Convent in Melbourne, the magnificent structure was sold by the diocese to a developer. The regrettable demolition of one of Newport's most notorious landmarks ensued; the site is now occupied by a K-Mart. (Courtesy Sisters of Divine Providence.)

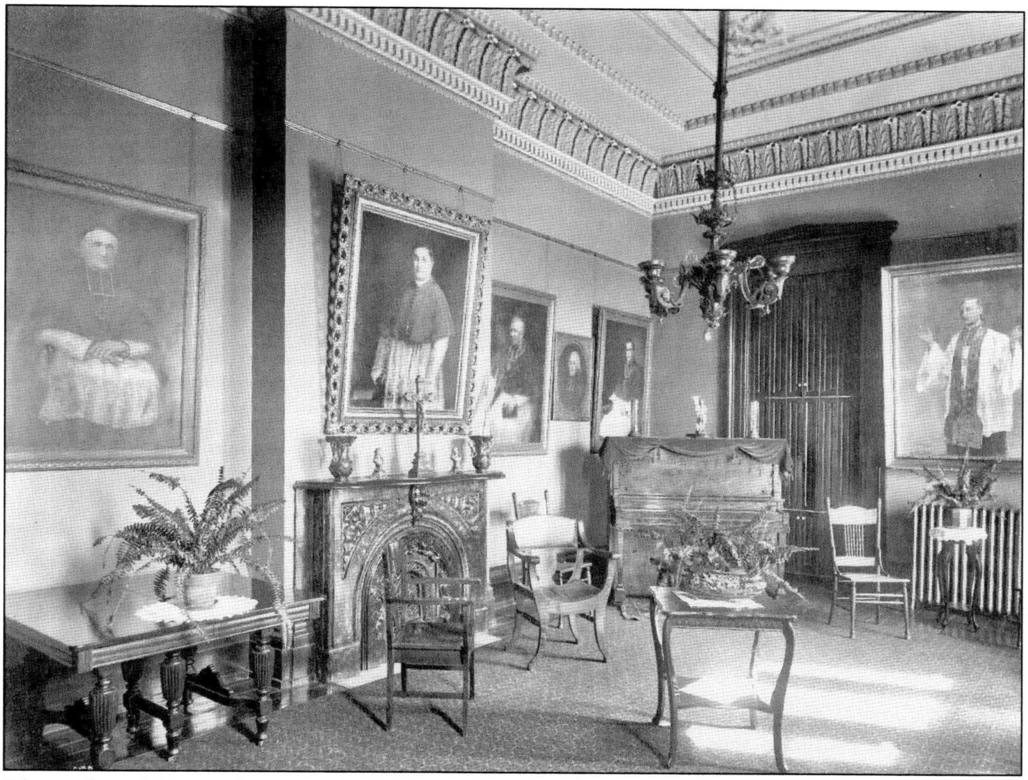

The parlor of Mount Saint Martin displays a painting above the fireplace of Bishop Maes of the Diocese of Covington and an image of Blessed Father Jean Martin Moye above the radiator. (Courtesy Sisters of Divine Providence.)

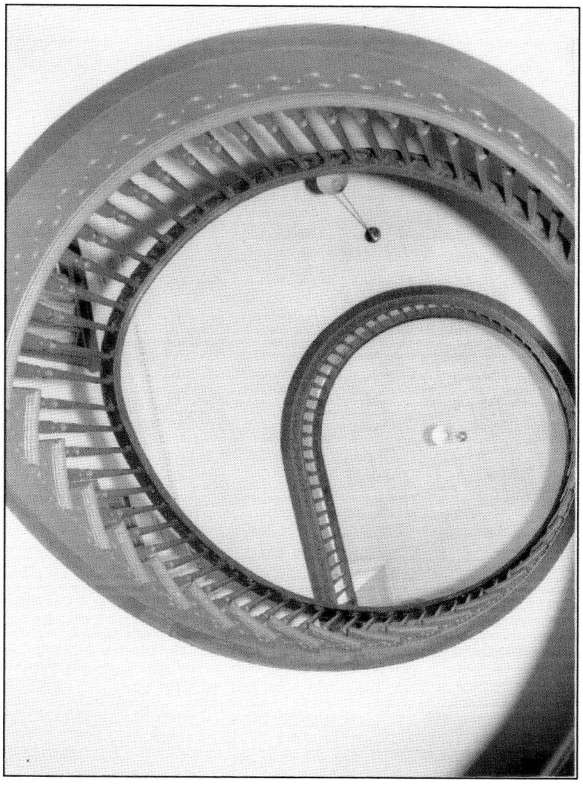

The circular staircase of 70 steps ascended three floors. In early years, a magnificent chandelier was suspended from the ceiling. (Courtesy Sisters of Divine Providence.)

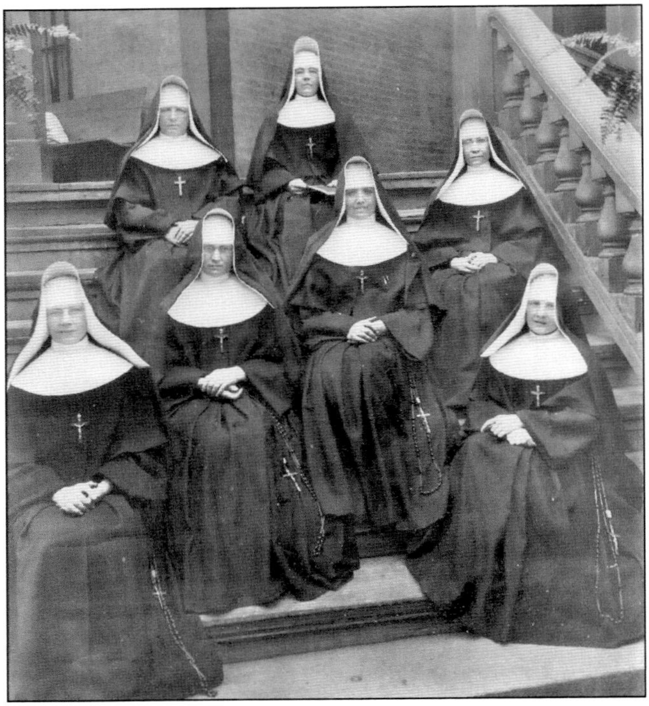

Photographed here are early sisters on the stairs of Mount Saint Martin, c. 1900. Pictured from left to right are (front row) an unidentified sister, Sr. Mary Kuntz, Sr. M. Rodriguez Steiner, and Sr. Justina Mary Tiller; (back row) Sr. M. Marthe Knab, Mother Mary Lucy Damidio, and Sr. M. Zaveria Molt. (Courtesy Sisters of Divine Providence.)

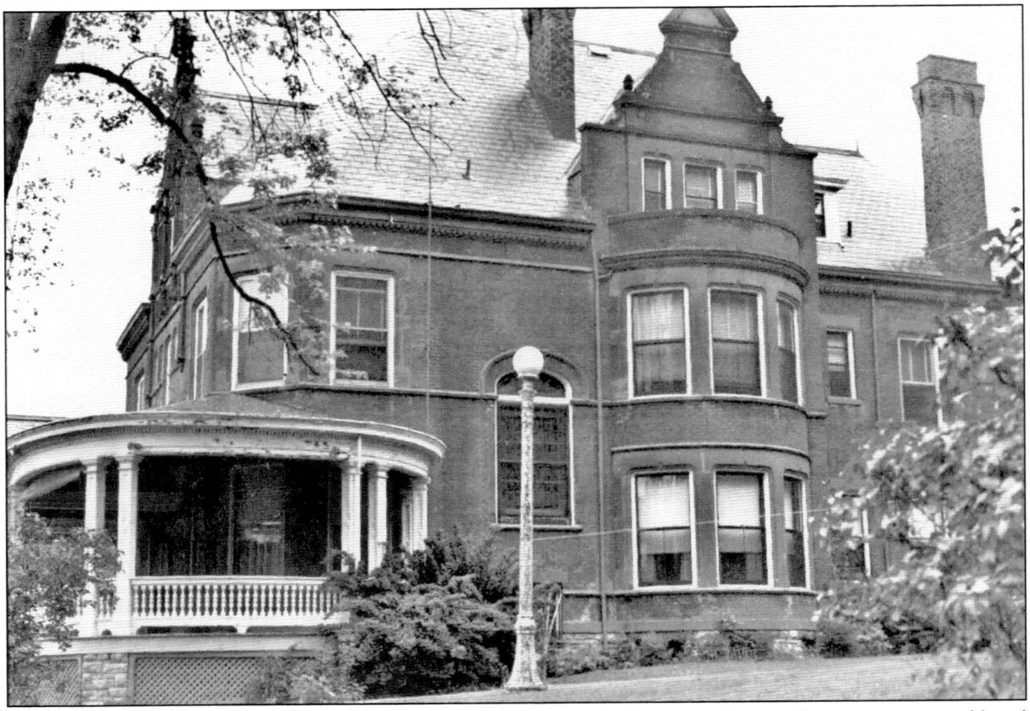

The Wiedemann Estate on upper Park Avenue was built 1893–1895 on a five-acre tract of land in Cote Brilliante. It housed George Wiedemann's widow Agnes, as well as their son Charles Wiedemann, for many years. The Diocese of Covington purchased the property in the 1950s, and for a time, Bishop William Mulloy resided here. It is currently a private residence. (Courtesy Sisters of Divine Providence.)

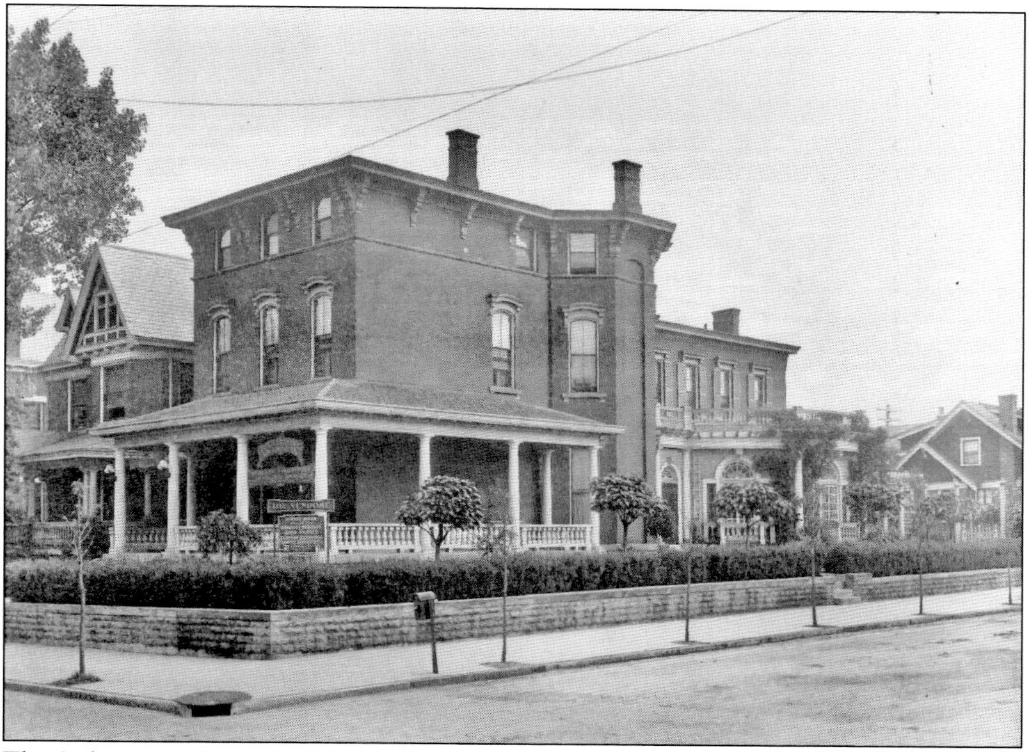

This Italianate-style home at 841 Washington Avenue, originally built for the John R. Anderson family, possesses a vibrant history. Hosting entertainers such as Frank Sinatra, Marilyn Monroe, and Dean Martin during their appearances at nearby clubs, it once earned the nickname of the "Beverly Hills barracks." In earlier years, owner Maggie Yeager ran a European restaurant and named her property the Vendome after the popular square in Paris, France. Later roles of this property include a finishing school for women, a daycare center, a nursing home, a boarding house, and a seven-unit apartment building. It is now a private residence, having been magnificently restored by the current owners in 1998. (Courtesy Donna and Roger Weddle.)

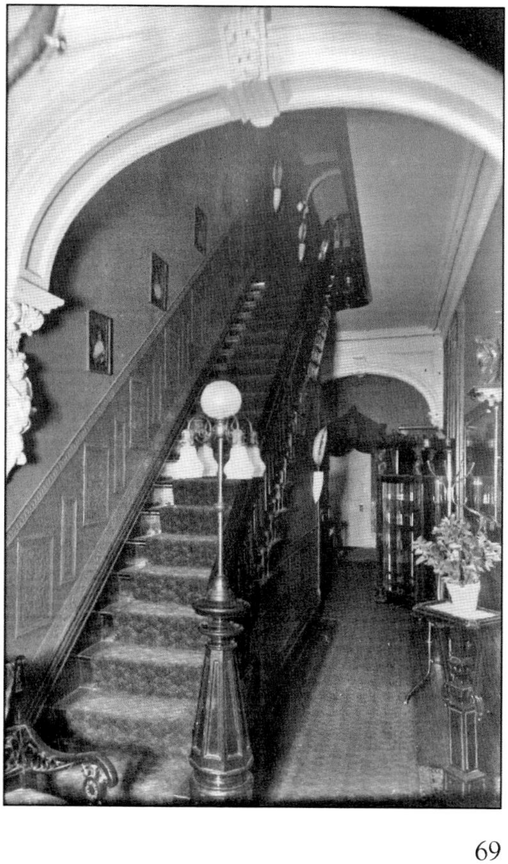

An interior view of the Vendome shows the elaborate staircase and first floor hallway as they appeared when owned by Maggie Yeager, c. 1918. In addition to housing the European restaurant, it also functioned as a luxury boarding house. The home features astounding 13-foot walls. (Courtesy Donna and Roger Weddle.)

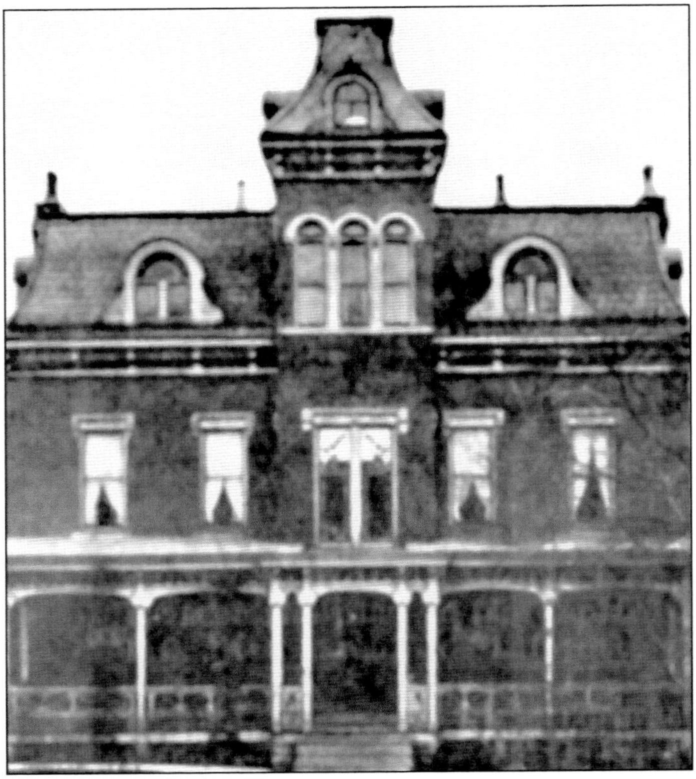

The Southgate House on East Third Street was built around 1814. British prisoners from the War of 1812 who were housed at the Newport Barracks reportedly participated in the construction. It was built for Richard Southgate, a Newport citizen and active politician. He was a state representative as well as a member of the senate, and he also served as Campbell County commonwealth's attorney. The home was passed down through many generations of the Southgate family. John Taliaferro Thompson, inventor of the Thompson machine gun (the Tommy Gun), was born here. (Courtesy Campbell County Historical Society.)

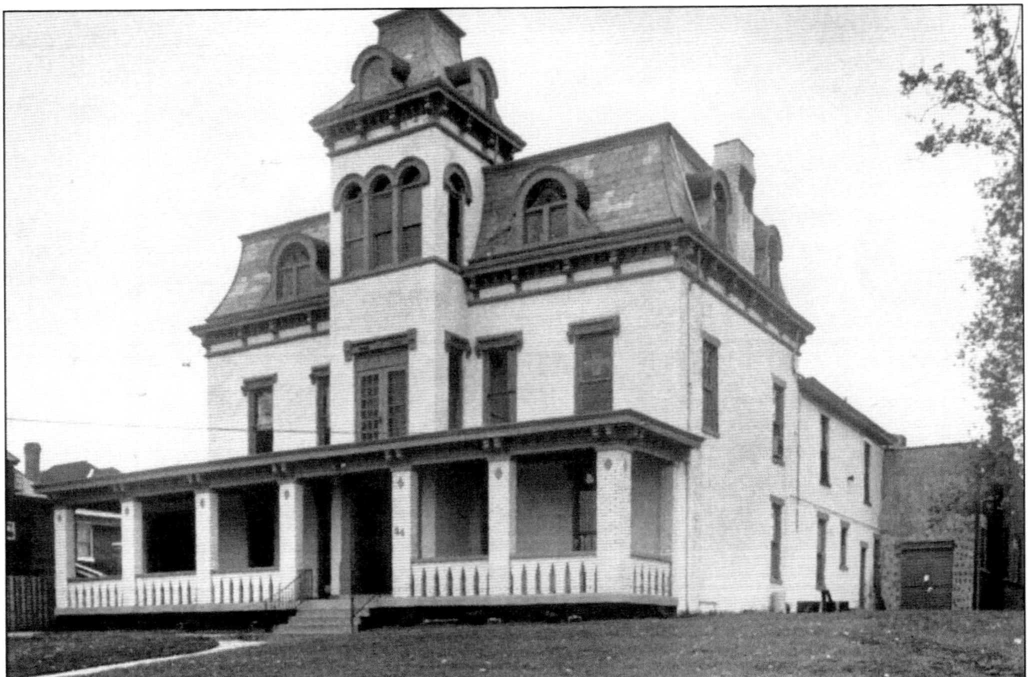

A later view of the Southgate House is portrayed. Occupied by the Knights of Columbus for many years, the structure now houses a bar and music venue. (Courtesy Campbell County Historical Society.)

Five

Religion and Education

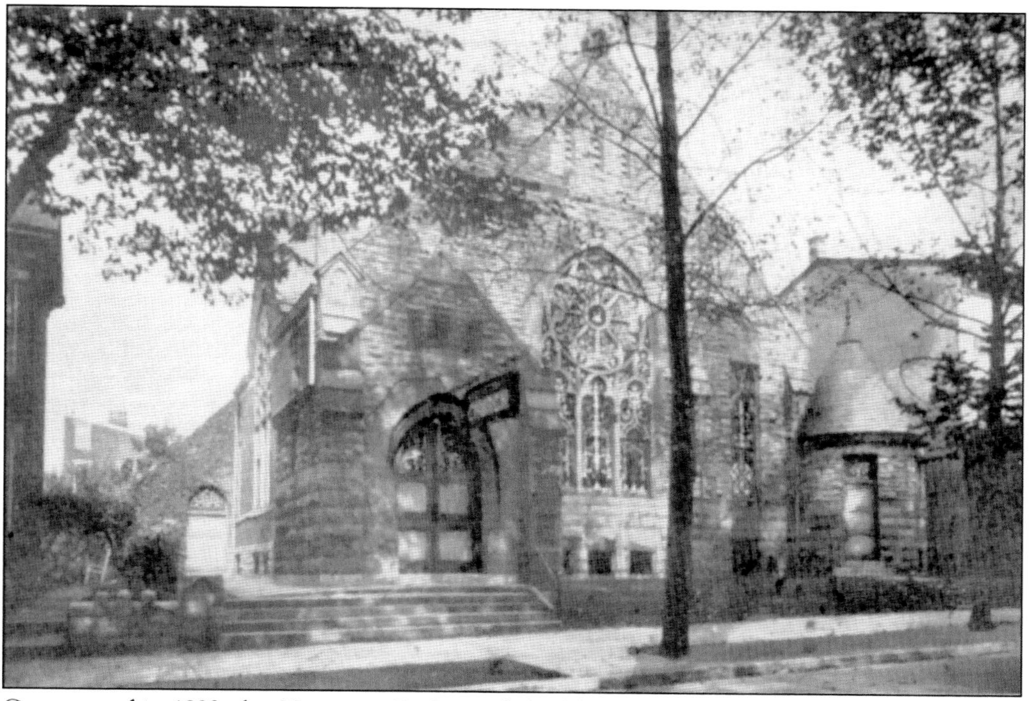

Constructed in 1893, this Victorian Gothic-style building at 625 Overton was home to the First Presbyterian Church of Newport. It has now been renovated into two condominiums. (Courtesy Kenton County Public Library.)

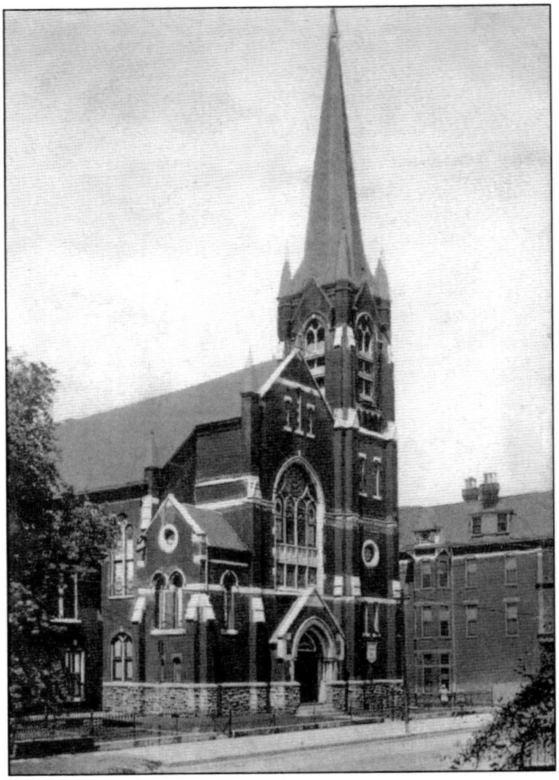

Salem Methodist-Episcopal Church stood at the southwest corner of Eighth and York Streets. Significant damage to the church during a tornado in 1986, coupled with declining membership, led the congregation to merge with Grace Methodist-Episcopal Church. The structure still stands and is now home to Footlighters, a community theatre group. (Courtesy Campbell County Historical Society.)

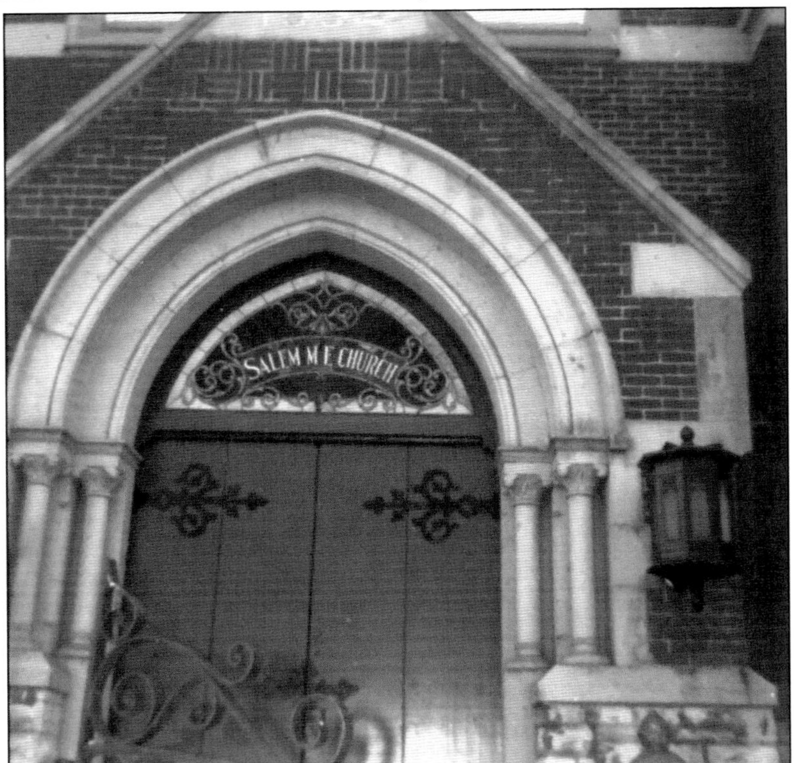

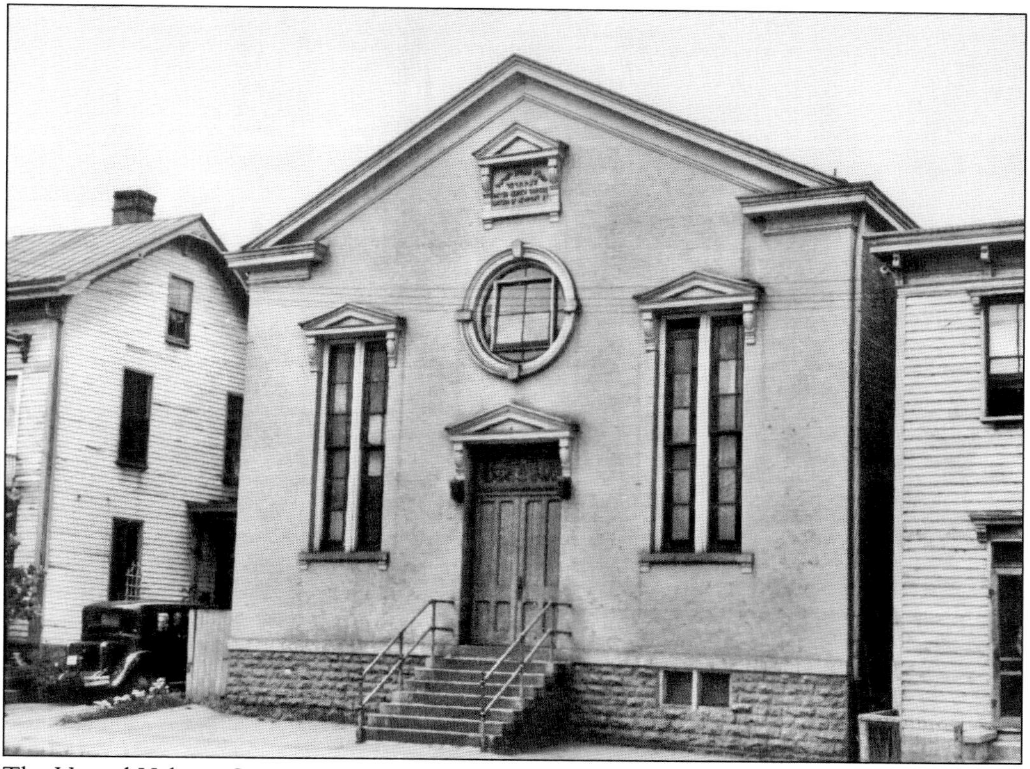

The United Hebrew Congregation was founded in 1897 and occupied this synagogue at 117 East Fifth Street in 1904. The Jewish community in Newport peaked in the 1920s, but the congregation began to decline thereafter. In 1969, the building was sold and became the Apostolic Temple. (Courtesy American Jewish Archives, Cincinnati, Ohio, through the City of Newport.)

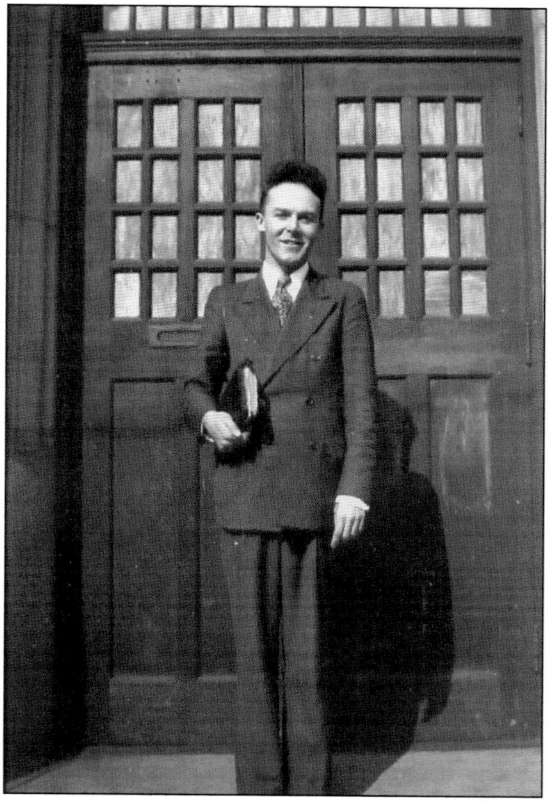

Pastor Jack Bishop stands in front of the doors of the Newport Gospel Tabernacle, now known as the Christian Tabernacle. Preaching at "street meetings" in his late teens, Reverend Bishop would establish this congregation shortly thereafter in 1931. (Courtesy Nicki Bishop.)

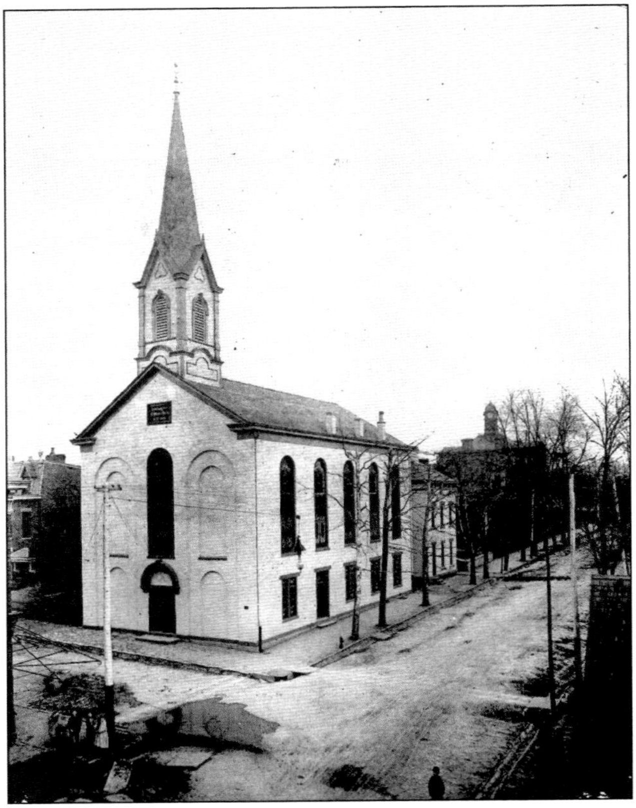

Saint John's United Church of Christ was initially organized as the First German Protestant Evangelical Church in 1847. The church established a German day school as well, with tuition costing 25¢ per month per pupil. This building at Seventh and Columbia Streets became home for the congregation in 1859. Fire destroyed the church in 1939; subsequently, the congregation relocated to their present location at Park and Nelson Streets. (Courtesy Saint John's United Church of Christ.)

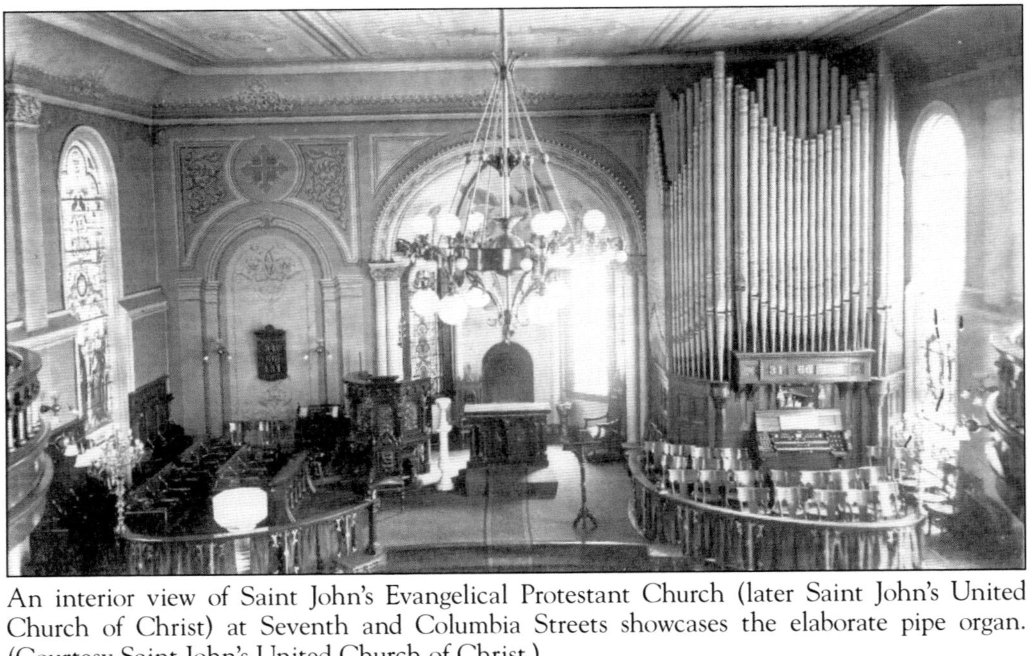

An interior view of Saint John's Evangelical Protestant Church (later Saint John's United Church of Christ) at Seventh and Columbia Streets showcases the elaborate pipe organ. (Courtesy Saint John's United Church of Christ.)

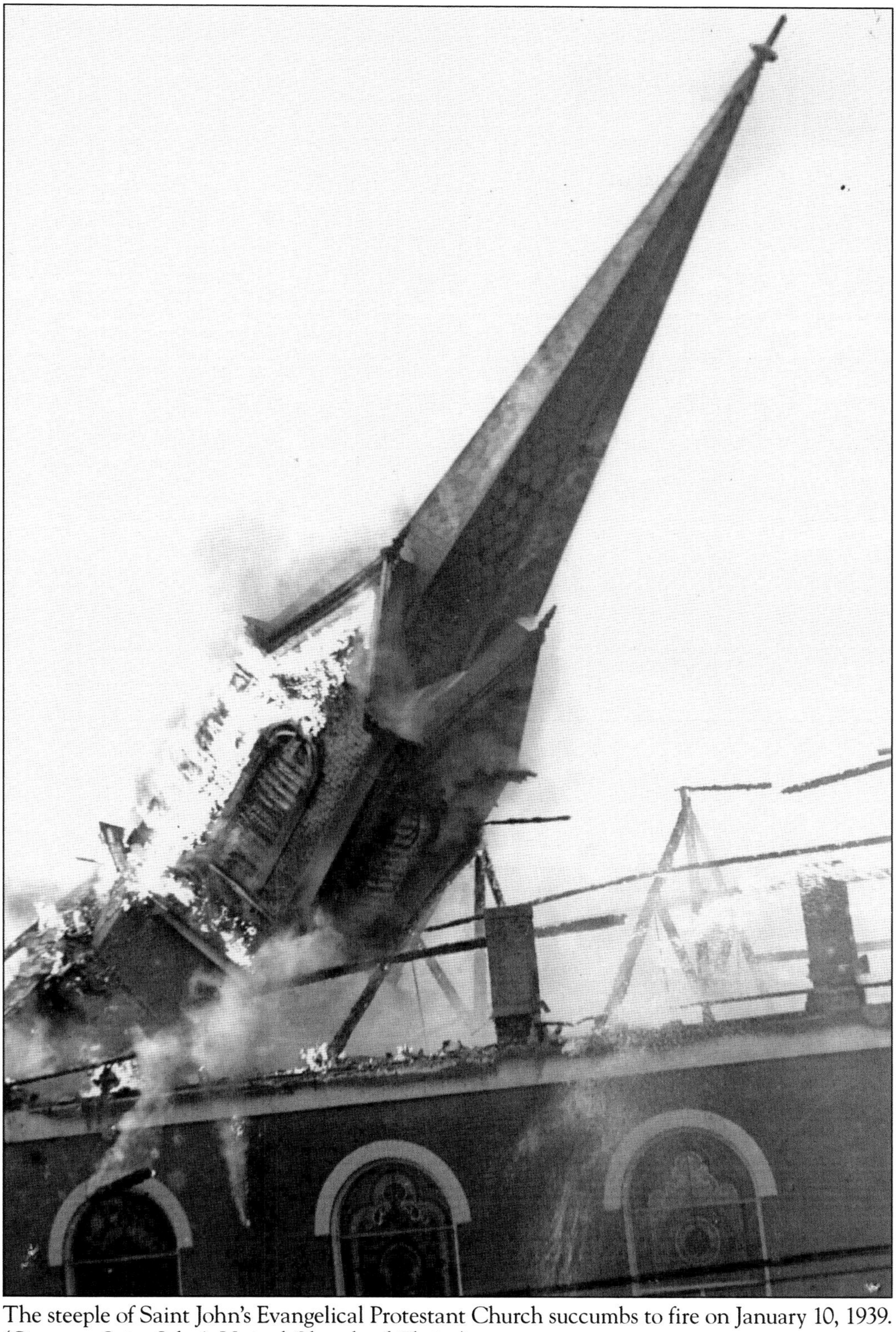

The steeple of Saint John's Evangelical Protestant Church succumbs to fire on January 10, 1939. (Courtesy Saint John's United Church of Christ.)

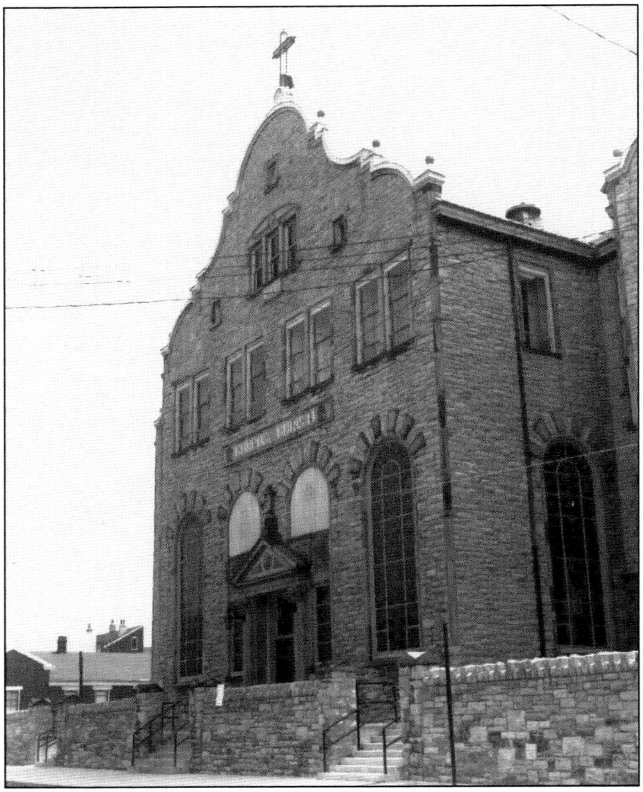

Corpus Christi was the first Catholic parish to be established in Campbell County. The original church lot was donated by Henry Goodman of Cincinnati in 1844. Mr. Goodman was a non-Catholic, but he was disturbed by the anti-Catholic demonstrations and riots taking place in other parts of the country. The cornerstone for this new church at Ninth and Isabella Streets was laid in 1902. Corpus Christi later closed and joined three other Newport parishes to form the Holy Spirit Parish. (Courtesy Campbell County Historical Society.)

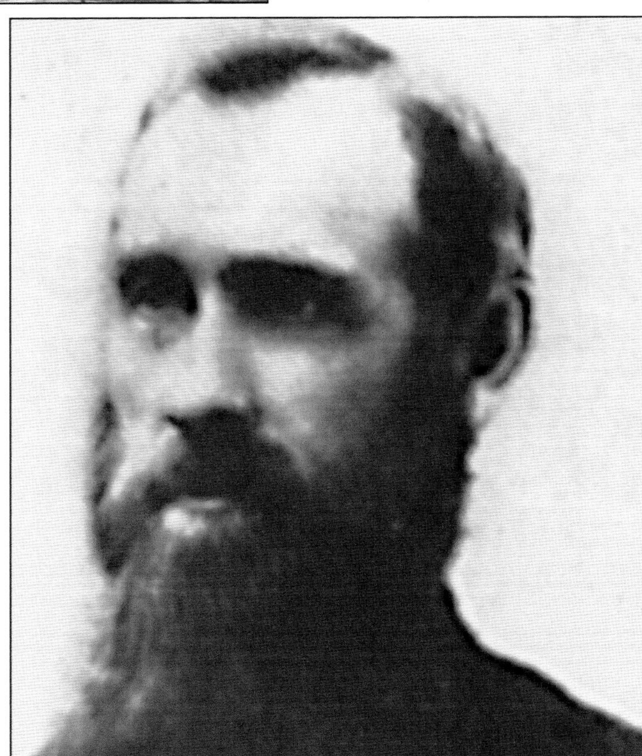

Rev. Charles Boeswald, a German native born in 1820, founded the Corpus Christi Parish in Newport. His life ended in 1855 after being struck in the head by a rock thrown by members of the "Know-Nothing Party," a nativist political movement whose targets included Catholics. (Courtesy Diocese of Covington.)

Although the church congregation had been founded earlier in 1844, the cornerstone for this home of Saint Paul's Episcopal Church was laid in 1871. Gen. James Taylor was one of the early church members. This historic limestone structure is one of Newport's most extraordinary architectural marvels remaining. (Courtesy Kenton County Public Library.)

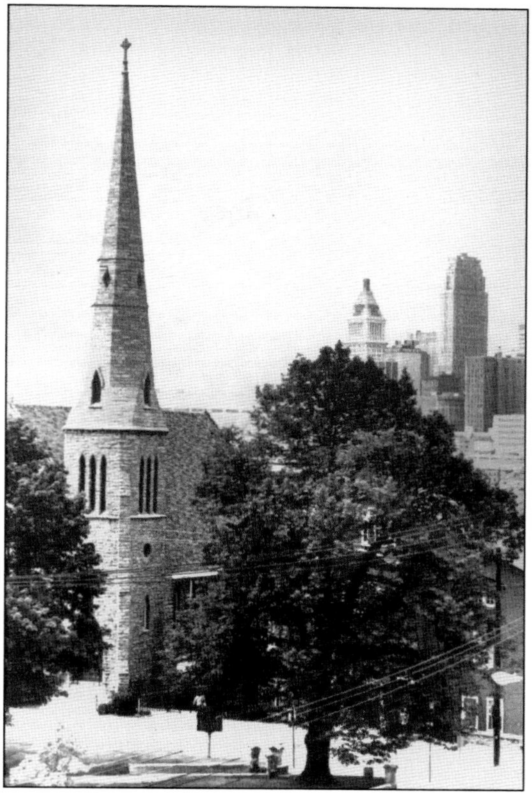

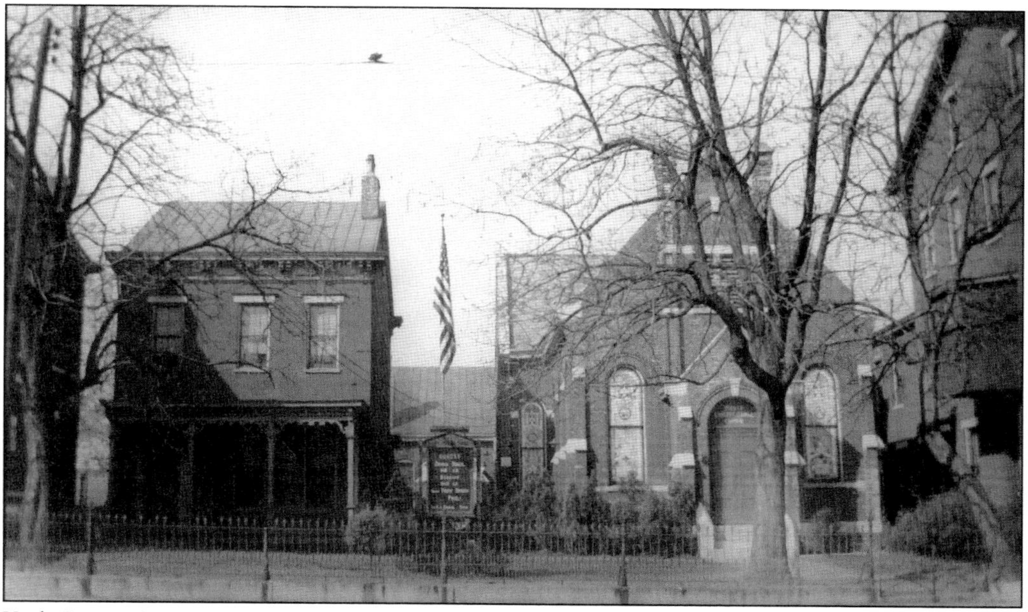

York Street Congregational Church, founded in 1877, was located at York and Ringgold (later Eighth) Streets. (Courtesy Campbell County Historical Society.)

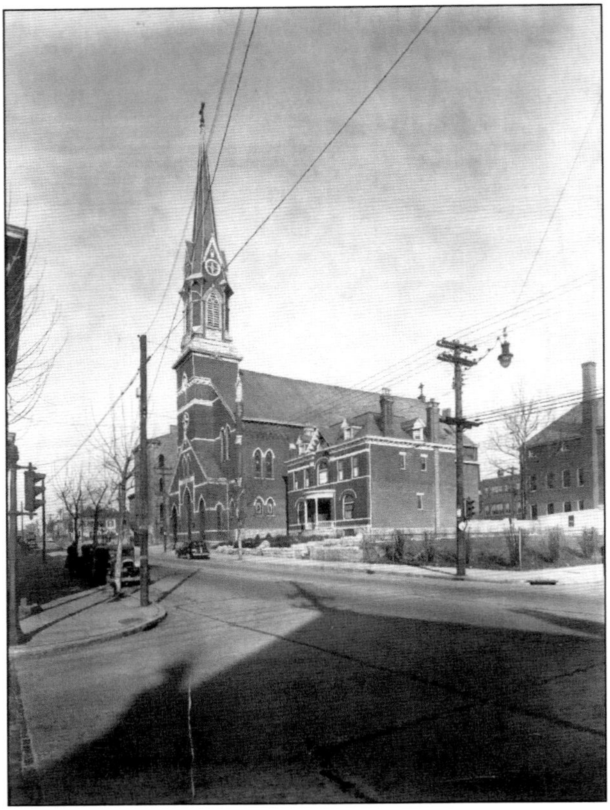

Immaculate Conception Church at 124 West Fifth Street was made up of a congregation of English-speaking Catholics, with their first mass celebrated on December 25, 1855. Parishioners would participate in their final mass in 1969; they subsequently merged with Corpus Christi Church. (Courtesy Campbell County Historical Society.)

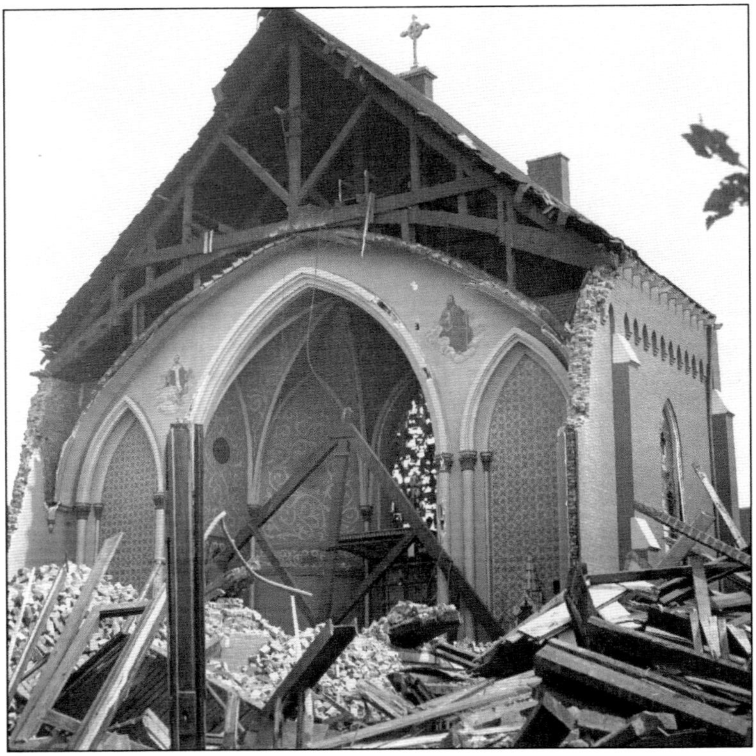

Somberly, demolition of Immaculate Conception Church took place in August of 1969. (Courtesy Campbell County Historical Society.)

Seven charter members organized the First Baptist Church of Newport in 1812. Initially gathering in the courthouse and various schoolhouses, they ultimately moved into this building at Eighth and York Streets, which was previously occupied by the Congregational Church. (Courtesy Kenton County Public Library.)

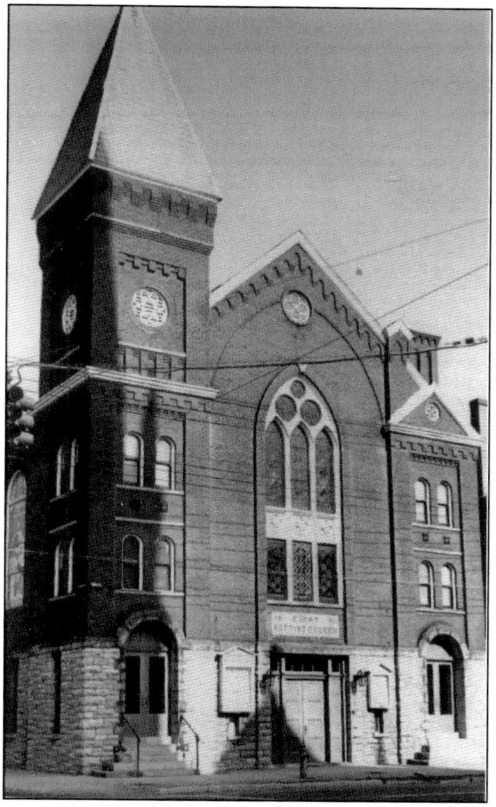

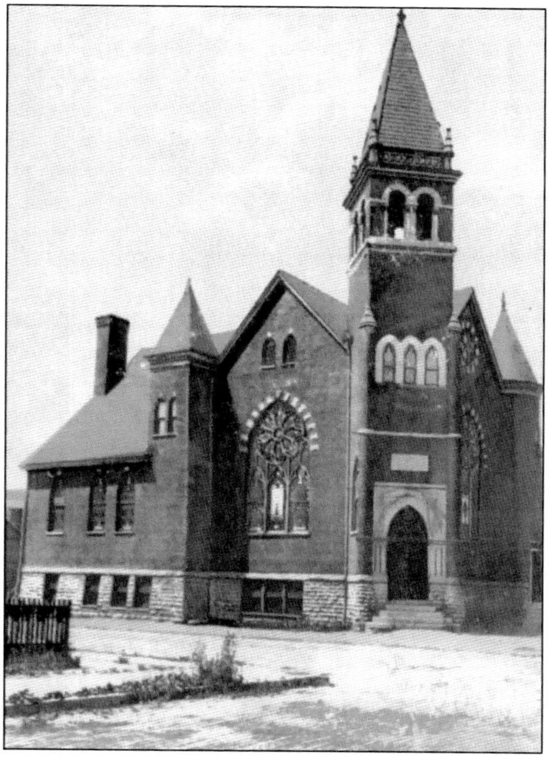

The congregation of Saint Mark's Lutheran Church moved into their new home at Eighth and Monroe Streets in 1897. Charles Wiedemann (son of Wiedemann Brewery founder) and August Helmbold (Newport mayor) were two well-known members of the church. (From the Collection of the Public Library of Cincinnati and Hamilton County.)

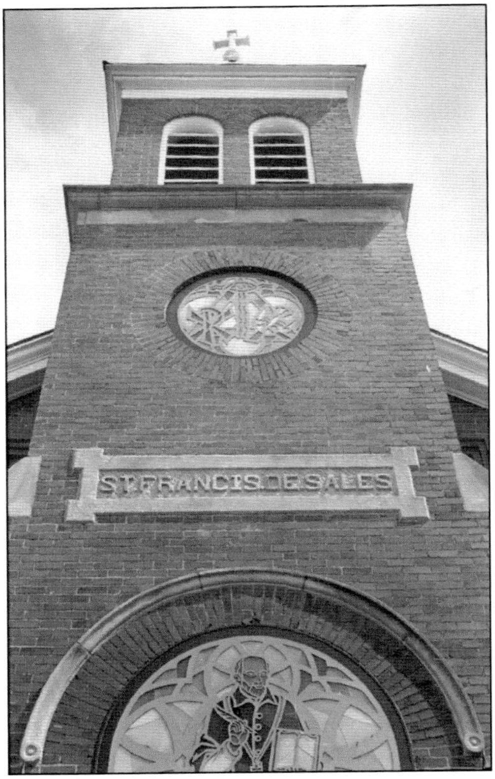

The Saint Francis de Sales Parish originated when a small number of families in the Cote Brilliante district of Newport broke off from Saint Stephen Parish. The dedication of the church took place in 1912. Saint Francis de Sales, Saint Vincent de Paul, Corpus Christi, and Saint Stephen Parishes have since unified to form the Holy Spirit Parish. (Courtesy Campbell County Historical Society.)

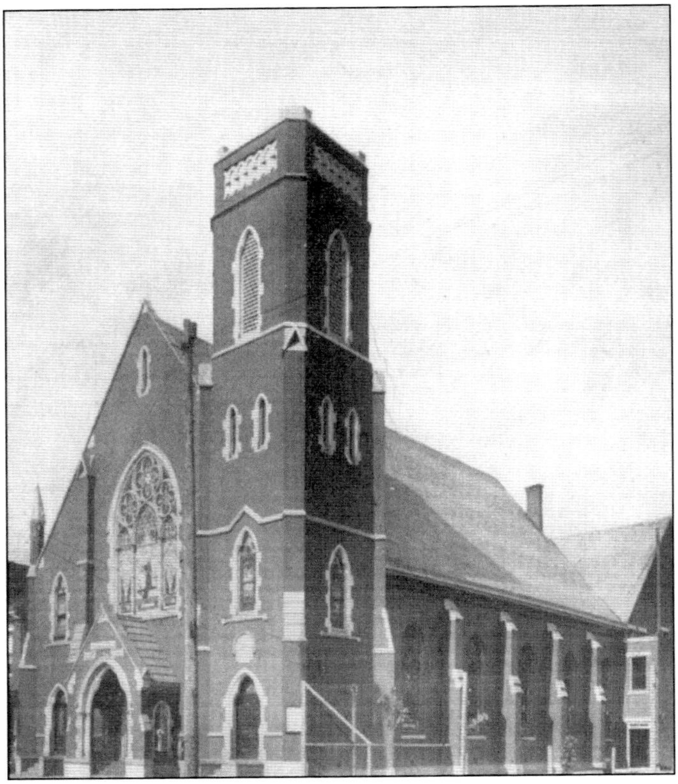

Grace Methodist-Episcopal Church at 111 East Sixth Street was built in 1866. In this photo, the steeple is gone. It was destroyed during the tornado of 1915 and never replaced. (Courtesy Special Collections and Archives, Northern Kentucky University.)

Seen here in this undated photo, the Saint Vincent de Paul School opened in September of 1916. The school enrollment at that time totaled 70 pupils. (Courtesy Sisters of Divine Providence.)

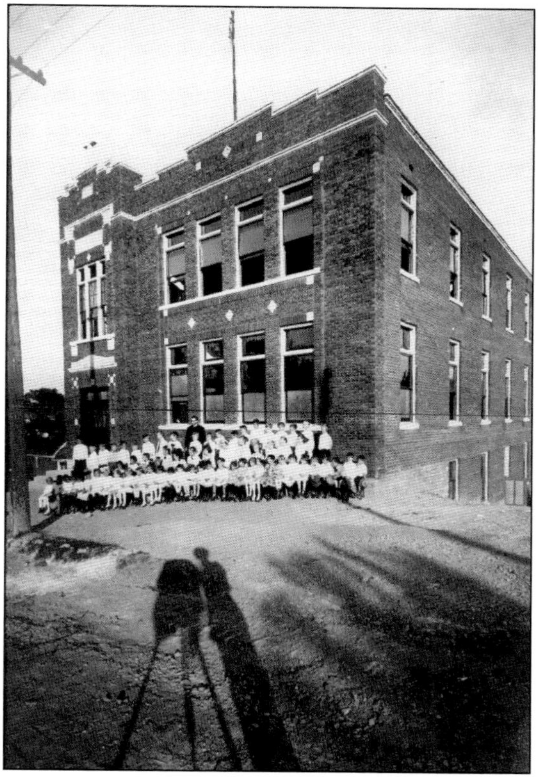

Sitting between Saratoga and Monmouth Streets, the Fourth Street School originated as the Newport Academy, established in 1798. The academy was built on land donated by Newport's founder Gen. James Taylor. Over the years, several school buildings have existed on this site. Newport children continue to attend school on this same site in a newer building that was completed in 1936. (Courtesy Paul Schuerman.)

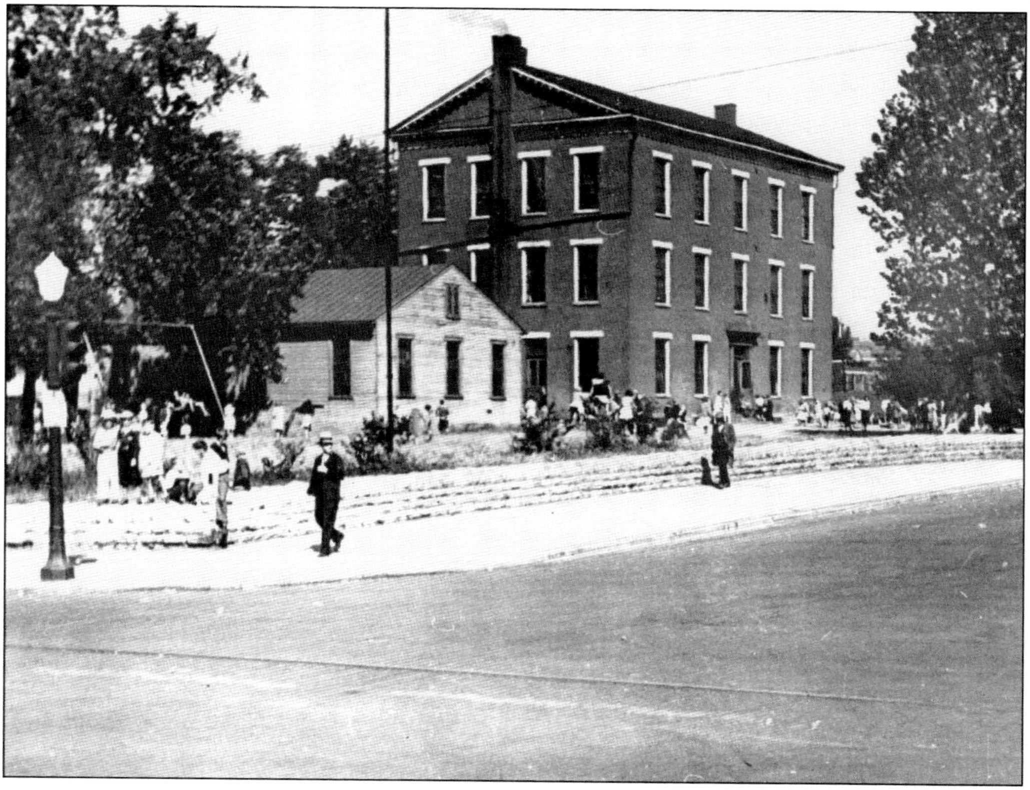

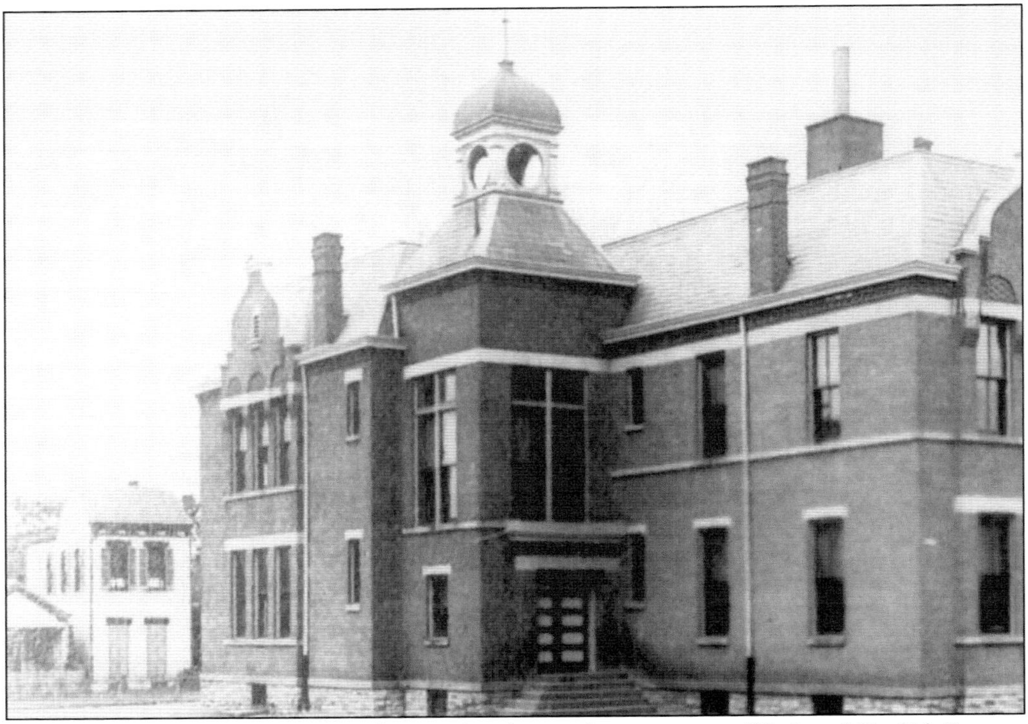

York Street School was constructed in 1886 at the northwest corner of York and Twelfth Streets. The structure was demolished in 1959, and the A.D. Owens School now occupies the site. (Courtesy Campbell County Historical Society.)

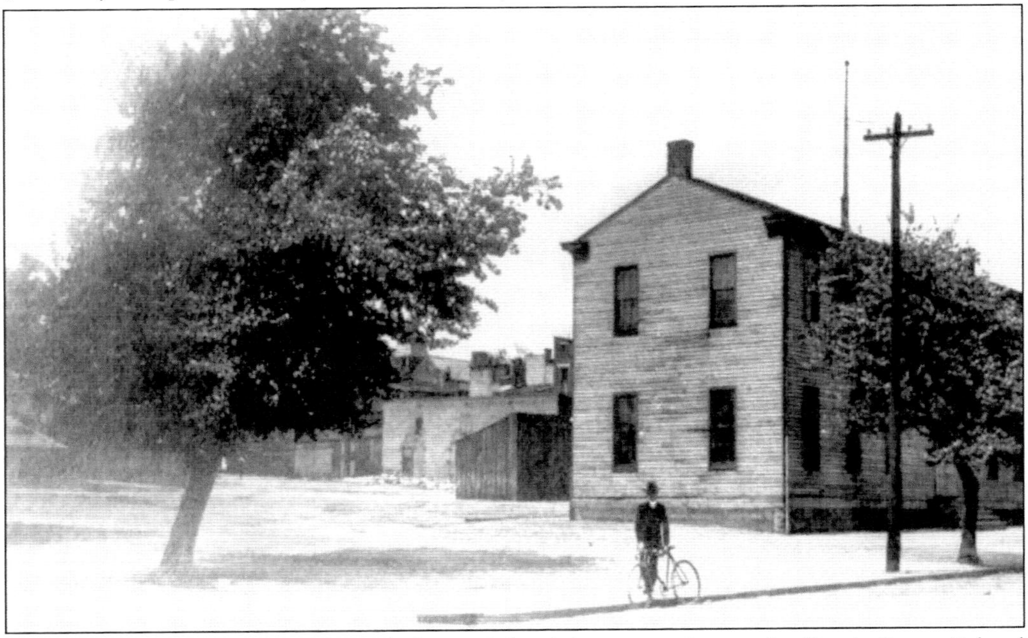

This is a 1904 view of the old Ninth Street School, known earlier as the Harris Street School (Harris Street was later renamed Ninth Street). Records identify the first principal as Emma B. Smith, earning an annual salary of $760 per year, with teachers receiving $500 per year. (Courtesy Campbell County Historical Society.)

Known as the Arnold Seminary in 1890, this school was previously called the Cabot Street School and the Central Avenue School. The earliest record of this school dates back to 1867. Located on Central Avenue, between Fifth and Sixth Streets, the building shown here in 1904 was torn down in 1927 to build the new Arnold School. It, too, was later razed; the Campbell County Jail was built on the site. (Courtesy Campbell County Historical Society.)

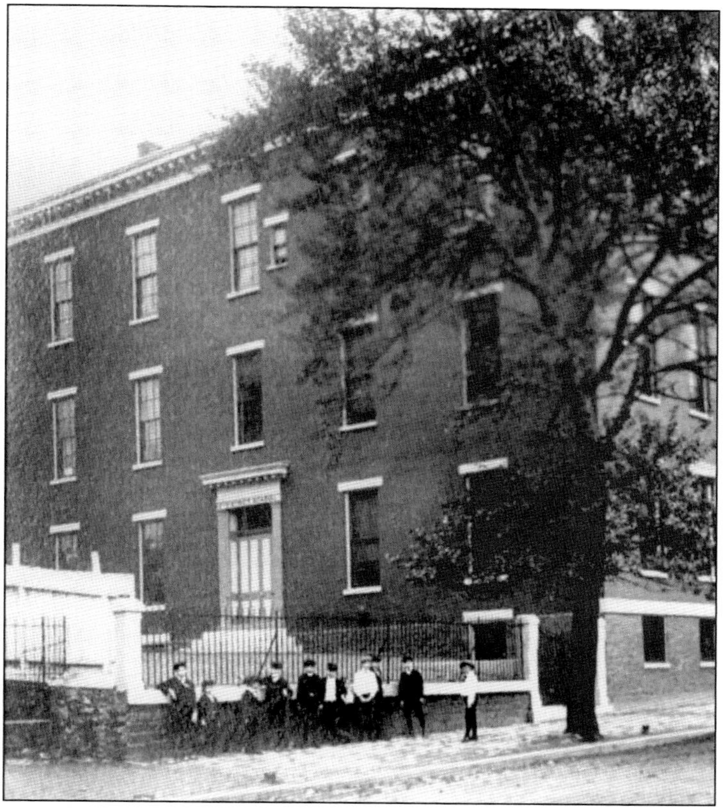

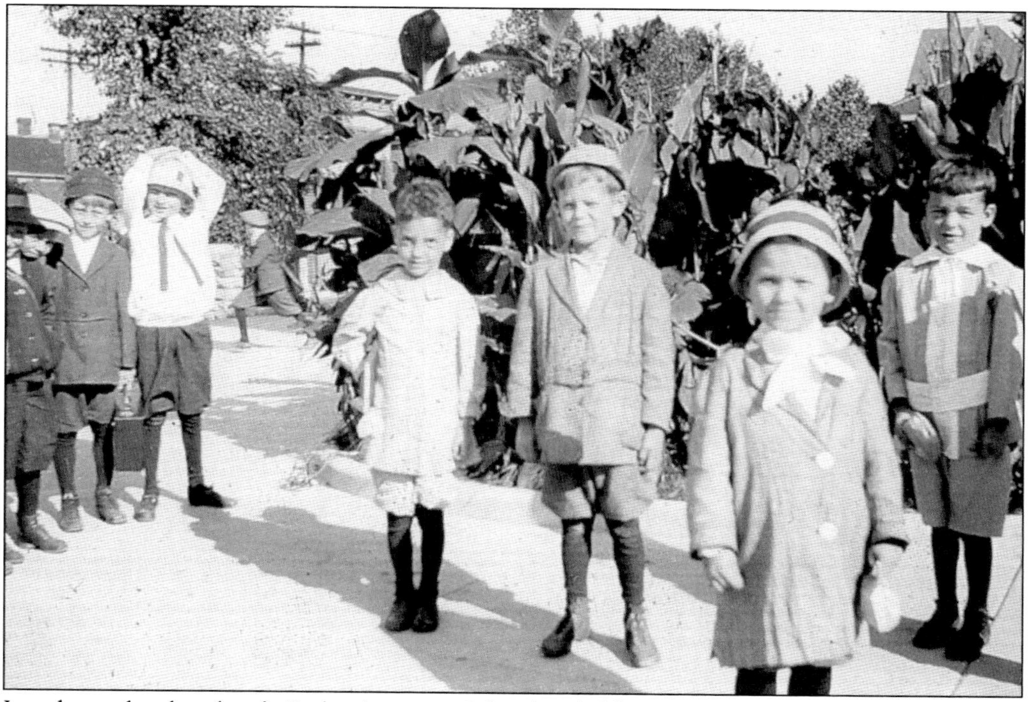

In the schoolyard of Park Avenue School, children pose in their school attire. (Courtesy Peter Garrett.)

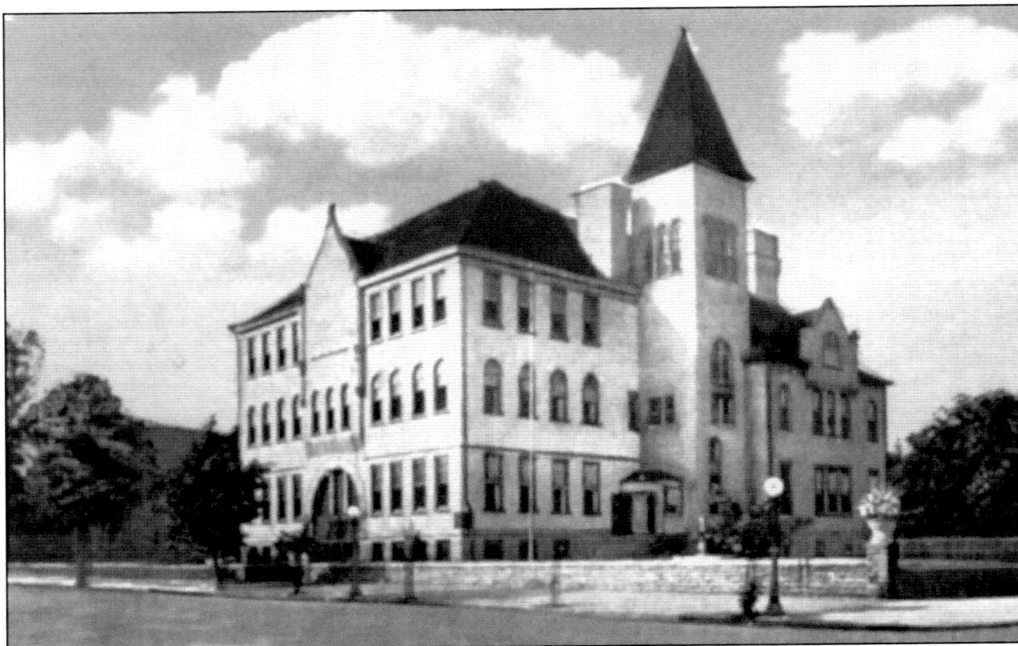

Park Avenue School opened in 1890. The building survived a significant fire in 1940, and it later became Dora Cummings Elementary School. It closed in 1980. (Courtesy Kenton County Public Library.)

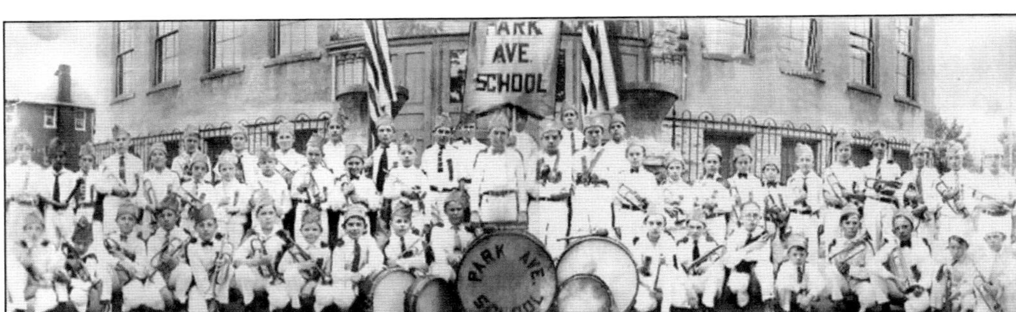

This 1929 image showcases the Drum and Bugle Corps of Park Avenue School, which was undoubtedly a popular diversion from classroom activities. (Courtesy Kirschner family.)

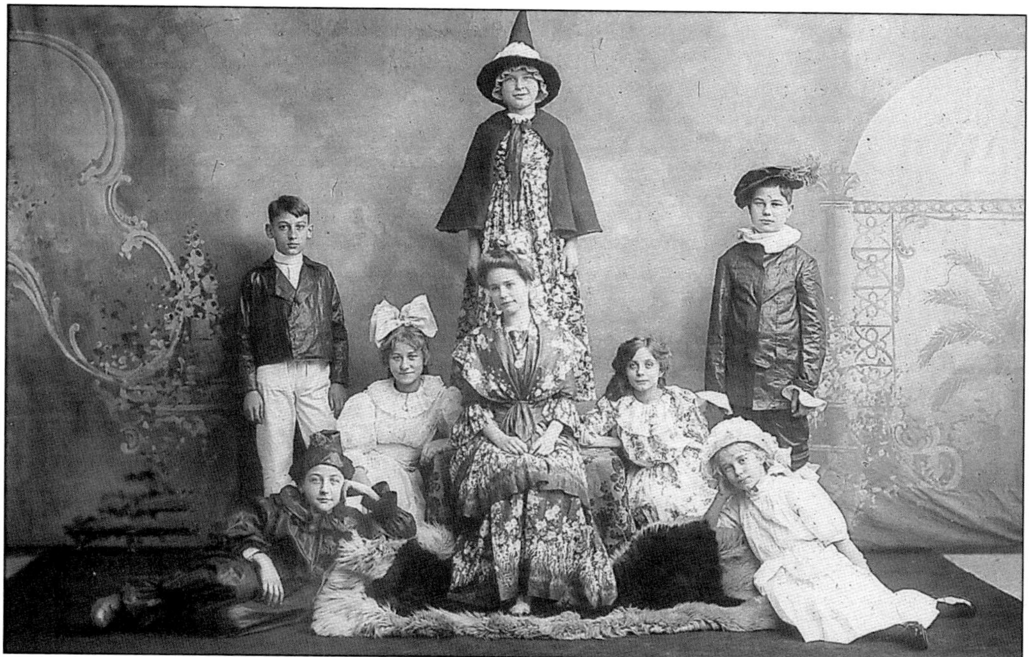

Pupils perform in a musical play at Park Avenue School on December 12, 1913. (Courtesy Peter Garrett.)

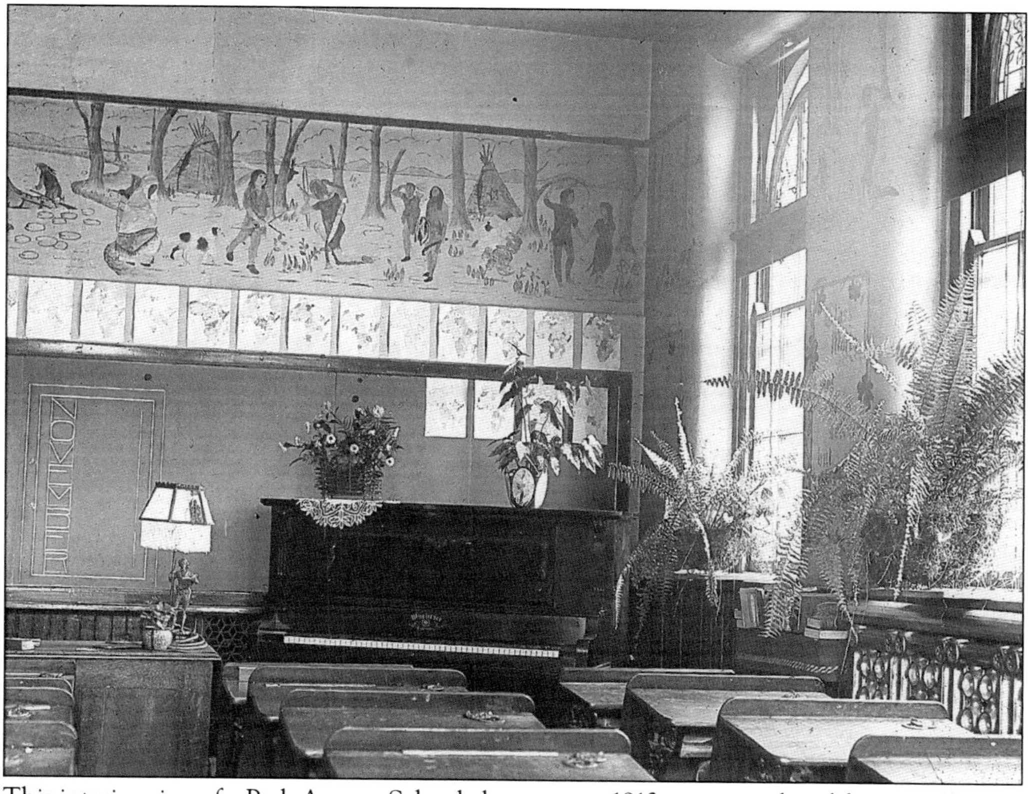

This interior view of a Park Avenue School classroom, c. 1913, was reproduced from a collection of glass slide images of the school. (Courtesy Peter Garrett.)

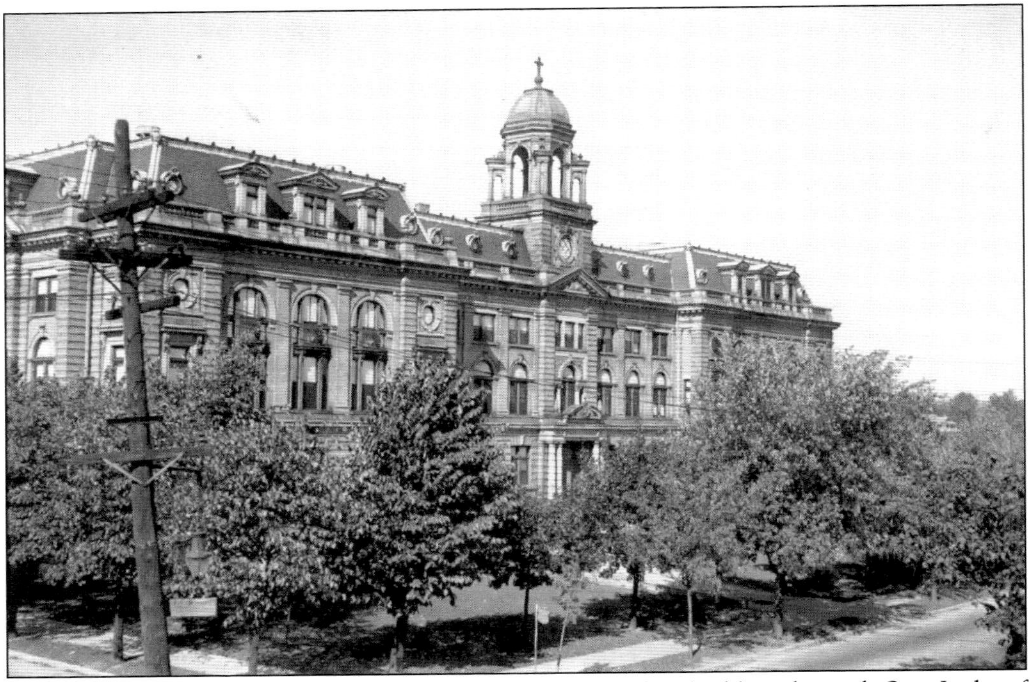

Designed by Cincinnati architect Samuel Hannaford, this building housed Our Lady of Providence, a Catholic girls' school. The school merged with Newport Catholic High School to form Newport Central Catholic in 1983. Originally called Academy Notre Dame of Providence, this building was dedicated in 1903 by Bishop Maes. It is now home to the Hannaford Suites. (Courtesy Sisters of Divine Providence.)

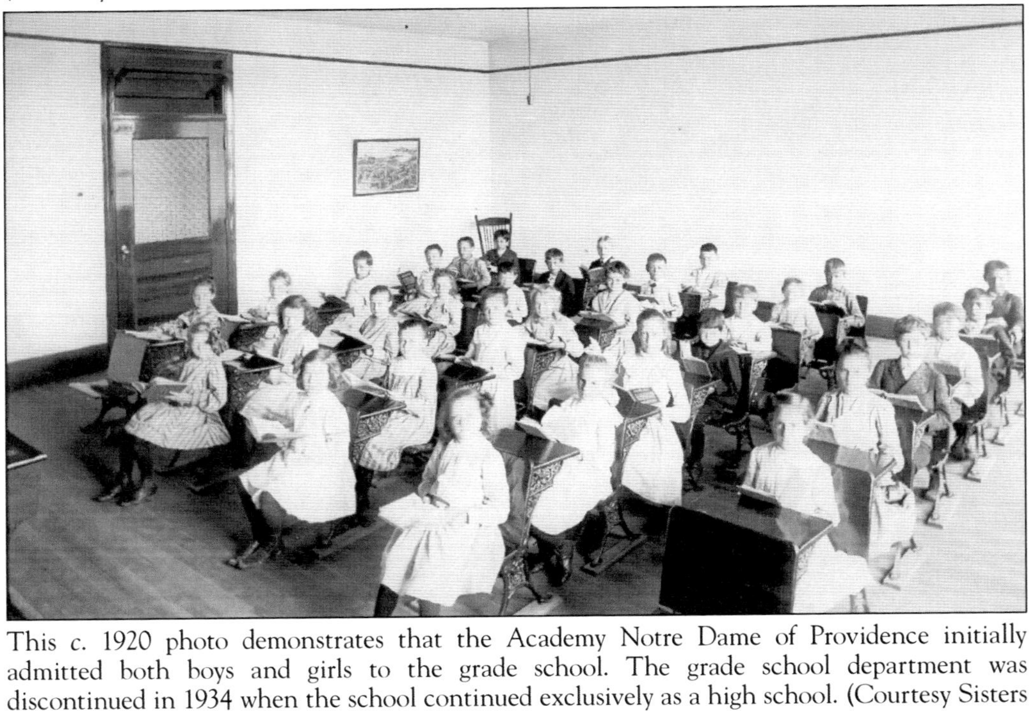

This c. 1920 photo demonstrates that the Academy Notre Dame of Providence initially admitted both boys and girls to the grade school. The grade school department was discontinued in 1934 when the school continued exclusively as a high school. (Courtesy Sisters of Divine Providence.)

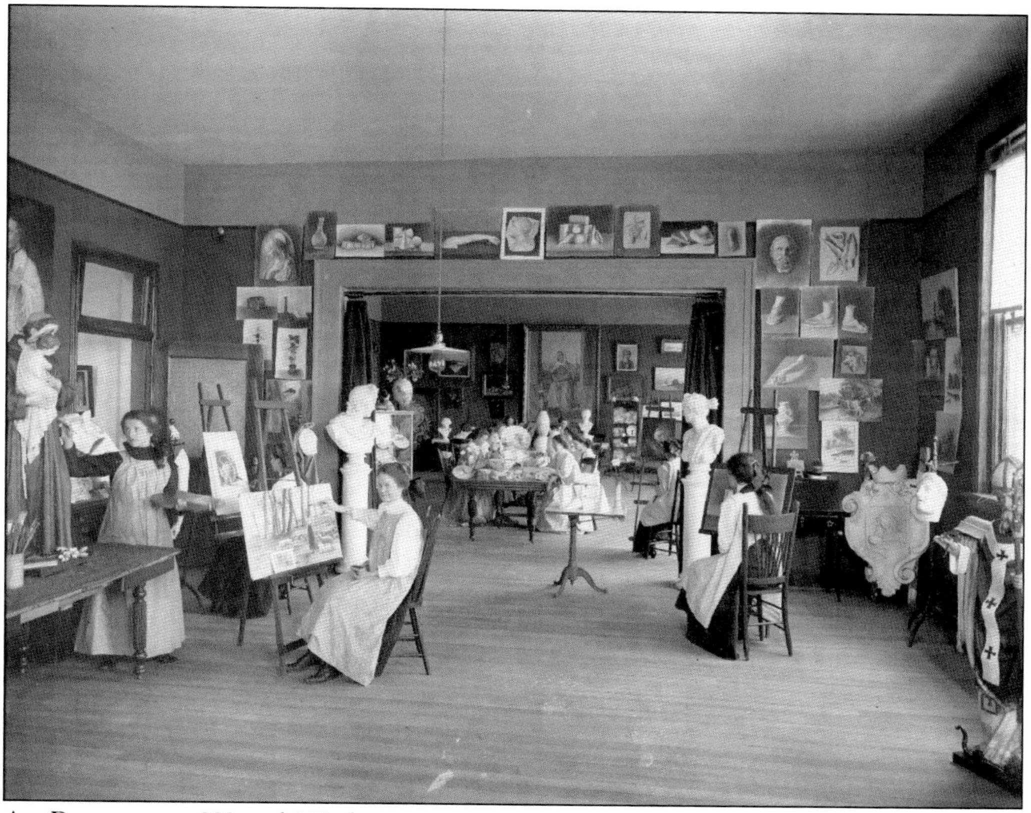

Art Departments 202 and 203 show some impressive products of the class. Sr. Marie du Sacre Coeur Houlne is seen on the far left; Sr. M. Adela Erpenbeck is on the far right. (Courtesy Sisters of Divine Providence.)

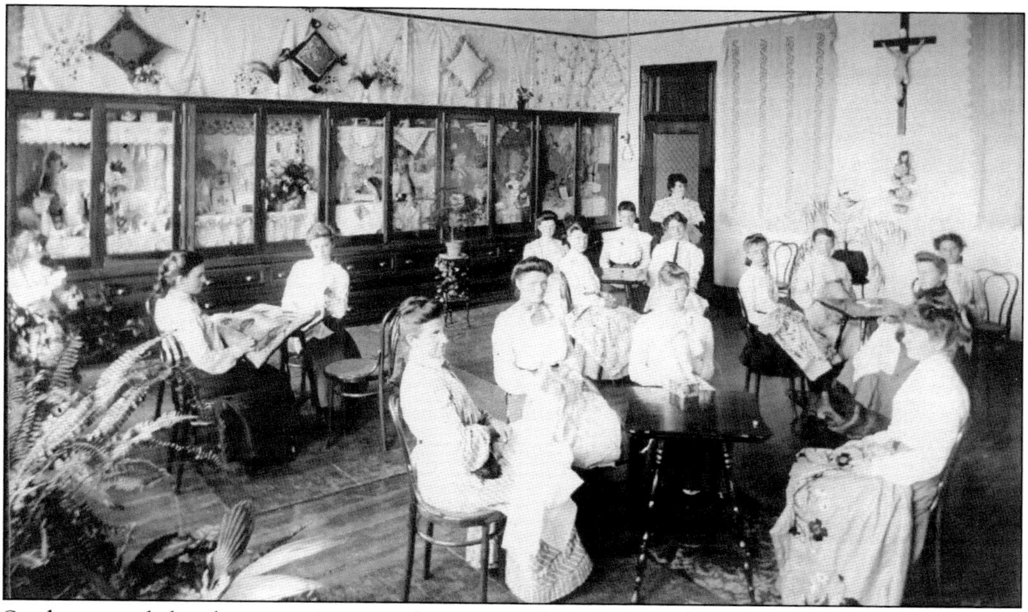

Students work busily on projects in the sewing department of the Academy Notre Dame of Providence, *c.* 1905. (Courtesy Sisters of Divine Providence.)

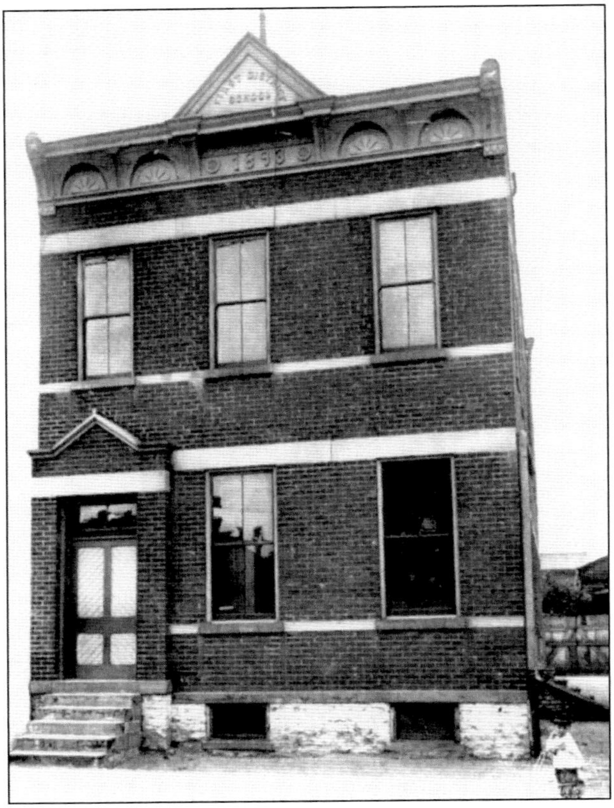

Commonly referred to as the "Colored School," the Southgate School was Newport's first educational facility for African Americans. Prior to public school availability for African Americans, their education oftentimes took place in secret locations or "underground schools." The Southgate School's history came to a conclusion in 1955 with the beginning of desegregation. (Courtesy Kenton County Public Library and Theodore H. Harris.)

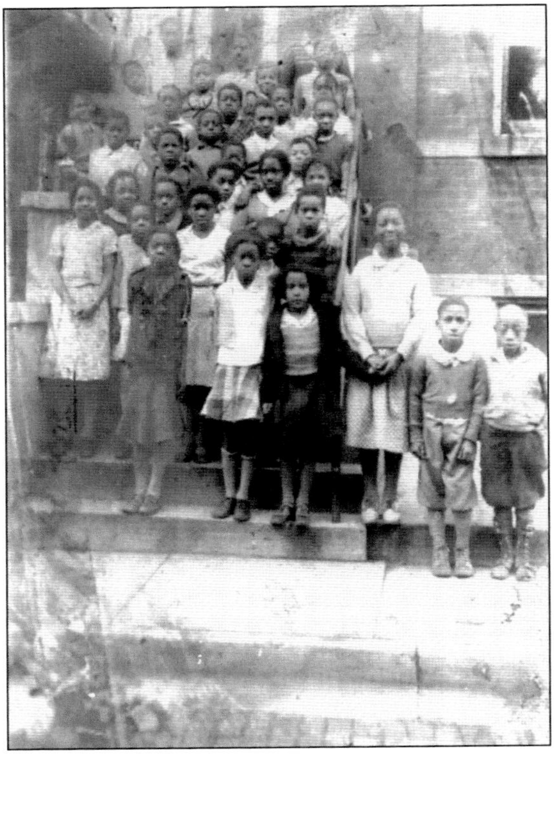

The pupils of the Southgate School in this c. 1900 photo are unidentified. (Courtesy Theodore H. Harris.)

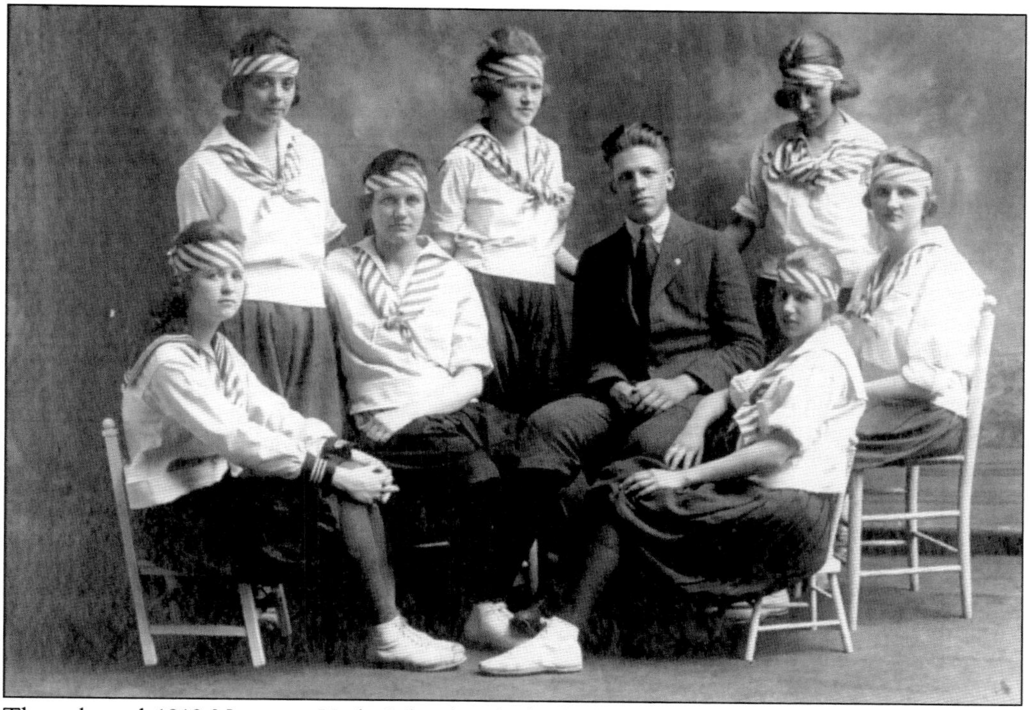

The talented 1919 Newport High School girls' basketball team suffered only one defeat that season. Pictured from left to right are (standing) Gertrude Rummell, May Jarvis, Marguerite Kountz; (sitting) Dorothy Listerman, Edna Wilhelmi, Herman Reed (coach), Wilma Reimert, and Dot Gilker. (Courtesy Mr. and Mrs. Richard Thompson.)

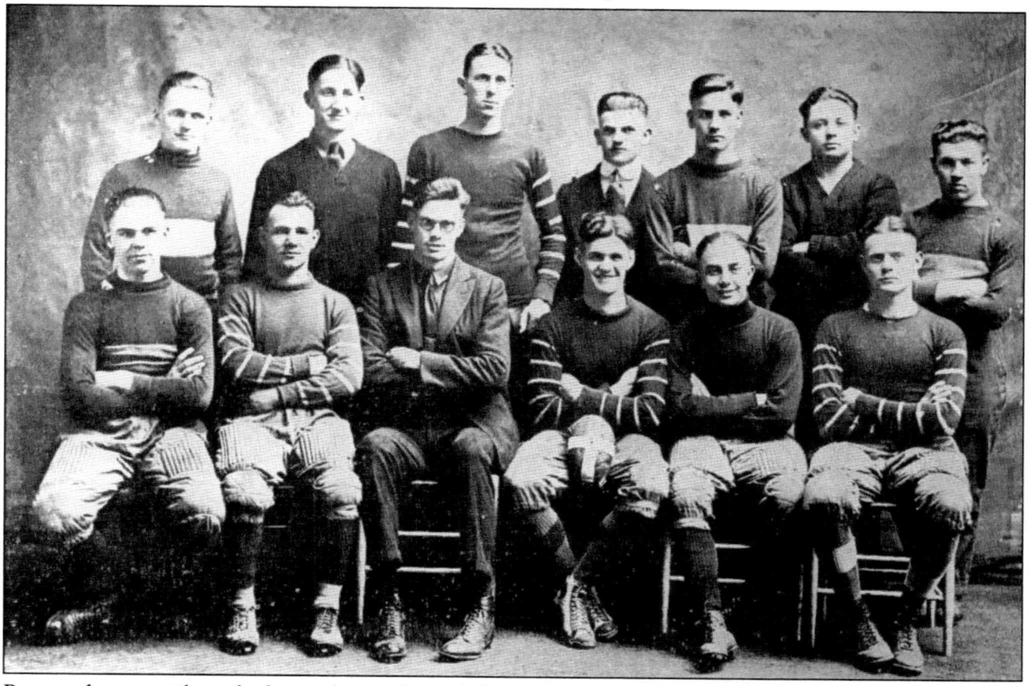

Pictured are unidentified members of the 1920 Newport High School football team. (Courtesy Campbell County Historical Society.)

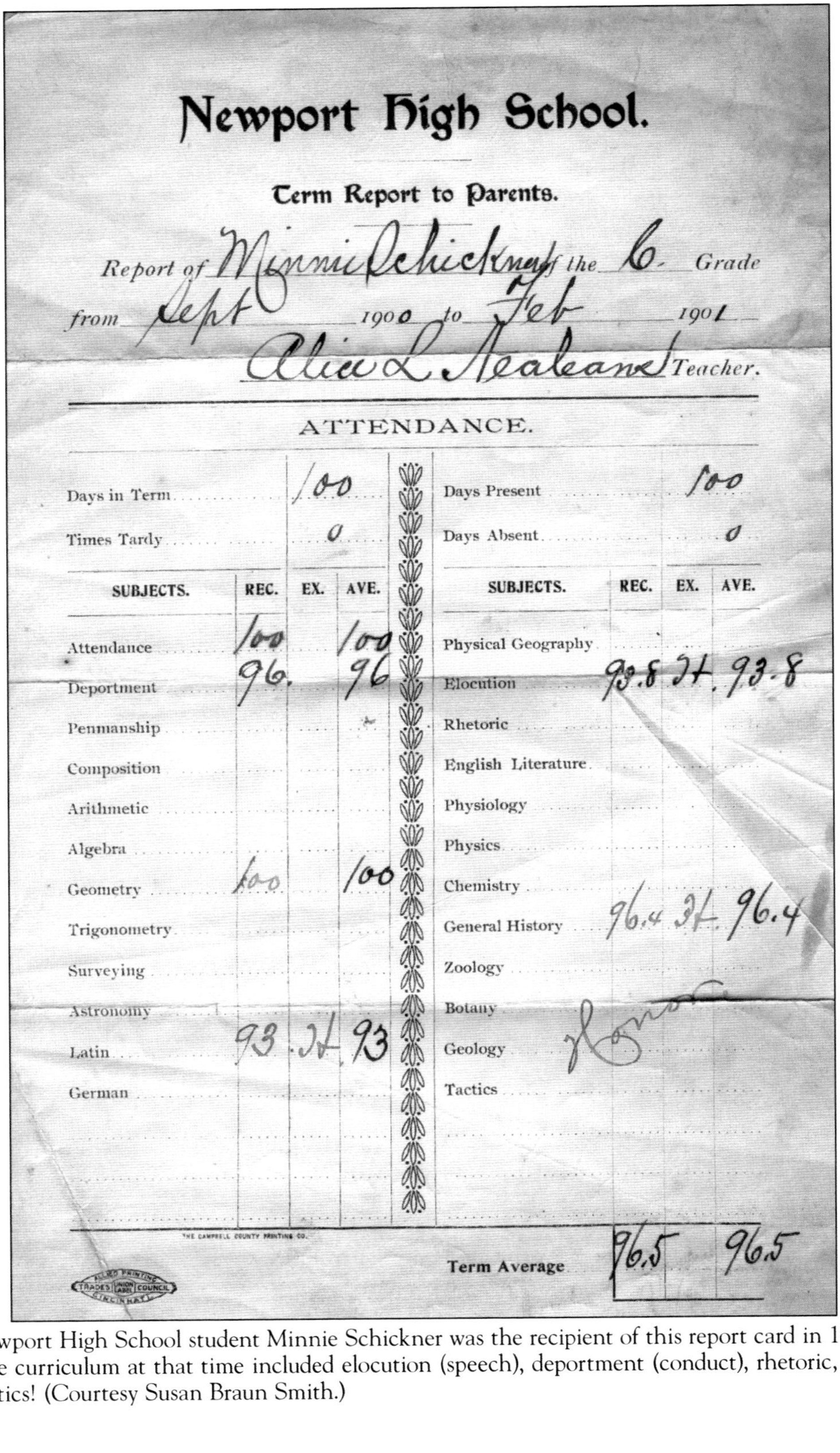

Newport High School.

Term Report to Parents.

Report of Minnie Schickner *of the* C *Grade*

from Sept *1900 to* Feb *1901*

Alice L. Nealeans *Teacher.*

ATTENDANCE.

Days in Term	100	Days Present	100
Times Tardy	0	Days Absent	0

SUBJECTS.	REC.	EX.	AVE.	SUBJECTS.	REC.	EX.	AVE.
Attendance	100		100	Physical Geography			
Deportment	96.		96	Elocution	93.8	Ft.	93.8
Penmanship				Rhetoric			
Composition				English Literature			
Arithmetic				Physiology			
Algebra				Physics			
Geometry	100		100	Chemistry			
Trigonometry				General History	96.4	Ft.	96.4
Surveying				Zoology			
Astronomy				Botany			
Latin	93	Ft.	93	Geology	Honor		
German				Tactics			

THE CAMPBELL COUNTY PRINTING CO.

Term Average	96.5	96.5

ALLIED PRINTING TRADES UNION LABEL COUNCIL CINCINNATI

Newport High School student Minnie Schickner was the recipient of this report card in 1900. The curriculum at that time included elocution (speech), deportment (conduct), rhetoric, and tactics! (Courtesy Susan Braun Smith.)

Here is Minnie Schickner at a younger age. The Schickner family resided in Newport for many years. (Courtesy Susan Braun Smith.)

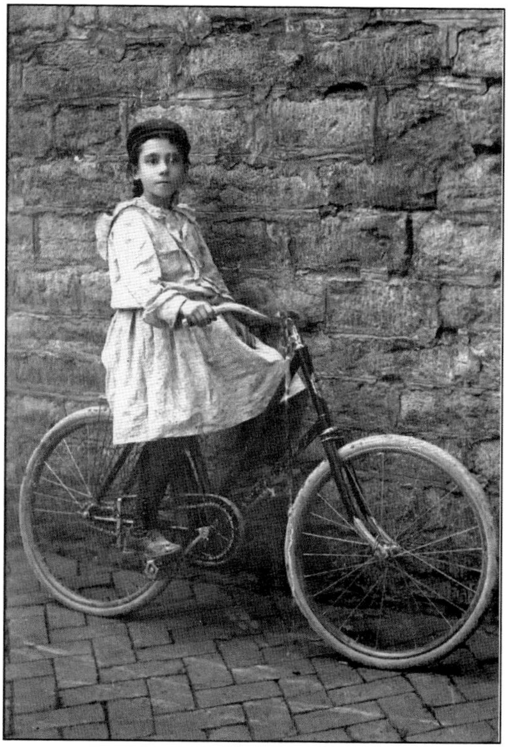

This Eighth Street School structure was built in 1872. With the site previously serving as the city cemetery, construction of an earlier building in 1847 necessitated movement of graves to Evergreen Cemetery. This building has also been known as the Ringgold Street School building (before Ringgold became Eighth Street) and the "old" Newport High School. (Courtesy Campbell County Historical Society.)

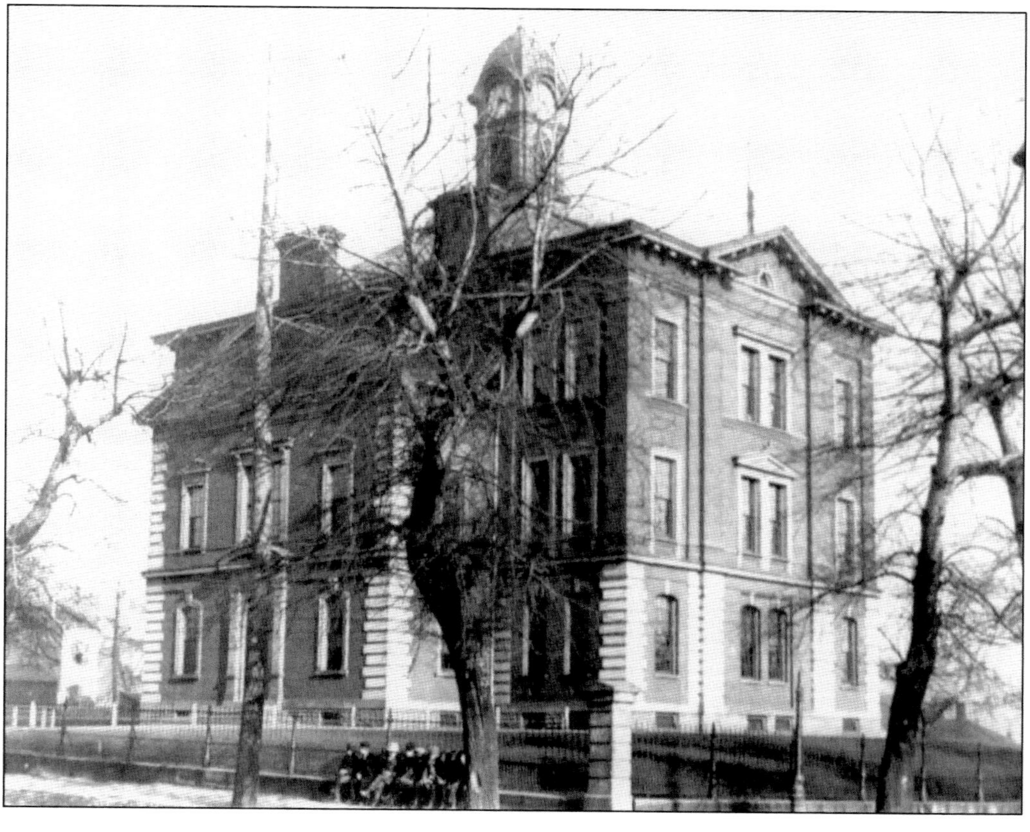

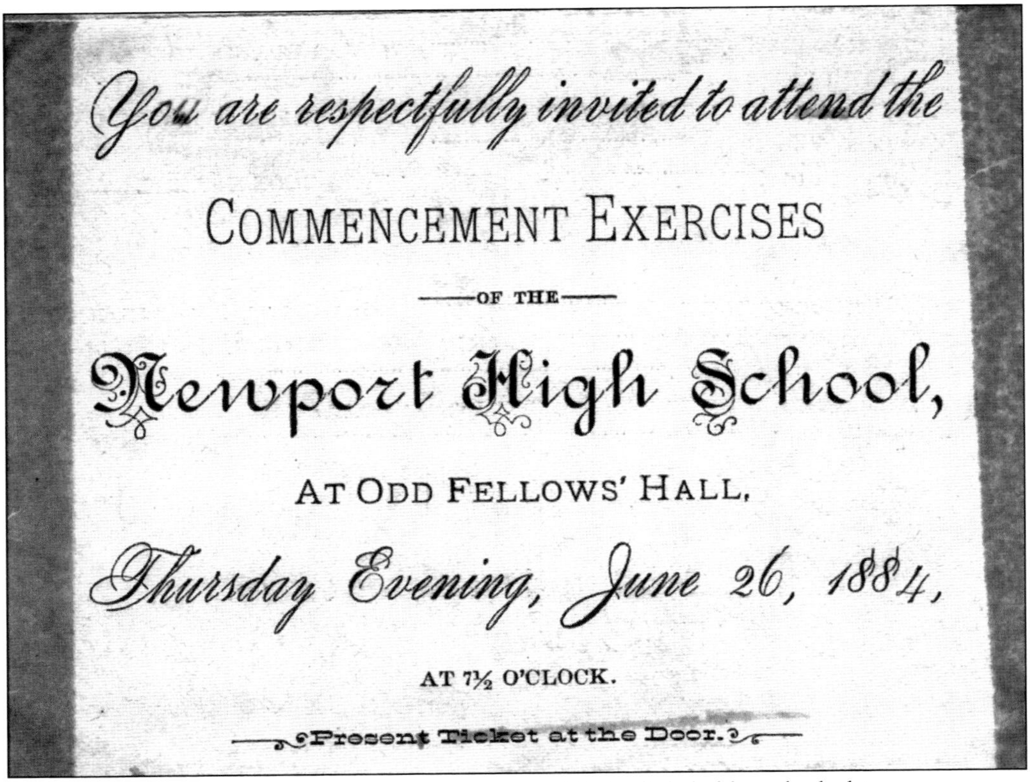

You are respectfully invited to attend the

COMMENCEMENT EXERCISES

—OF THE—

Newport High School,

AT ODD FELLOWS' HALL,

Thursday Evening, June 26, 1884,

AT 7½ O'CLOCK.

—Present Ticket at the Door.—

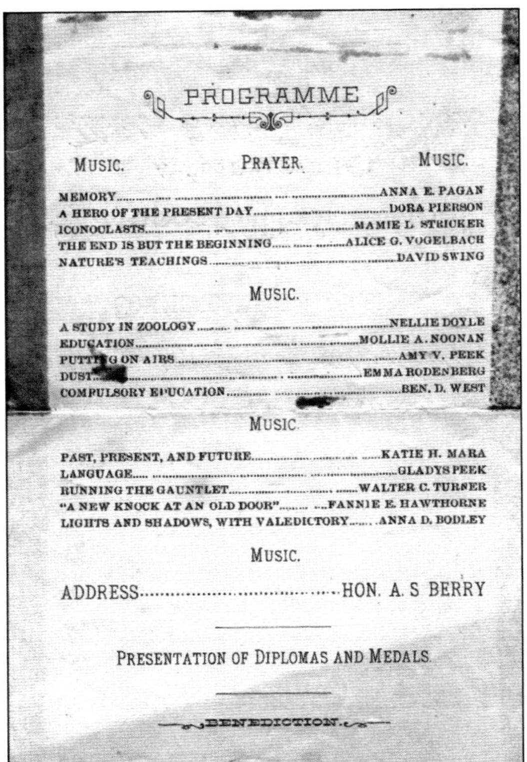

PROGRAMME

MUSIC. PRAYER. MUSIC.

MEMORY..........ANNA E. PAGAN
A HERO OF THE PRESENT DAY..........DORA PIERSON
ICONOCLASTS..........MAMIE L. STRICKER
THE END IS BUT THE BEGINNING..........ALICE G. VOGELBACH
NATURE'S TEACHINGS..........DAVID SWING

MUSIC.

A STUDY IN ZOOLOGY..........NELLIE DOYLE
EDUCATION..........MOLLIE A. NOONAN
PUTTING ON AIRS..........AMY V. PEEK
DUST..........EMMA RODENBERG
COMPULSORY EDUCATION..........BEN. D. WEST

MUSIC.

PAST, PRESENT, AND FUTURE..........KATIE H. MARA
LANGUAGE..........GLADYS PEEK
RUNNING THE GAUNTLET..........WALTER C. TURNER
"A NEW KNOCK AT AN OLD DOOR"..........FANNIE E. HAWTHORNE
LIGHTS AND SHADOWS, WITH VALEDICTORY..........ANNA D. BODLEY

MUSIC.

ADDRESS..........HON. A. S BERRY

PRESENTATION OF DIPLOMAS AND MEDALS.

—BENEDICTION.—

Albeit slightly blemished, this program from Newport High School's 1884 commencement exercises has survived well over a century. (Courtesy Campbell County Historical Society.)

Six

THE RIVERS

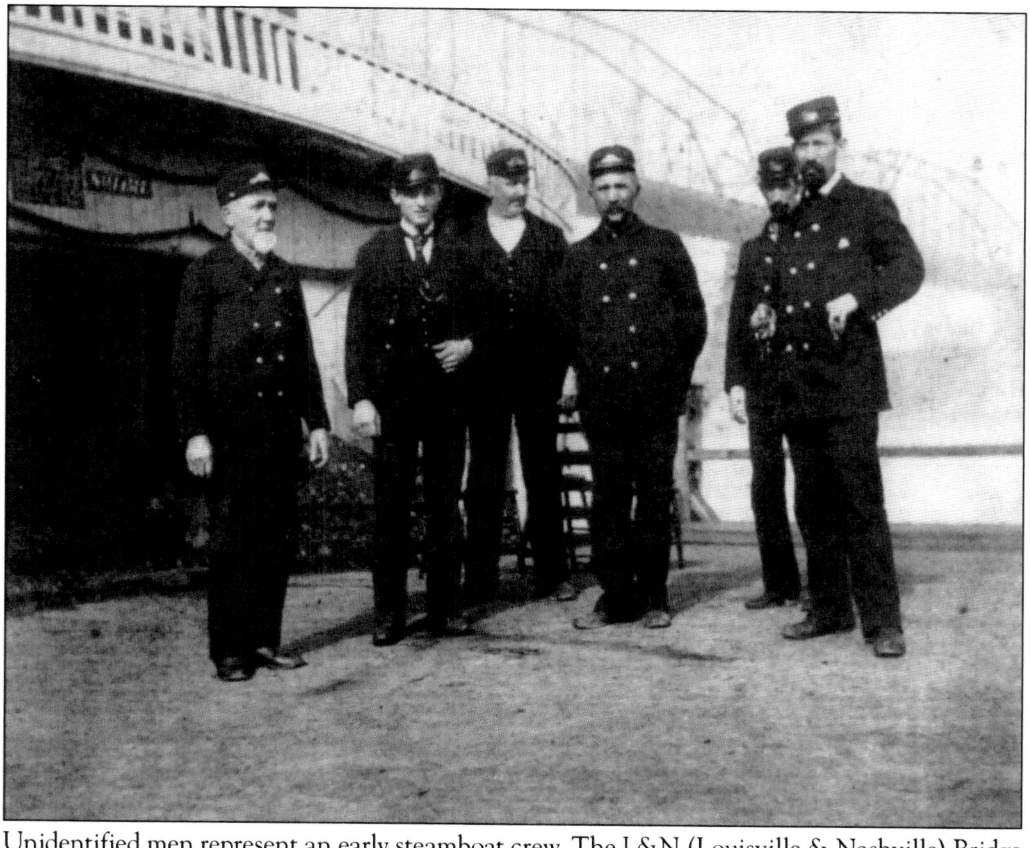

Unidentified men represent an early steamboat crew. The L&N (Louisville & Nashville) Bridge can be seen in the background. (Courtesy Kenton County Public Library.)

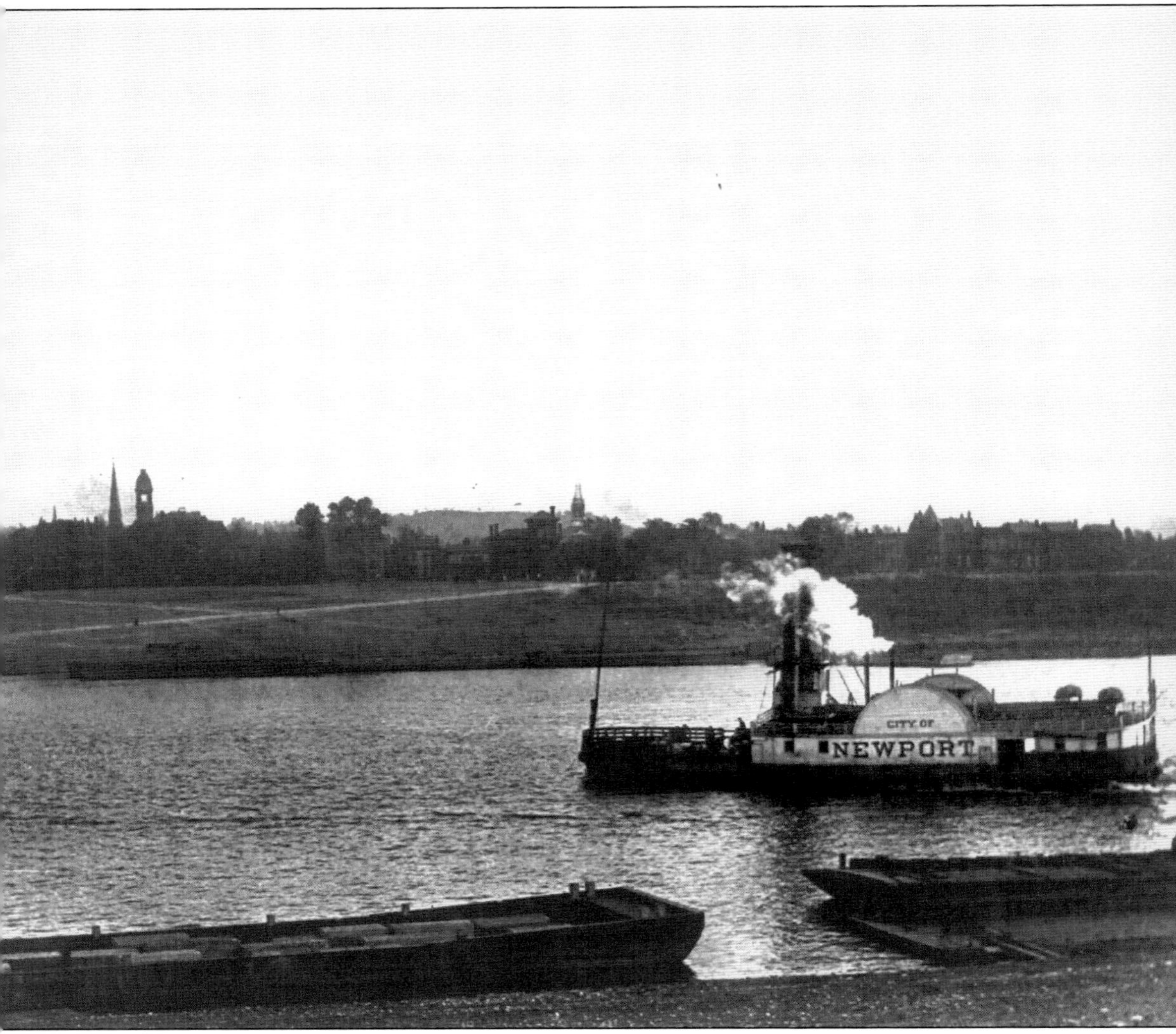

Although the rivers were undoubtedly the lifeline of many early cities, they also hindered access to other areas. Before the bridges, ferry service was a common way to circumvent this barrier. The ferry pictured here ran service between the foot of York Street in Newport to the foot of Broadway in Cincinnati. Newport is seen in the background. (Courtesy Earl Clark Collection.)

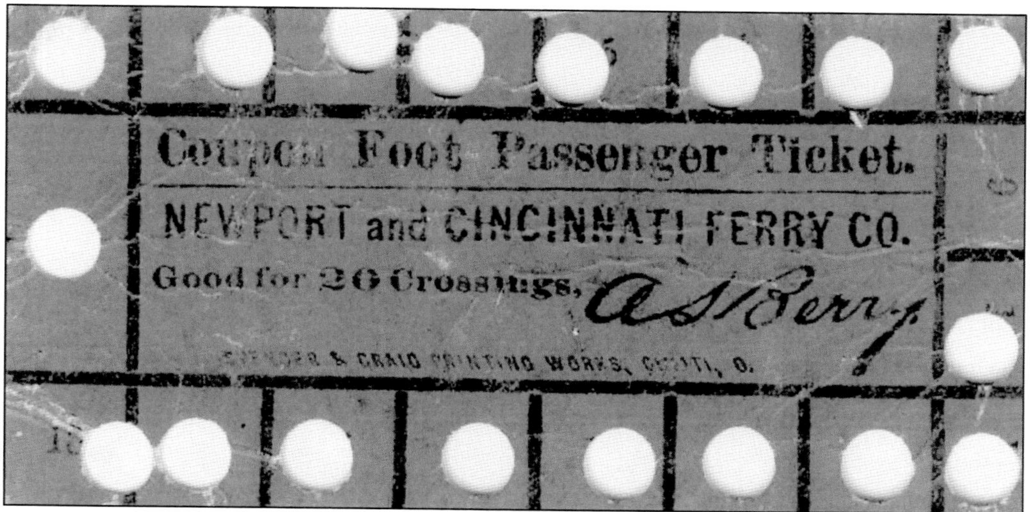

In 1892, 10¢ would buy a coupon good for 20 ferry crossings for a foot passenger traveling between Newport and Cincinnati. (Courtesy Behringer Crawford Museum, Covington, Kentucky.)

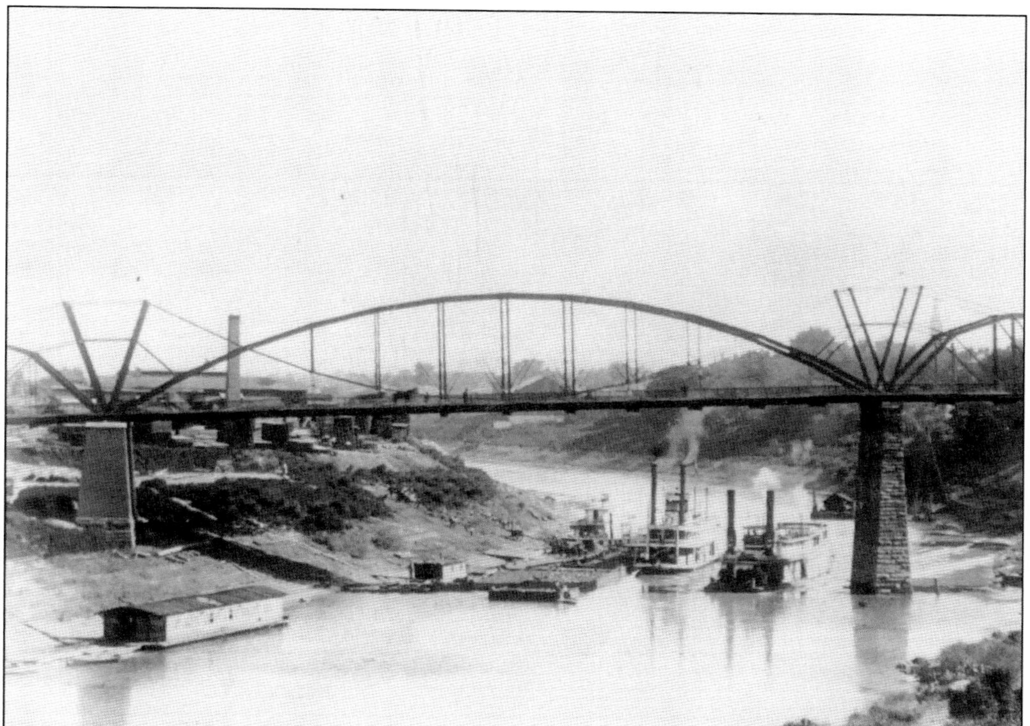

Steamboats on the Licking River cross underneath the Fourth Street Bridge in 1887. This structure was completed in 1886 and replaced the suspension bridge that preceded it. Pedestrian tolls were lifted in 1923; automobile tolls would persist until 1926. After undergoing several renovations over the years, the bridge was replaced again in 1936 by the World War Veterans Memorial Bridge. (From the Collection of the Public Library of Cincinnati and Hamilton County.)

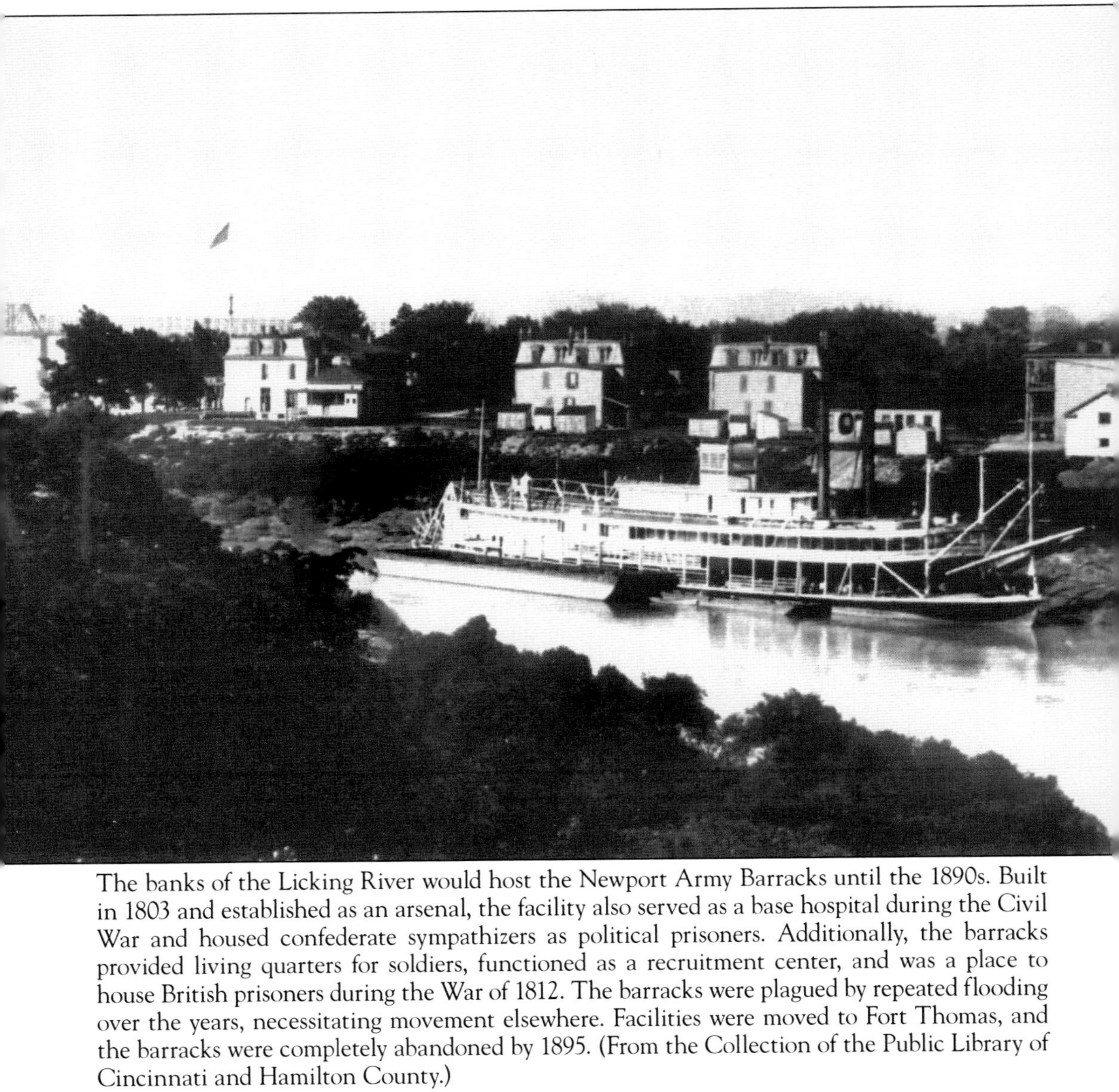

The banks of the Licking River would host the Newport Army Barracks until the 1890s. Built in 1803 and established as an arsenal, the facility also served as a base hospital during the Civil War and housed confederate sympathizers as political prisoners. Additionally, the barracks provided living quarters for soldiers, functioned as a recruitment center, and was a place to house British prisoners during the War of 1812. The barracks were plagued by repeated flooding over the years, necessitating movement elsewhere. Facilities were moved to Fort Thomas, and the barracks were completely abandoned by 1895. (From the Collection of the Public Library of Cincinnati and Hamilton County.)

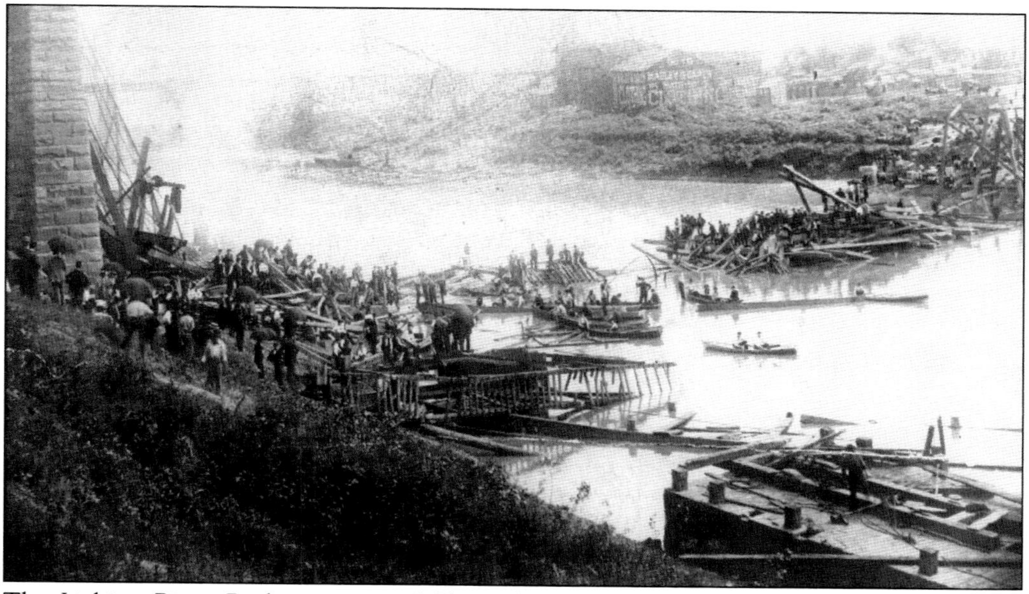

The Licking River Bridge connected Eleventh Street in Newport with Twelfth Street in Covington. The structure collapsed during construction on June 15, 1892, reportedly killing 31 people. Following the catastrophe, the bridge went on to be completed and opened in December of the same year. The bridge was replaced in 1915 with what became known as the Shortway Bridge, where tolls would persist until 1986. The Licking Valley Girl Scout Bridge now occupies the site. (Courtesy Kenton County Public Library.)

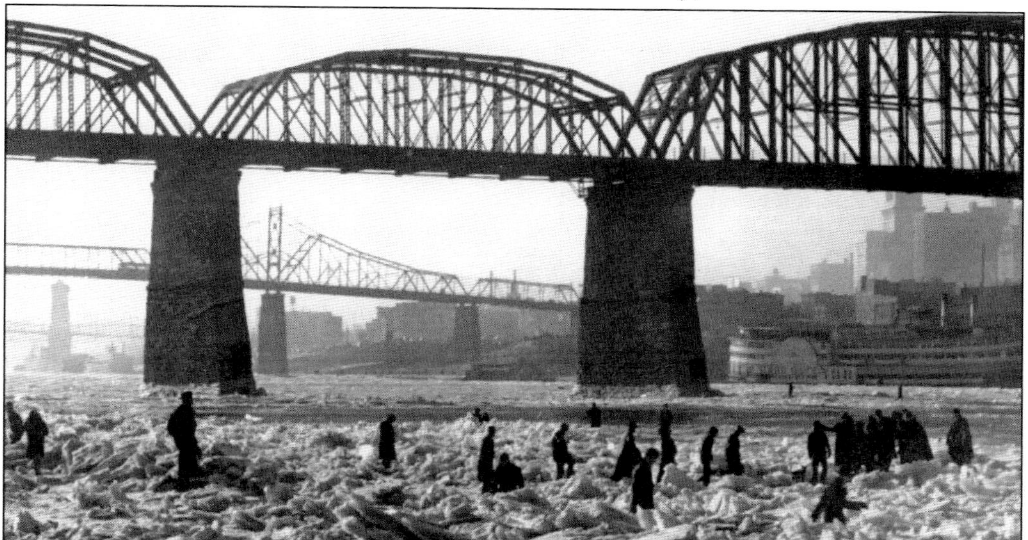

Some brave individuals accessed Cincinnati without the aid of bridges by walking over the frozen Ohio River in this January 28, 1940 photo. The L&N (Louisville & Nashville) Bridge, seen in the foreground, opened in 1872 as the first railroad bridge over the Ohio River. It was also known at one time as the Pennsylvania Bridge. Streetcar tracks were subsequently appended in 1896. In 1987, the last train would cross; the bridge was closed to automobiles in 2001. The structure was painted purple and reopened exclusively as a pedestrian bridge in 2003. Although formally renamed the Newport Southbank Bridge, it is commonly referred to as the "Purple People Bridge." (Courtesy Virginia Bennett.)

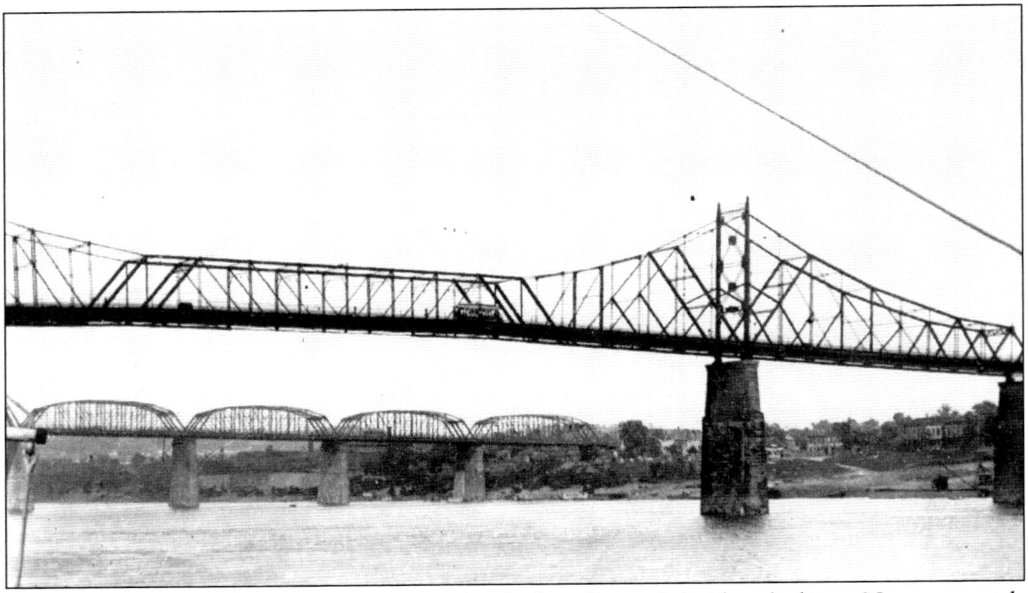

The Green Line electric streetcars utilized the Central Bridge linking Newport with Cincinnati, as seen in this 1897 photo. The Central Bridge would maintain this connection until it was imploded in 1992 to be replaced by the Taylor-Southgate Bridge. Remnants of the Central Bridge do still exist. Some of the railing can be seen at the Port of Entry at Riverboat Row. Decorative medallions were also incorporated into the floodwall near the Bellevue side. (Courtesy Earl Clark Collection.)

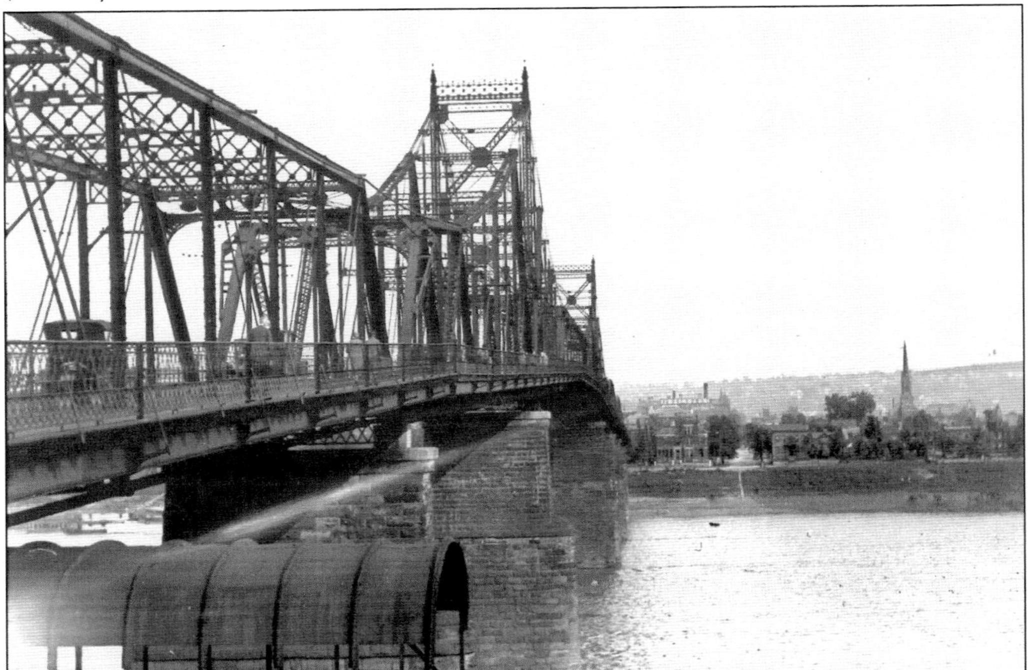

Cars cross the Central Bridge, heading for Newport, c. 1925. Built in 1890, the Central Bridge was Newport's second bridge to span the Ohio River, with the L&N Bridge predating it by 18 years. (Courtesy Kenton County Public Library.)

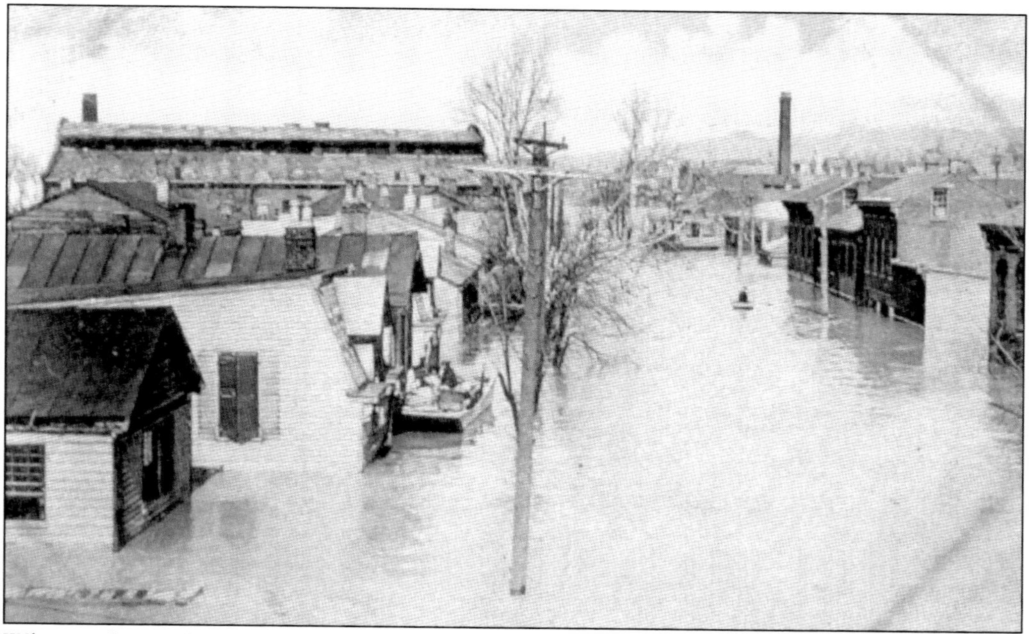

Whereas future floods were extensively photographed, not many images are found of the Flood of 1913. This time, the Ohio River crested at 69.9 feet on April 1, 1913. (Courtesy Kenton County Public Library.)

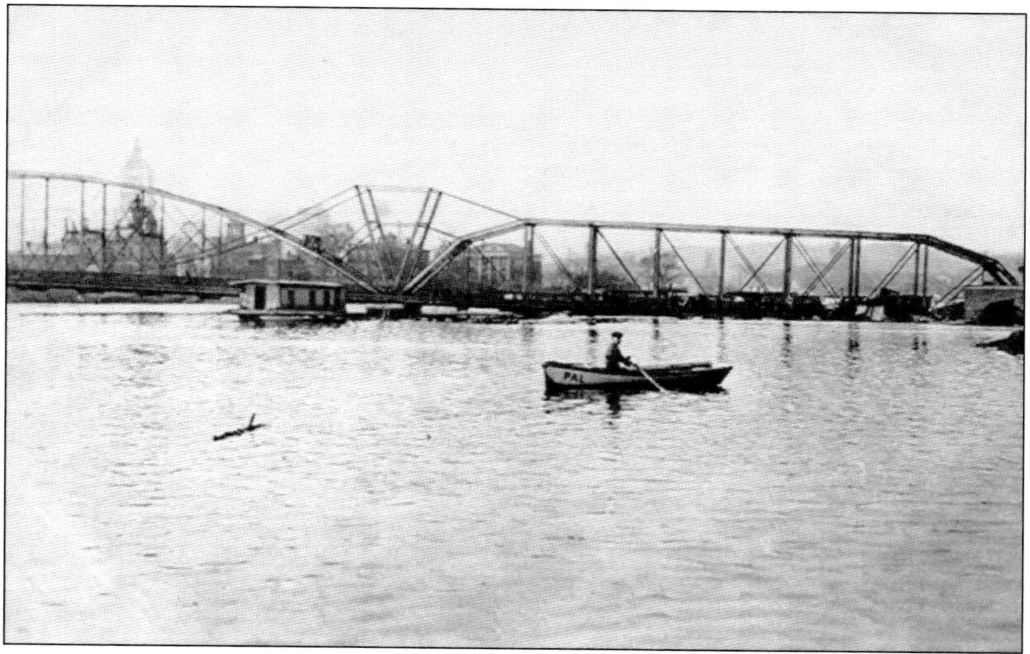

A man floats upon the Licking River during the Flood of 1913, with the Fourth Street Bridge in the background. (Courtesy Campbell County Historical Society.)

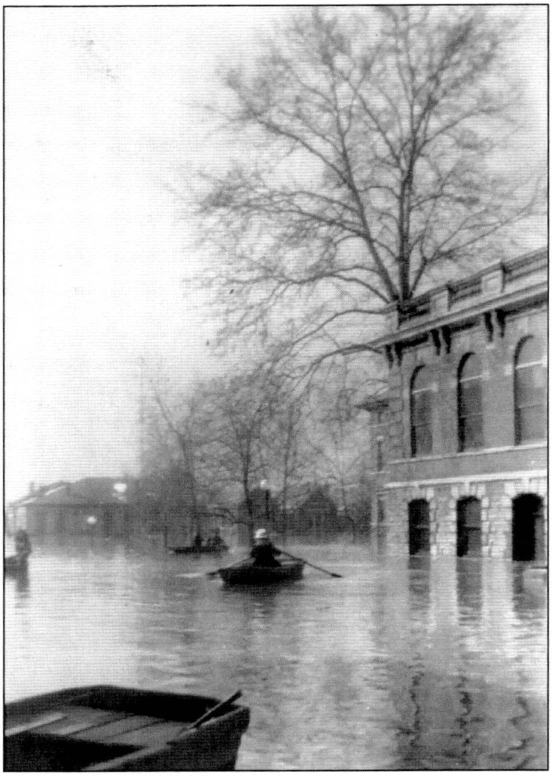

Flooding during 1937 even necessitated the closure of the Campbell County Courthouse at Fourth and York Streets. (Courtesy Rick Parker.)

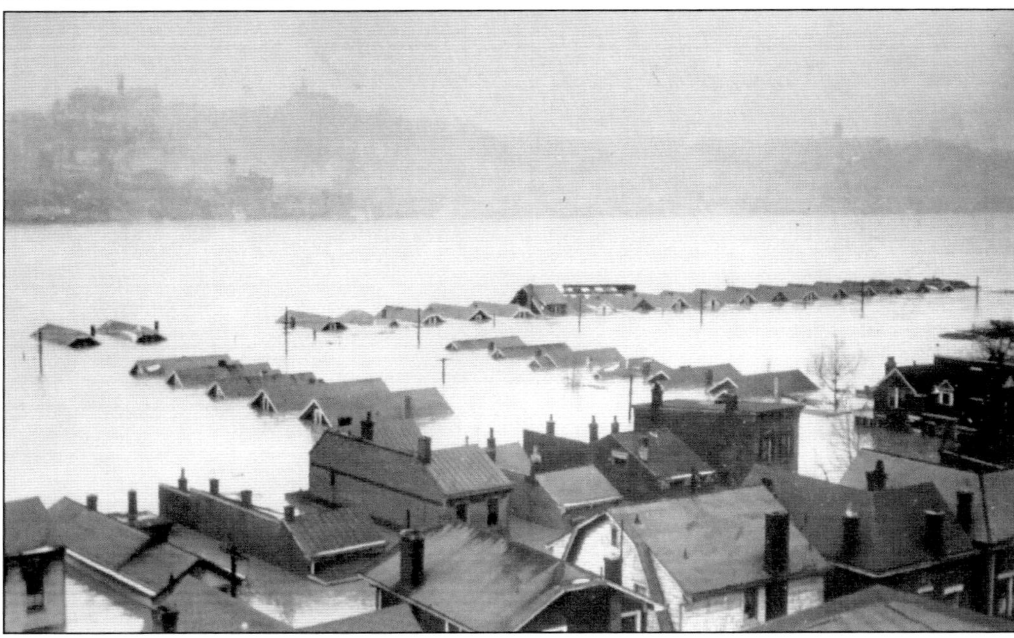

The Flood of 1937 became the worst in Northern Kentucky's history, with the Ohio River reaching a peak elevation of 79.9 feet on January 26, 1937. Over 2,500 Newport homes were flooded, many filled to the rooftops. In sharp contrast, the river's record low is recorded at 1 foot 7 inches, descending to this level during the drought of 1881. (Courtesy LeRoy Hoffman and the City of Newport.)

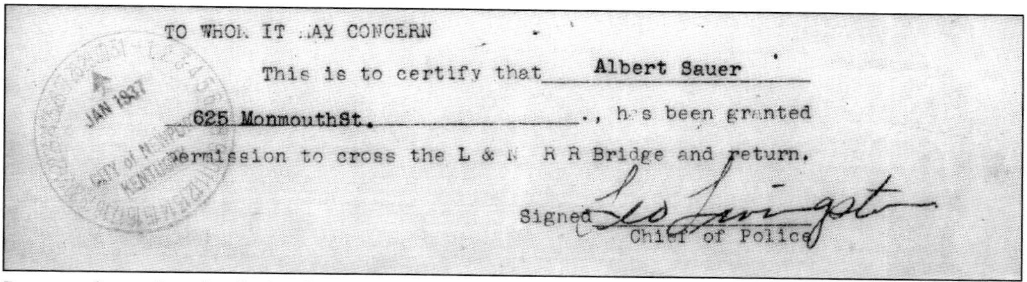

TO WHOM IT MAY CONCERN

This is to certify that Albert Sauer

625 Monmouth St., has been granted

permission to cross the L & N R R Bridge and return.

Signed

Chief of Police

JAN 1937

CITY of NEWPORT

KENTUCKY

Permits from the chief of police were required in order to be granted access to the L&N Bridge during the 1937 flood. (Courtesy Al Sauer.)

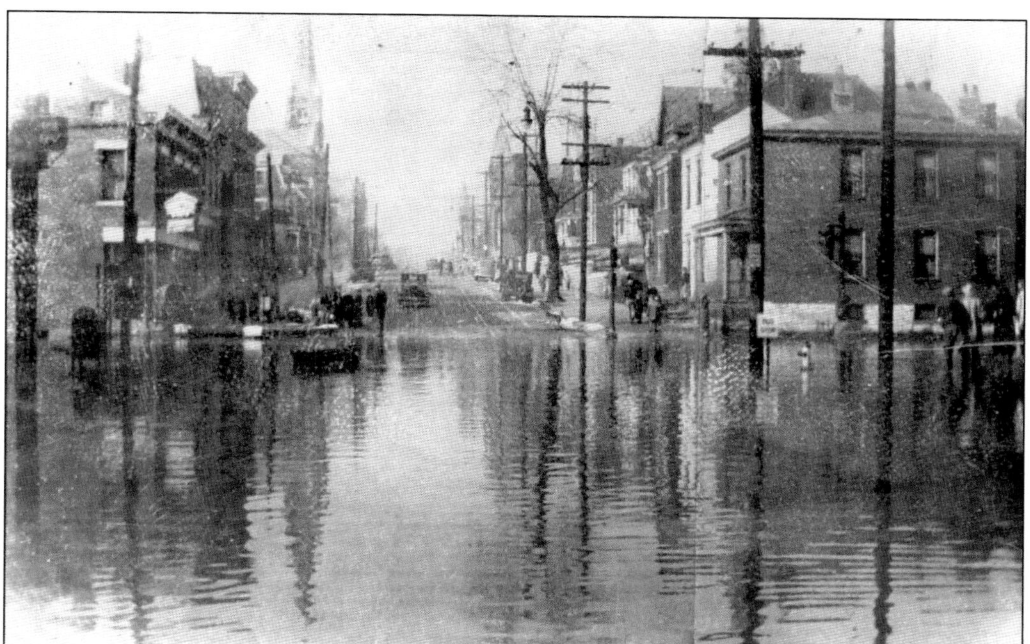

A typical neighborhood view during the flooding in January of 1937 is shown here at Ninth and York Streets. (Courtesy Kenton County Public Library.)

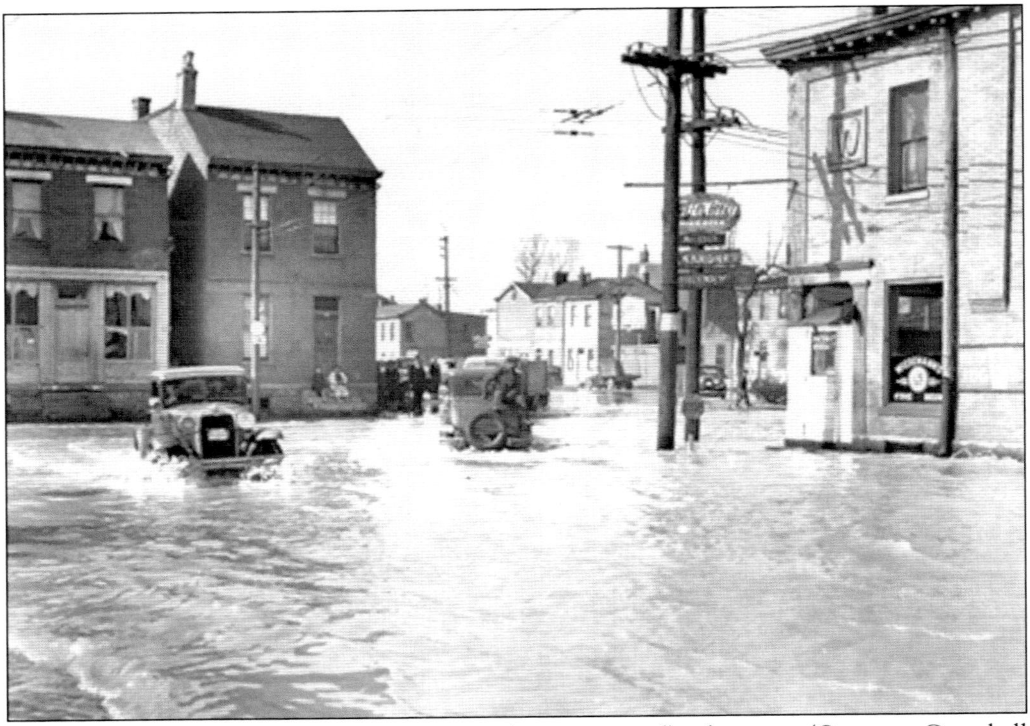

Automobiles attempt to navigate the streets despite rising flood waters. (Courtesy Campbell County Historical Society.)

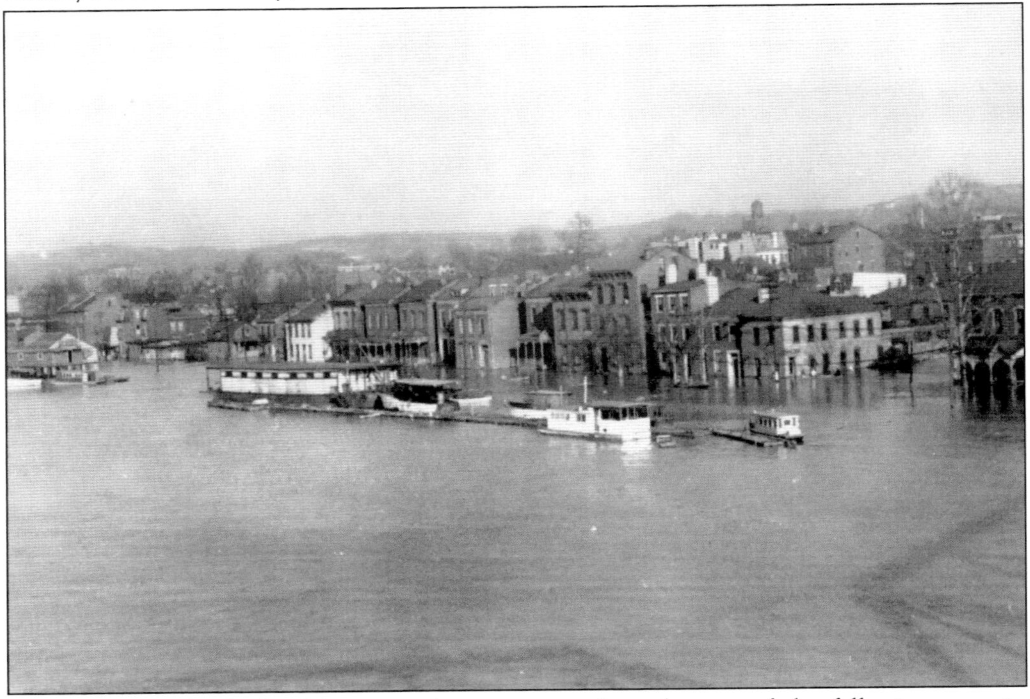

Although the Flood of 1936 receives less attention than the one of the following year, its consequences were also quite significant, as seen in this riverfront picture. The water peaked at 60.6 feet this time. (Courtesy Kenton County Public Library.)

Seven

SIN CITY

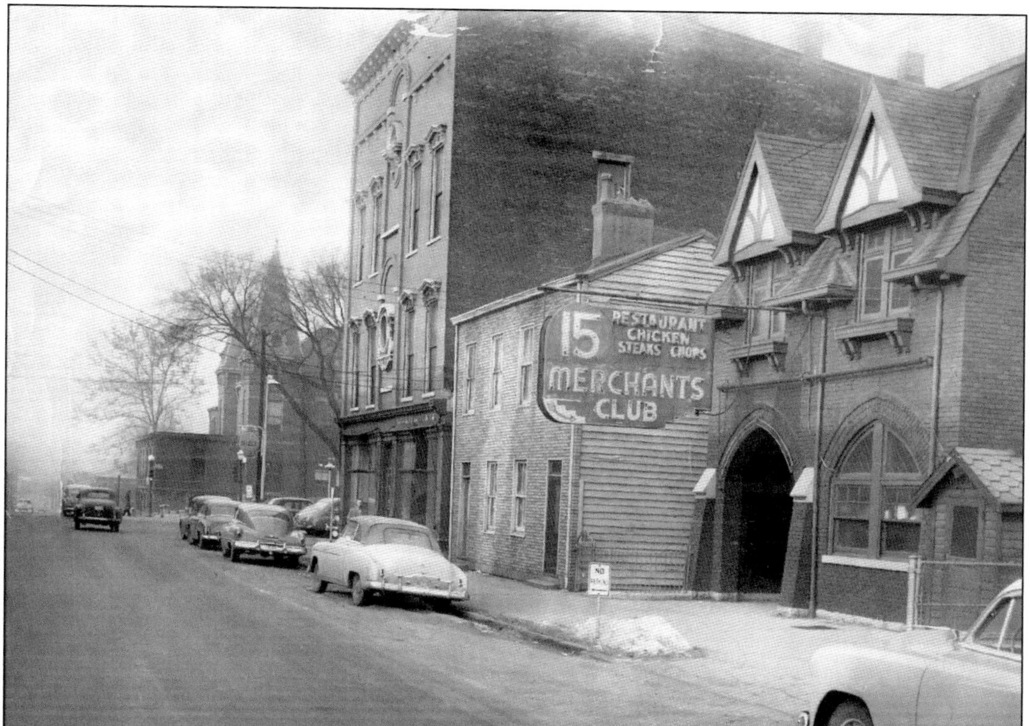

The Merchants Club was located at 15 East Fourth Street. A dining room occupied the front of the building, while the casino in the rear included craps, blackjack, roulette, and slots. At a time when officials turned a blind eye to gambling, the proximity to the courthouse did not inhibit the illegal activities going on inside the establishment. The site is currently occupied by a Goodyear Automobile Service Center. (Courtesy Kenton County Public Library.)

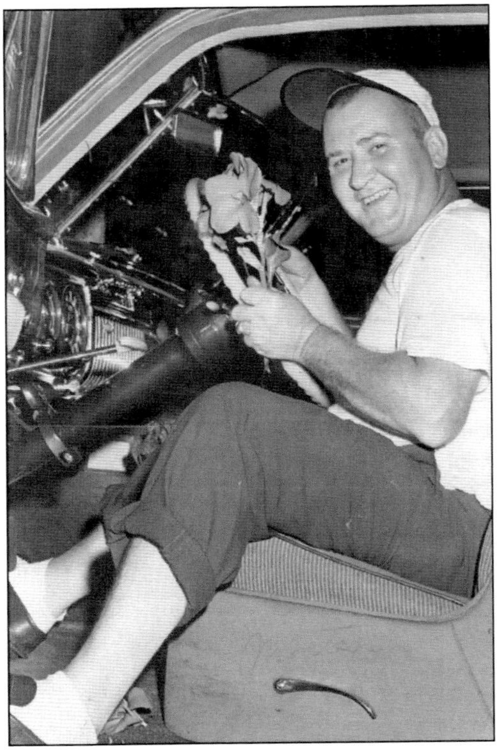

As an associate of the Cleveland Syndicate, Albert "Red" Masterson, shown here in 1946, operated the Merchants Club. He was known as "The Enforcer." Numerous suspicious fires were attributed to Masterson, including the first fire at the Beverly Hills Club in 1936. He died in 1972 at the age of 66. (Courtesy Campbell County Historical Society.)

"Screw" Andrews (born Frank Andriello), second from left, is pictured in 1962 with Gus Postel, James Cobb, and Willard Whitley. Screw Andrews controlled many clubs, including the Sportsman's Club and the Alibi Club. Once charged with the murder of competitor Melvin Clark, he was acquitted after a self defense plea. However, tax evasion charges and an eventual conviction for running a gambling establishment led to his prison time. He is reported to have died after falling from the fourth-story window of a hospital in 1973. (Courtesy Kenton County Public Library.)

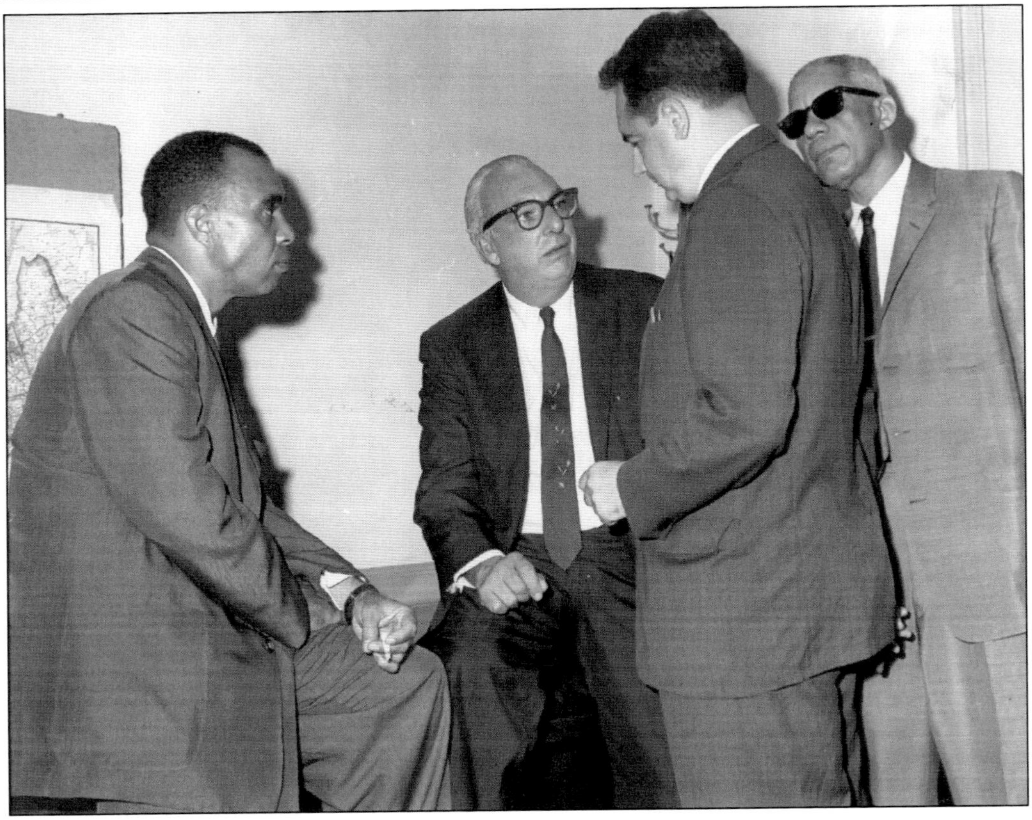

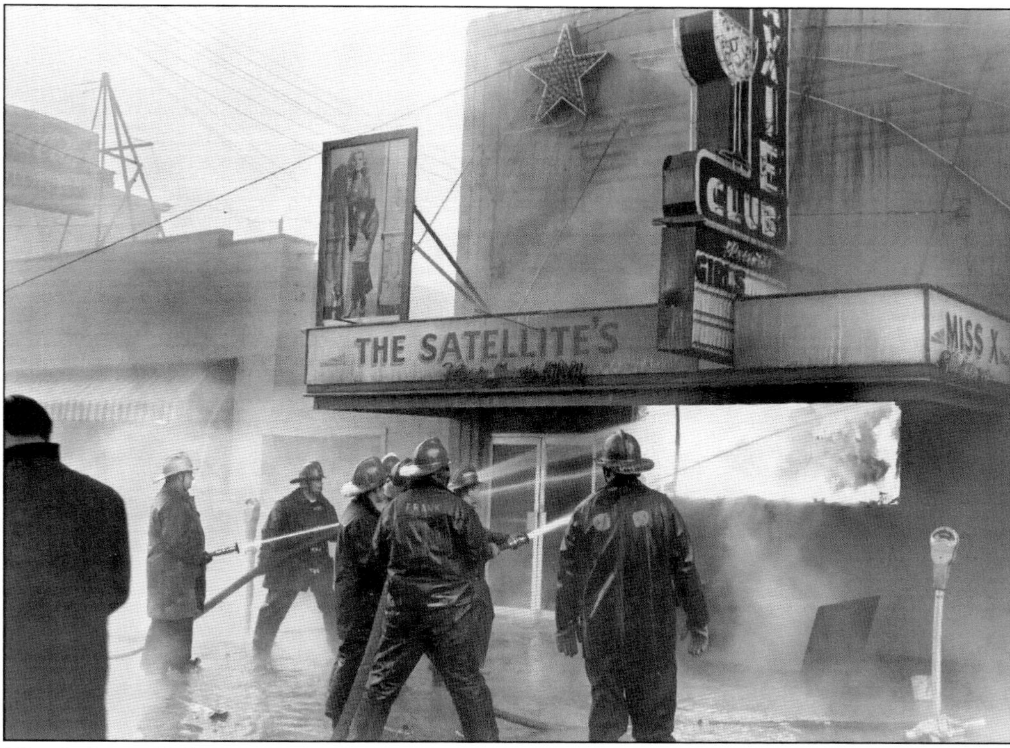

The Galaxie Club at 613 Monmouth Street burned in March of 1970. This property played a major role in Newport's gambling history as home to several casinos, including the Stark Club, the Stardust, and the Silver Slipper. It later became the site of the Brass Mule. (Courtesy Campbell County Historical Society.)

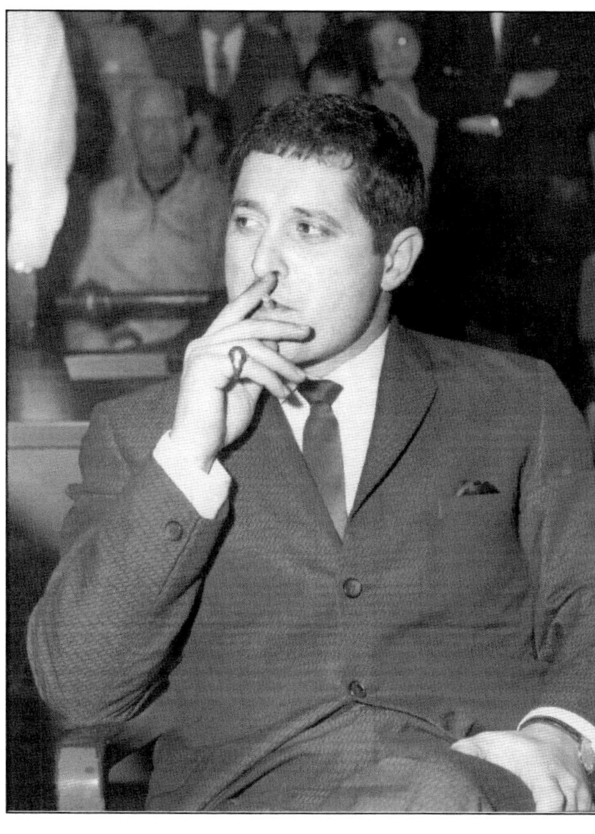

Tito Carinci, a former football star at Xavier University, operated the Glenn Rendezvous, later renamed the Tropicana, at 928 Monmouth Street. In an attempt to keep Newport corrupt, he engineered the unsuccessful set-up of George Ratterman, the reform party's candidate for sheriff. Subsequently, after a failed run for mayor of Newport, Carinci moved to Miami where income tax evasion charges and bookmaking charges would catch up with him. (Courtesy *The Kentucky Post.*)

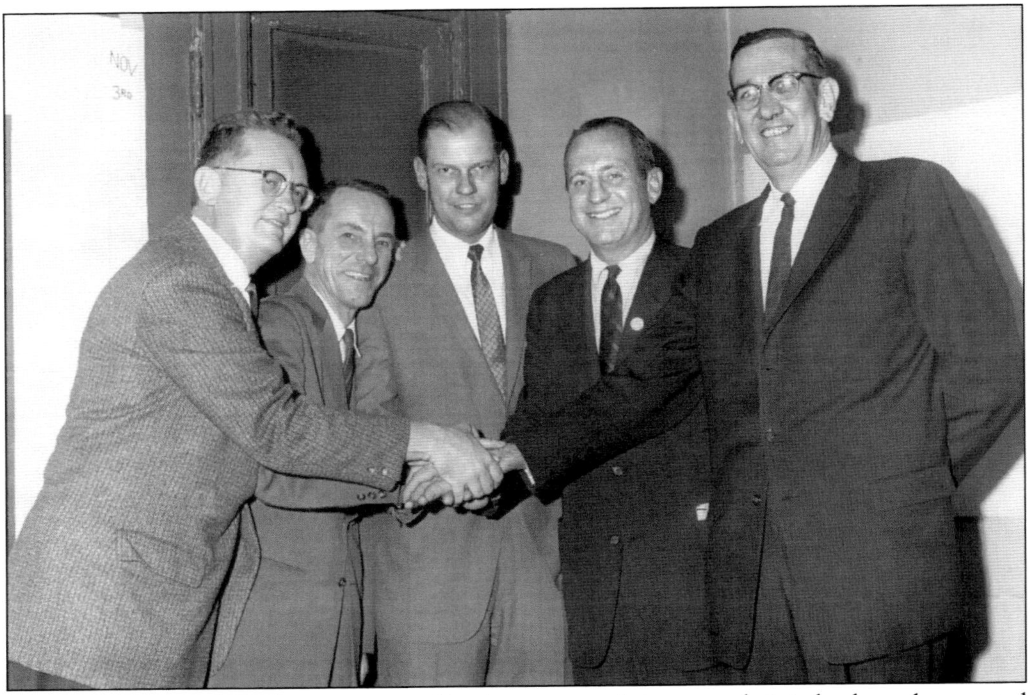

The "Committee of 500" was a group of businessmen, ministers, and civic leaders who wanted to clean up Newport, making gambling and political corruption their primary targets. Shown from left to right are the following five key members of this group: Claude Johnson (committee president), Francis (Bud) Herzog, George Ratterman, Jack Wadsworth, and Henry Cook. (Courtesy *The Kentucky Post*.)

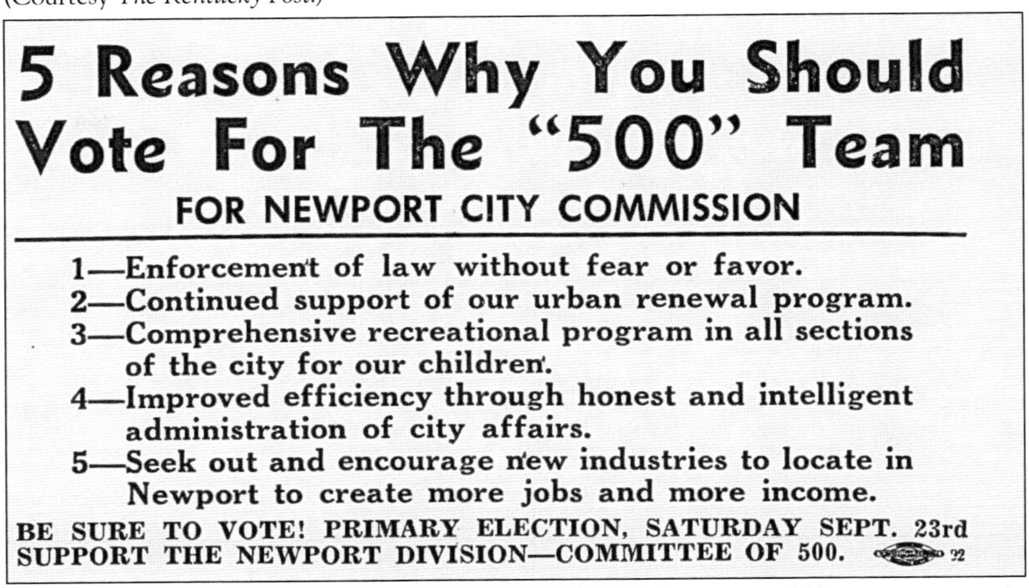

5 Reasons Why You Should Vote For The "500" Team

FOR NEWPORT CITY COMMISSION

1—Enforcement of law without fear or favor.
2—Continued support of our urban renewal program.
3—Comprehensive recreational program in all sections of the city for our children.
4—Improved efficiency through honest and intelligent administration of city affairs.
5—Seek out and encourage new industries to locate in Newport to create more jobs and more income.

BE SURE TO VOTE! PRIMARY ELECTION, SATURDAY SEPT. 23rd
SUPPORT THE NEWPORT DIVISION—COMMITTEE OF 500.

With this handout, the "Committee of 500" asked for the support of Newport citizens in an attempt to get honest candidates into key political positions. Their goal of "enforcement of law without fear or favor" pointed a finger at the widely accepted practice of bribery and payoffs that had become too familiar in Newport. (Courtesy Special Collections and Archives, Northern Kentucky University.)

Rita Desmond was one of two Tropicana strippers who participated in the botched attempt to tarnish the reputation of George Ratterman. On the night of the event, her assignment was to distract Ratterman's friend Thomas Paisley while the set-up proceeded. (Courtesy *The Kentucky Post*.)

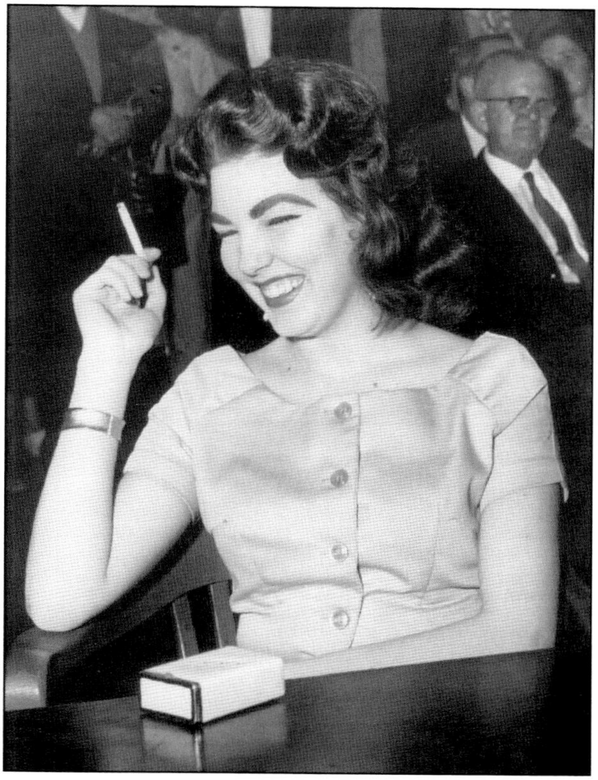

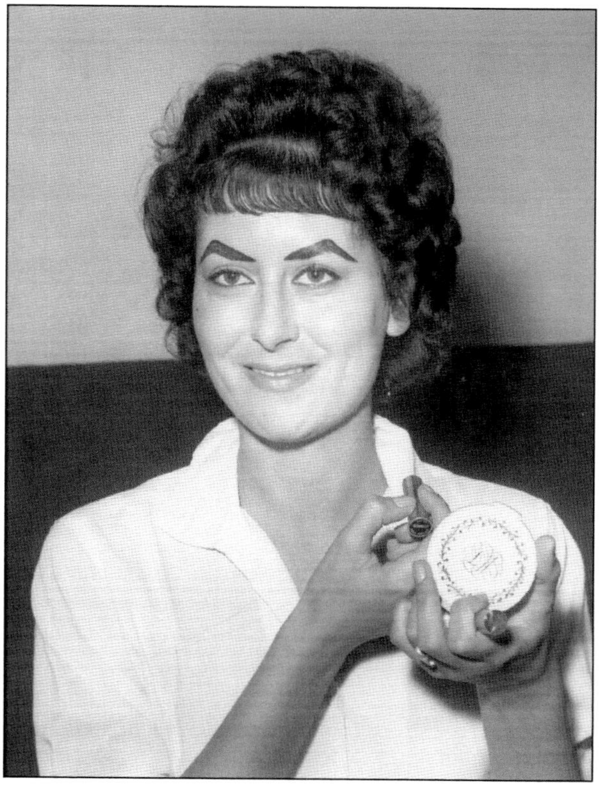

"April Flowers" (Juanita Jean Hodges) was a headline stripper at the Tropicana. Her role in the framing of George Ratterman was to position herself next to the partially clad reform party candidate after he had been drugged. She upheld the fabricated tale of Tito Carinci during the Ratterman trial but later admitted that she had perjured herself during that trial after being promised a trip to Puerto Rico in exchange for her distorted testimony. (Courtesy *The Kentucky Post*.)

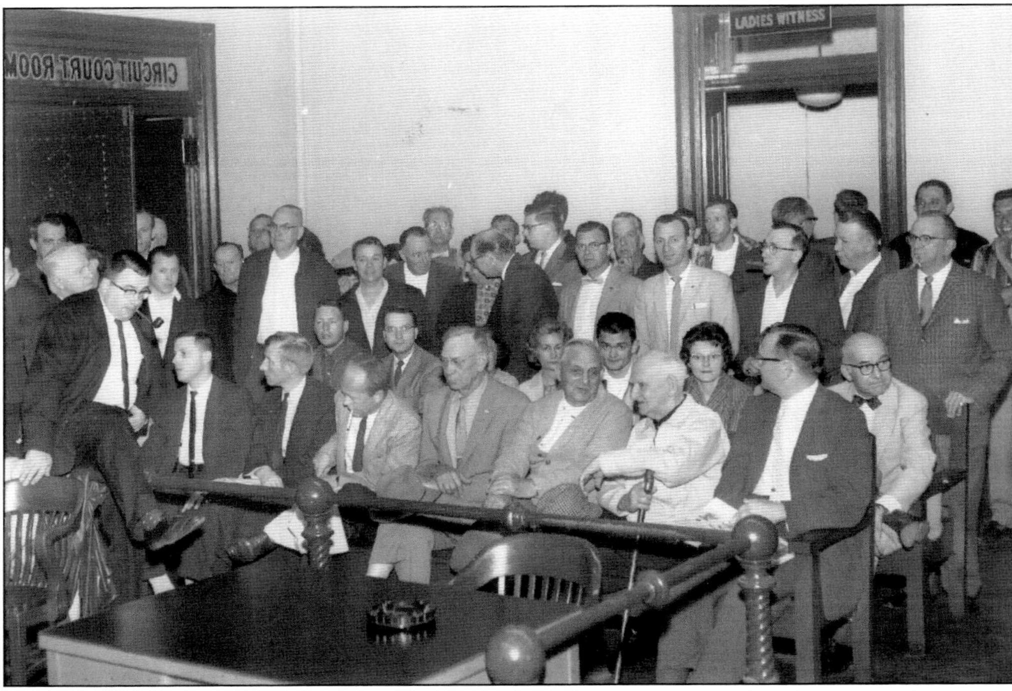

The trial of George Ratterman not only sparked the curiosity of local citizens, but it also attracted the attention of national media. This view of the courtroom demonstrates the circus-like atmosphere that existed. (Courtesy *The Kentucky Post*.)

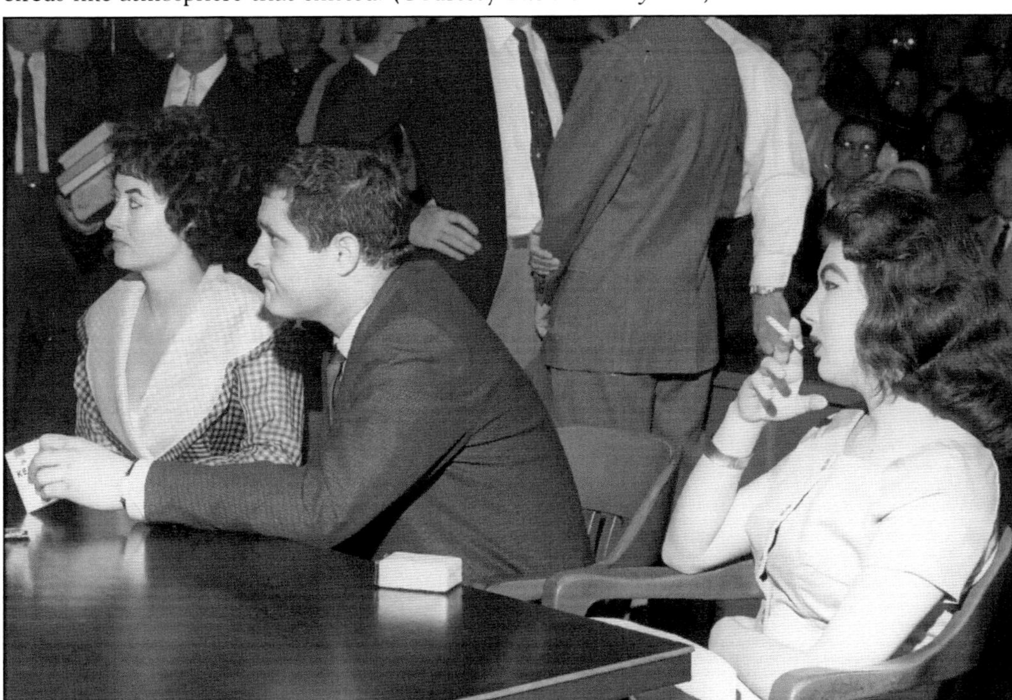

From left to right, April Flowers, Tito Carinci, and Rita Desmond are seated inside the courtroom. Their testimonies were discredited during the trial. (Courtesy *The Kentucky Post*.)

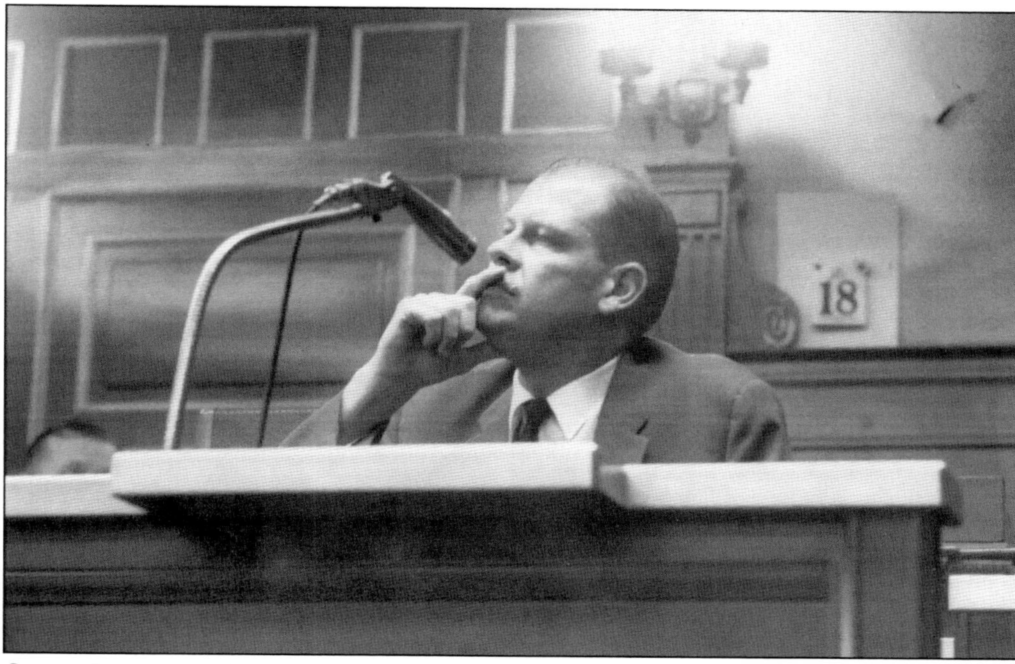

George Ratterman thoughtfully testifies. Ratterman easily won his bid for county sheriff in 1961. He is credited with the ensuing exodus of organized crime from the city of Newport, bringing an end to the era of gambling and corruption. After serving as sheriff, he moved to Colorado where he worked as an investment counselor. (Courtesy *The Kentucky Post.*)

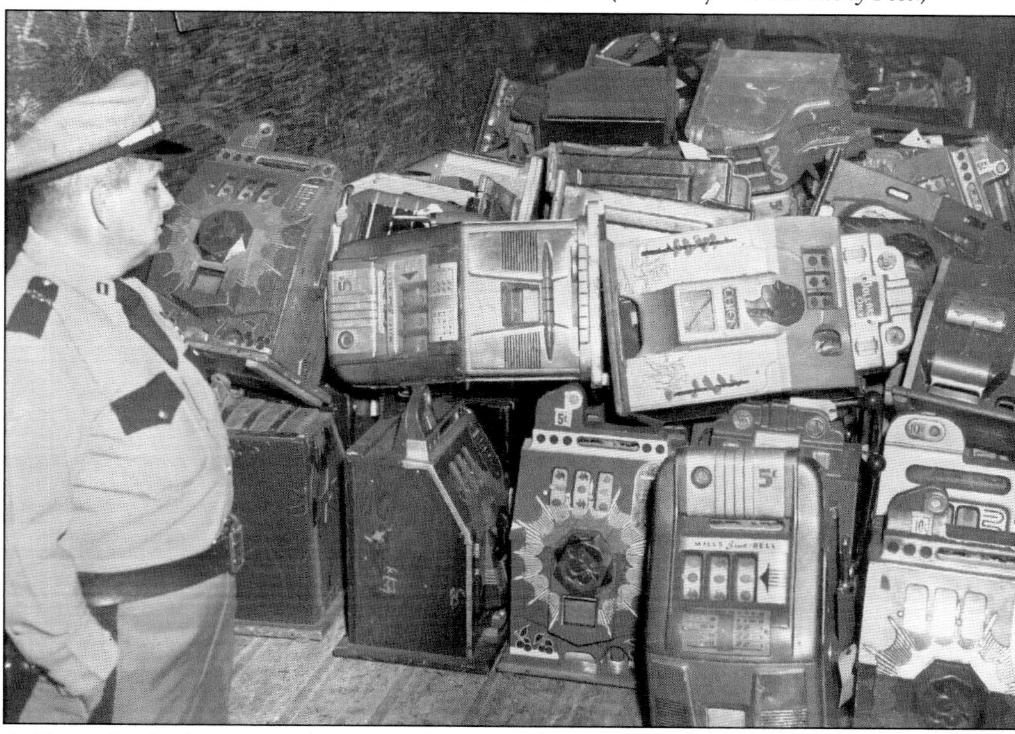

A Kentucky highway patrolman watches over slot machines seized from Newport casinos. (Courtesy *The Kentucky Post.*)

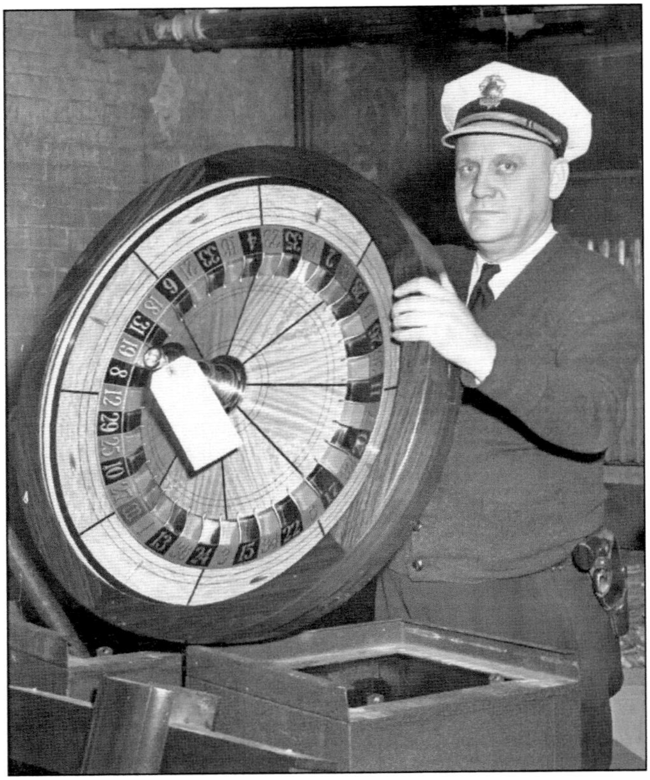

Lt. Kenneth Collins of the Newport Police Department holds a product of a police raid, a roulette wheel from the Glenn Rendezvous Casino. (Courtesy *The Kentucky Post.*)

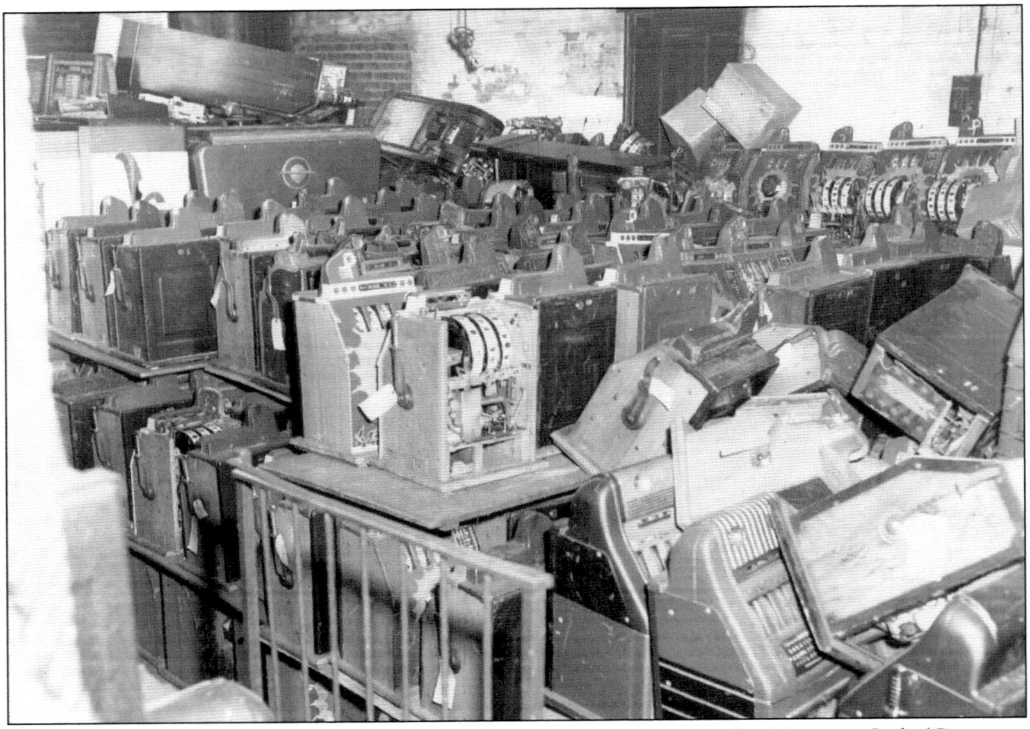

Confiscated slot machines were "imprisoned" in a storage area at the Newport Jail. (Courtesy *The Kentucky Post.*)

Eight

TIDBITS

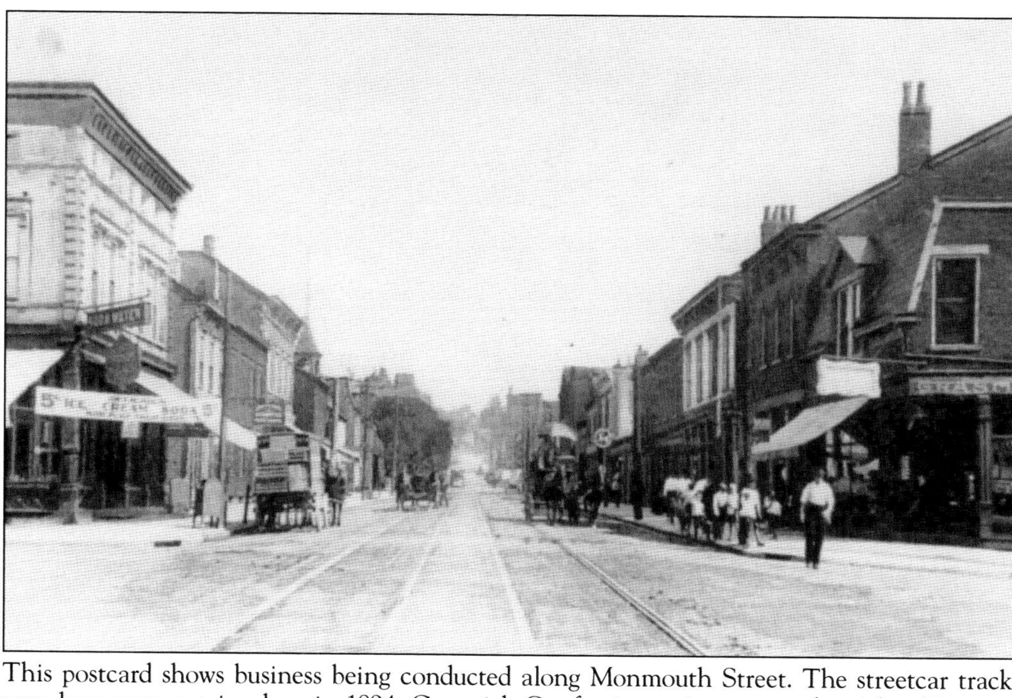

This postcard shows business being conducted along Monmouth Street. The streetcar tracks seen here were put in place in 1894. Grasmick Confectioners is seen on the right. (Courtesy Earl Clark Collection.)

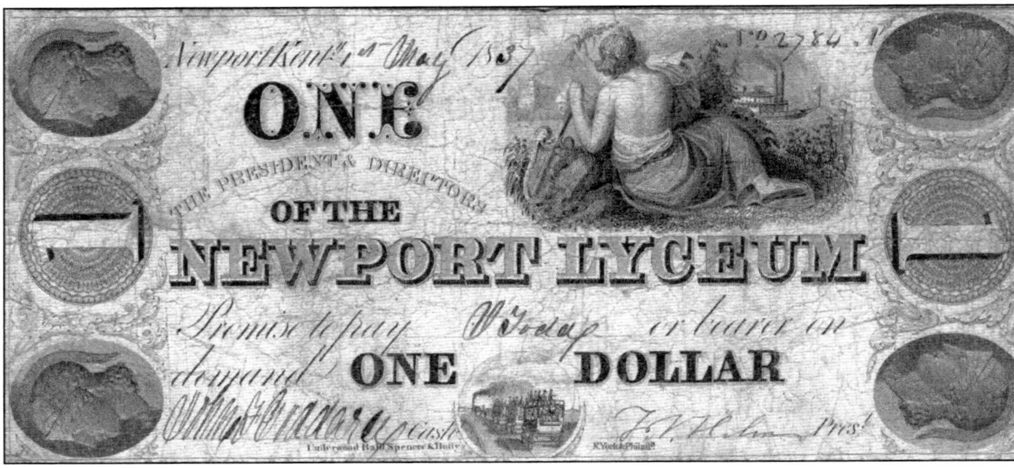

This $1 note from the Newport Lyceum is dated May 1, 1837. Little specifics are known about the lyceum; it appears to have been established in 1832. The organization functioned as an early library as well as a sponsor of lectures and other educational programs for the community. The four heads in each corner of this note were anti-counterfeiting marks. (Courtesy Peter Garrett.)

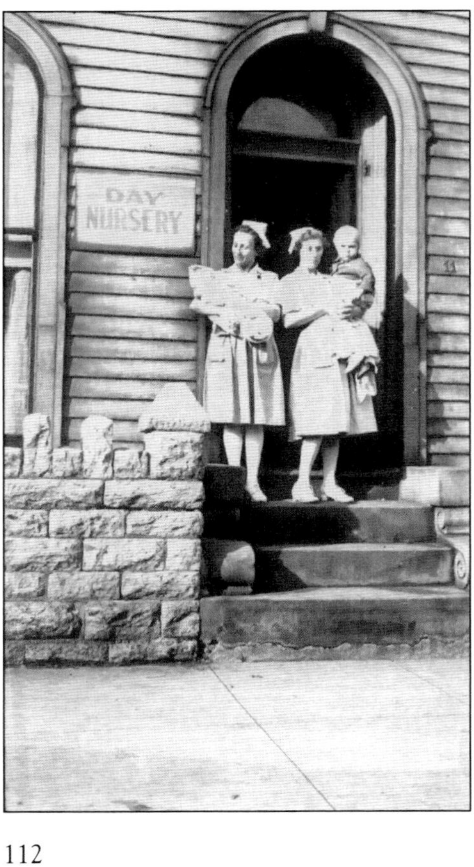

The City of Newport operated the Newport Day Nursery for children of working mothers. Initially located in the city building, the nursery later moved to 11 East Fifth Street. At the time of this photo, c. 1930, Agnes Hearn was the matron. It is not known if she is one of the ladies in the photo. The city abolished the nursery in 1946. (Courtesy Peter Garrett.)

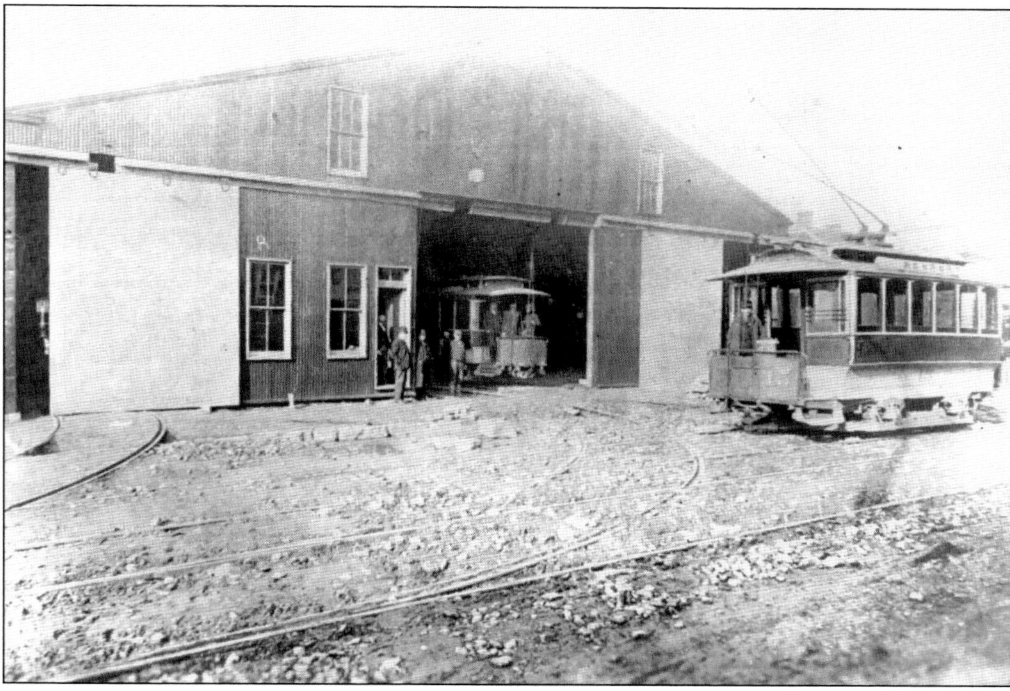

This is a picture of the Newport Carbarn as it appeared in 1893. (Courtesy Special Collections and Archives, University of Kentucky Libraries.)

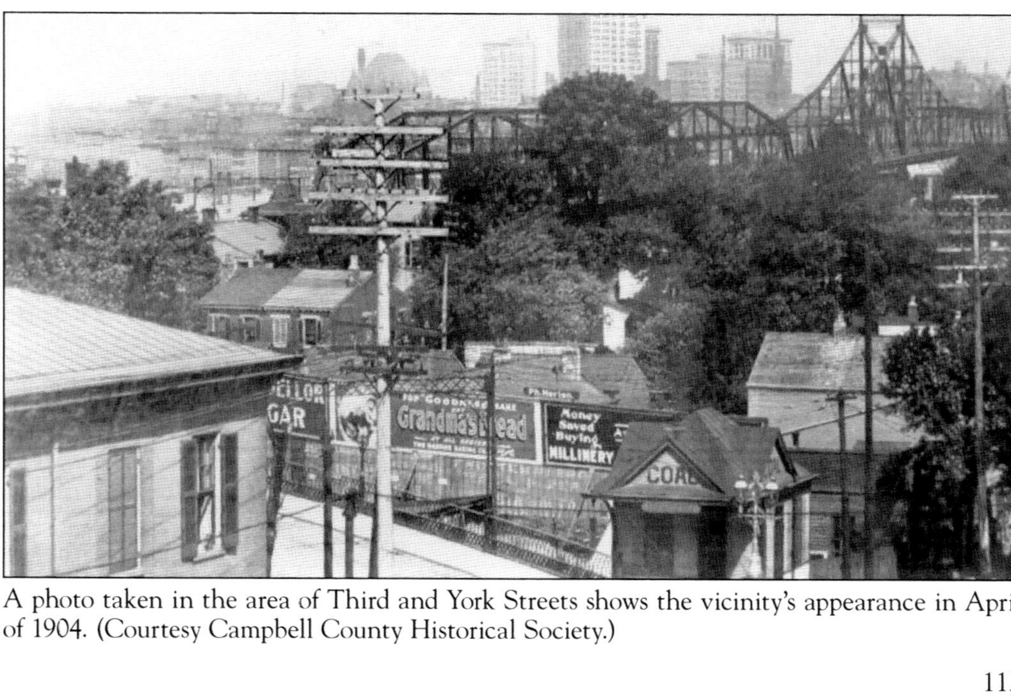

A photo taken in the area of Third and York Streets shows the vicinity's appearance in April of 1904. (Courtesy Campbell County Historical Society.)

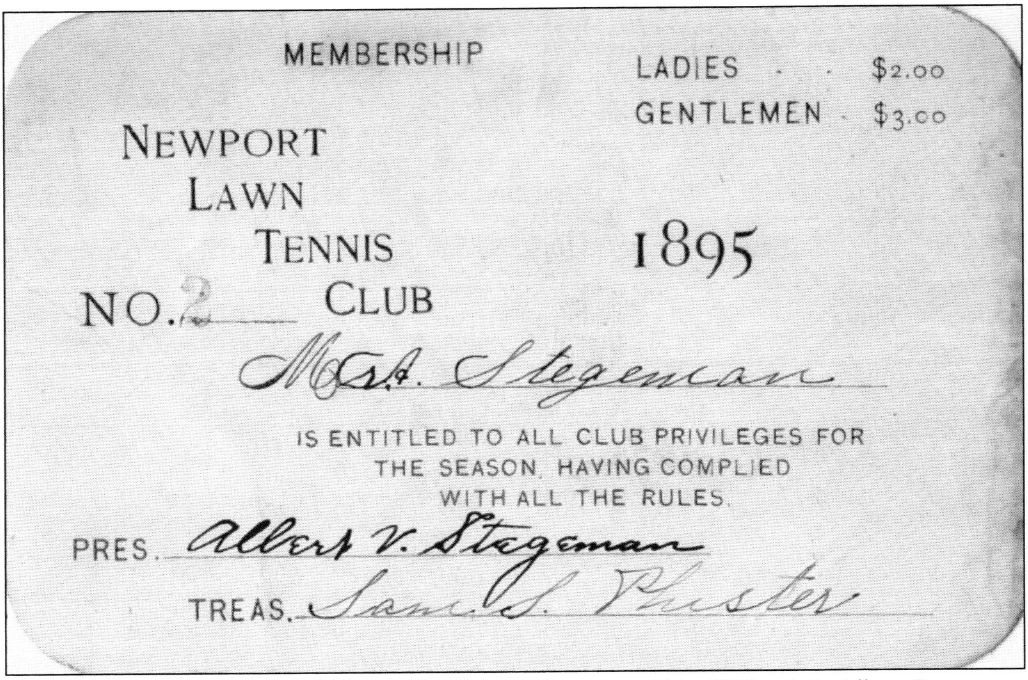
MEMBERSHIP

LADIES . . $2.00
GENTLEMEN . $3.00

NEWPORT
LAWN
TENNIS
CLUB

1895

NO. 2

Mr. A. Stegeman

IS ENTITLED TO ALL CLUB PRIVILEGES FOR THE SEASON, HAVING COMPLIED WITH ALL THE RULES.

PRES. Albert V. Stegeman

TREAS. Sam S. Phister

This Newport Lawn Tennis Club membership card was issued in 1895 to Mr. Albert Stegeman, member No. 2, who was also the president of the club. (Courtesy Behringer Crawford Museum, Covington, Kentucky.)

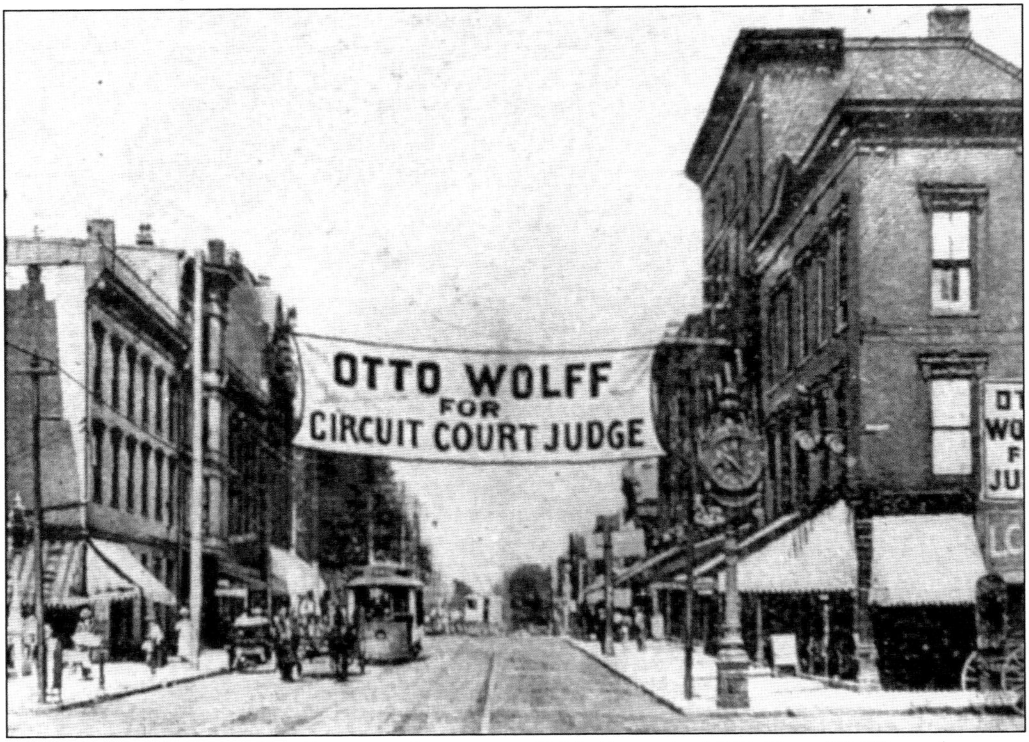

Streetcars glide along York Street in this view at Fifth Street in 1908. Otto Wolff sought votes in his successful bid for circuit court judge. (Courtesy Kenton County Public Library.)

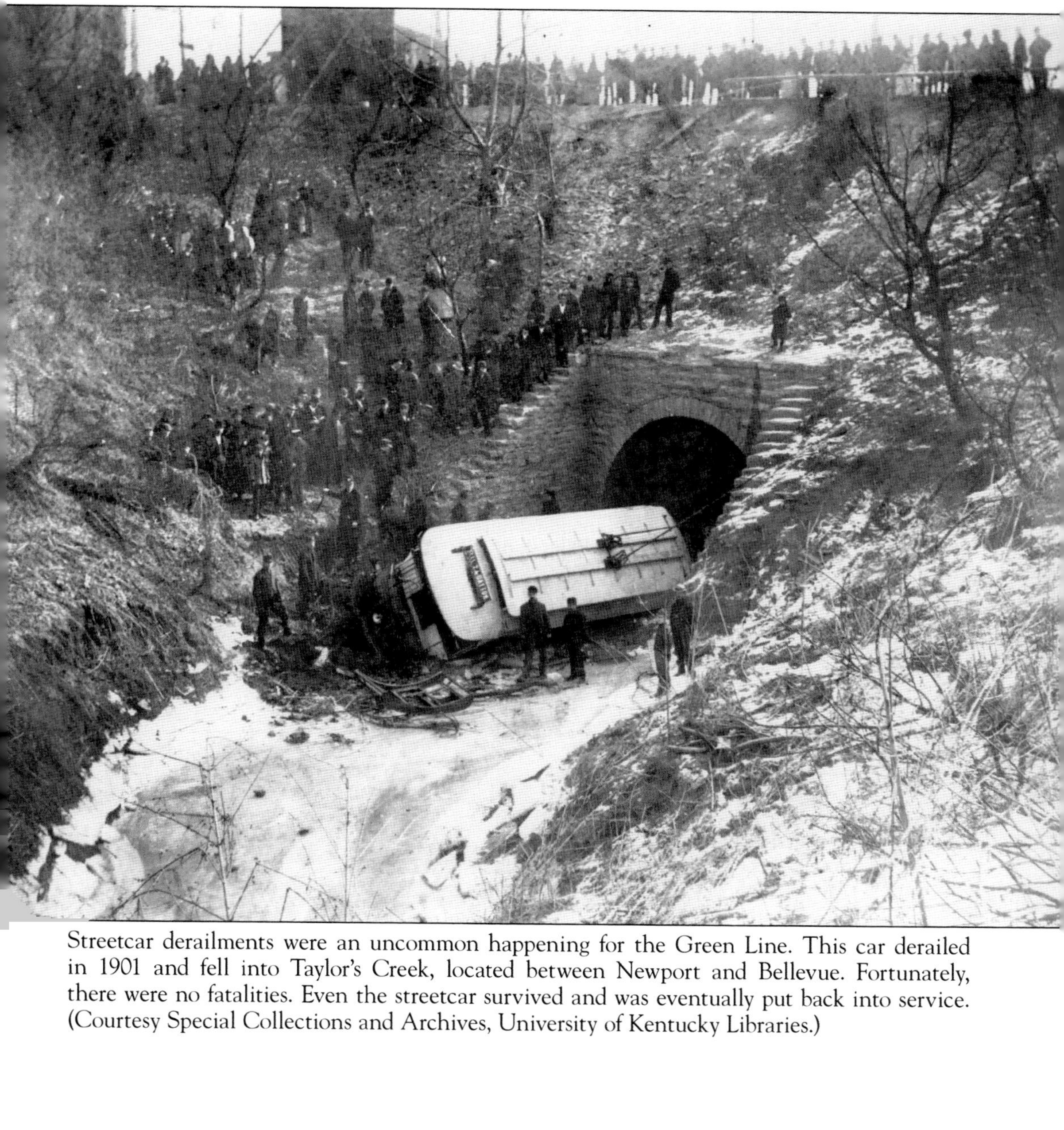

Streetcar derailments were an uncommon happening for the Green Line. This car derailed in 1901 and fell into Taylor's Creek, located between Newport and Bellevue. Fortunately, there were no fatalities. Even the streetcar survived and was eventually put back into service. (Courtesy Special Collections and Archives, University of Kentucky Libraries.)

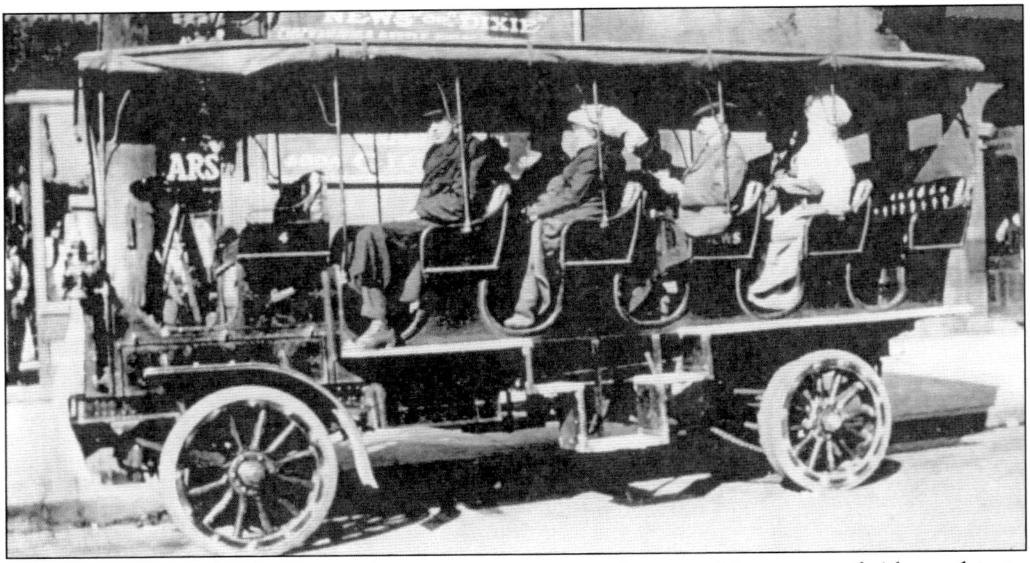

Passengers first took advantage of a new omnibus route between Newport and Alexandria in 1892. The omnibus was owned by the Gosney Transfer Company and left Newport daily at 7:00 a.m., arriving in Alexandria at 9:30 a.m. Its return service left Alexandria at 3:00 p.m. and arrived in Newport at 5:30 p.m. The vehicle pictured above is believed to have been in service at a later date, likely around 1910. (Courtesy Cliff B. Gosney Jr., through Mr. and Mrs. Richard Thompson.)

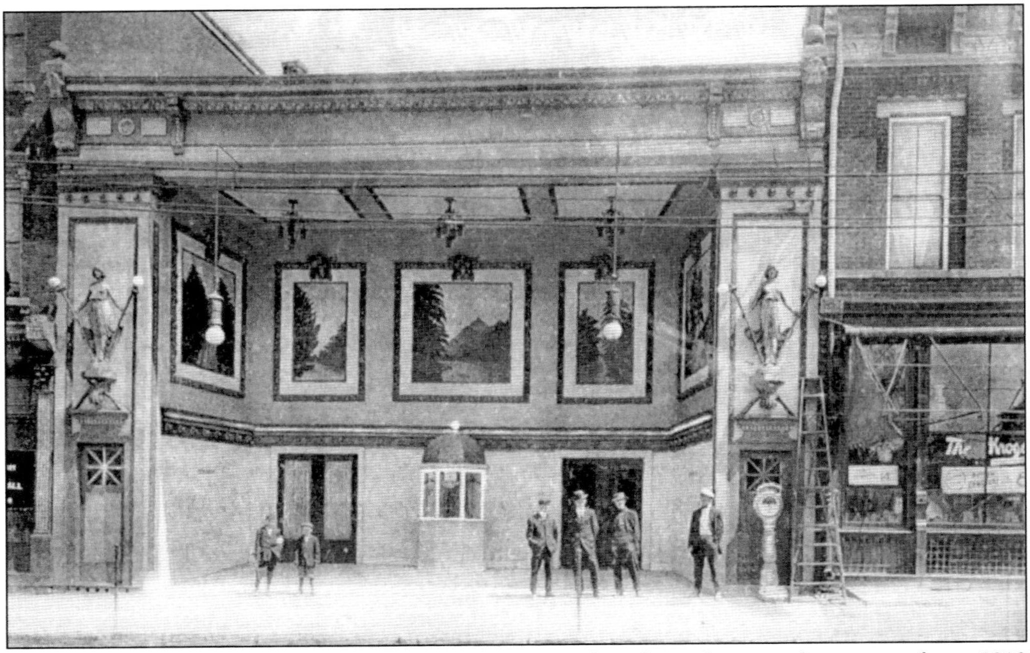

The Colonial Theater at 943 Monmouth Street is found in the city directories from 1910 until 1921. Various proprietors included Isaac Frankel and Daniel Worth. The Kroger Grocery and Baking Company can be seen next door. Now a huge multi-state grocery chain, Kroger's first store was located in Newport. (From the Collection of the Public Library of Cincinnati and Hamilton County.)

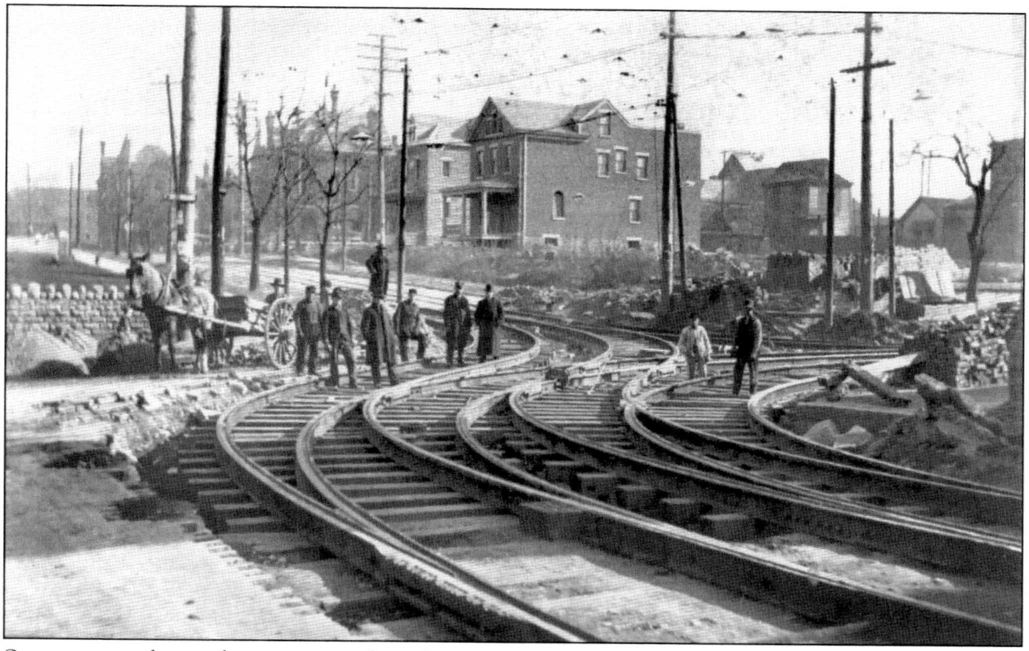

Streetcar tracks are being repaired in the vicinity of Third Street and Washington Avenue, *c.* 1900. (Courtesy Special Collections and Archives, University of Kentucky Libraries.)

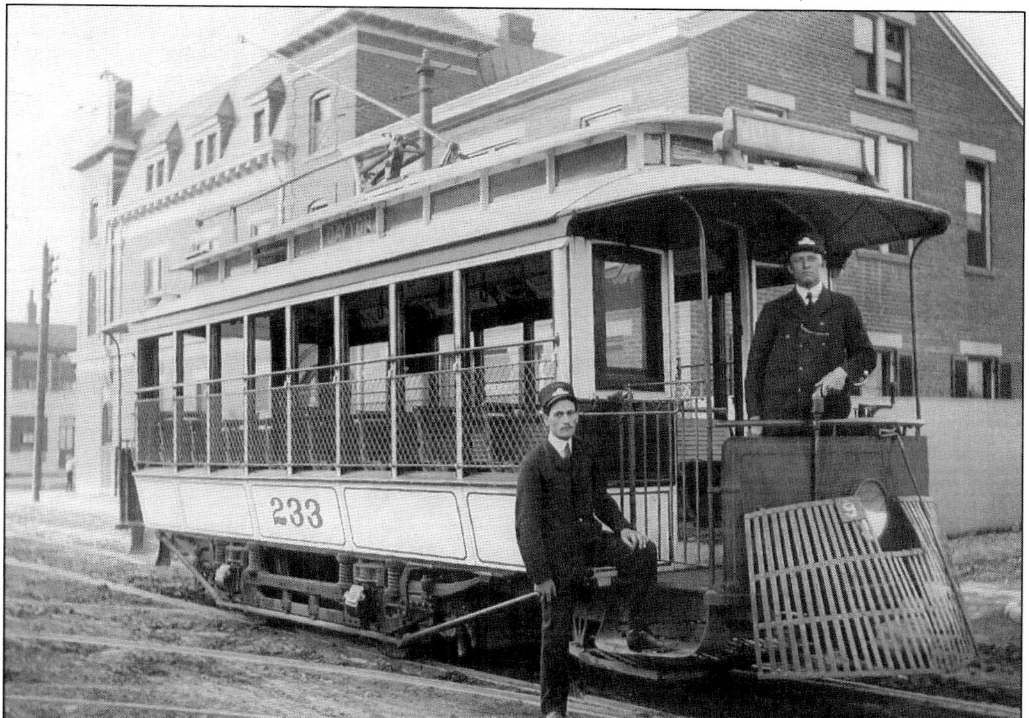

Outside the Newport Carbarn in 1901, motorman John M. Ravenscraft (pictured inside the streetcar) and an unidentified conductor prepare to head to Fort Thomas via the Green Line route No. 9. Mr. Ravenscraft was one of four family members to dedicate over 140 years of combined service to The Green Line. (Courtesy Terry W. Lehmann Collection.)

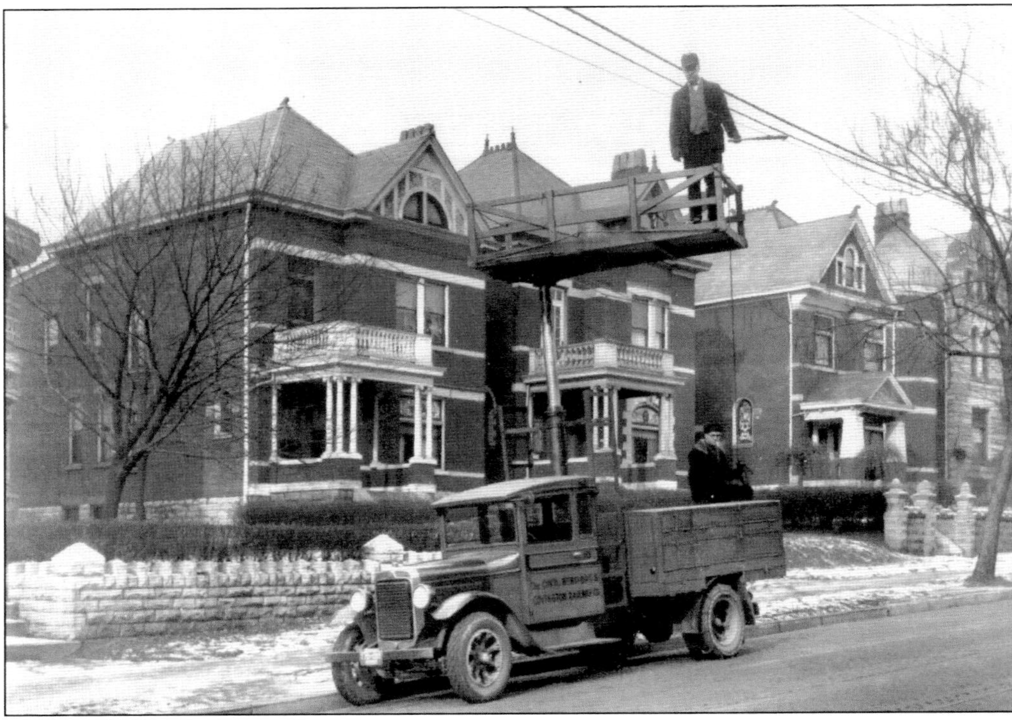

Greasing the lines was part of the routine maintenance performed by streetcar crews. A graphite-based substance was used to decrease friction and prolong the life of the lines. (Courtesy Terry W. Lehmann Collection.)

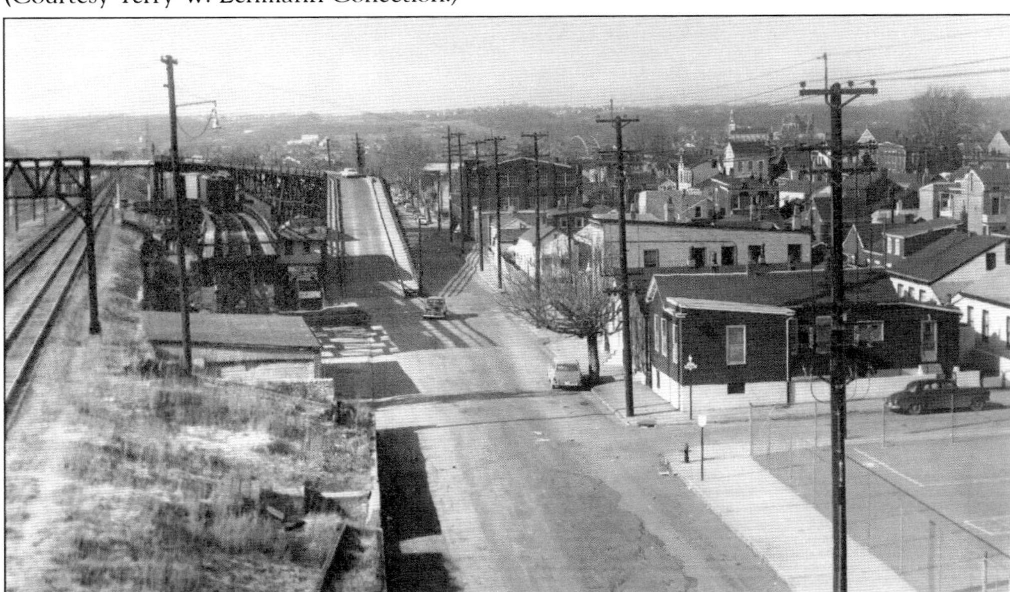

The Wagon Wheel Bridge was built in 1919 over four sets of railroad tracks and connected South Newport with West Newport. It was torn down due to safety reasons and rebuilt as the Berning-Jordan Bridge. The bridge was named in honor of L/Cpl Tom Berning and PFC Gary Jordan. Both young men were U.S. Marines killed in action in Vietnam, and both had attended Newport Catholic High School. (Courtesy Campbell County Historical Society.)

The 1938 bus schedule is outlined on this Monmouth Street Merchants' Association ticket worth 2¢ off. (Courtesy Terry W. Lehmann Collection.)

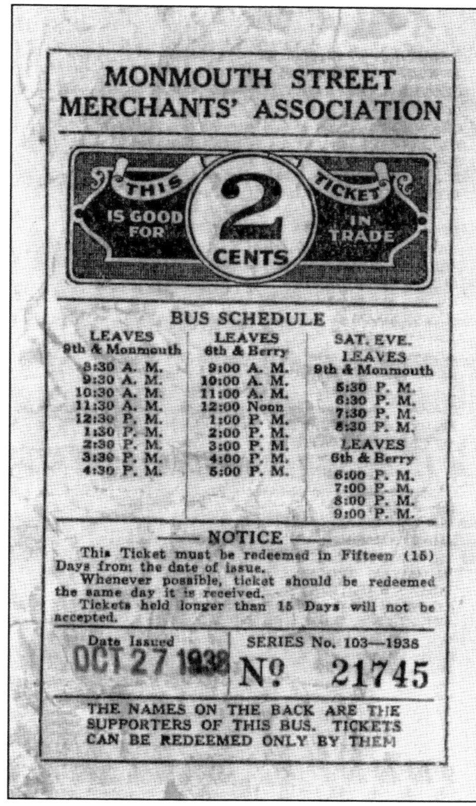

MONMOUTH STREET MERCHANTS' ASSOCIATION

THIS TICKET IS GOOD FOR 2 CENTS IN TRADE

BUS SCHEDULE

LEAVES 9th & Monmouth	LEAVES 6th & Berry	SAT. EVE. LEAVES 9th & Monmouth
8:30 A. M.	9:00 A. M.	5:30 P. M.
9:30 A. M.	10:00 A. M.	6:30 P. M.
10:30 A. M.	11:00 A. M.	7:30 P. M.
11:30 A. M.	12:00 Noon	8:30 P. M.
12:30 P. M.	1:00 P. M.	LEAVES 6th & Berry
1:30 P. M.	2:00 P. M.	6:00 P. M.
2:30 P. M.	3:00 P. M.	7:00 P. M.
3:30 P. M.	4:00 P. M.	8:00 P. M.
4:30 P. M.	5:00 P. M.	9:00 P. M.

NOTICE

This Ticket must be redeemed in Fifteen (15) Days from the date of issue.

Whenever possible, ticket should be redeemed the same day it is received.

Tickets held longer than 15 Days will not be accepted.

Date Issued OCT 27 1938 | SERIES No. 103—1938 | No 21745

THE NAMES ON THE BACK ARE THE SUPPORTERS OF THIS BUS. TICKETS CAN BE REDEEMED ONLY BY THEM

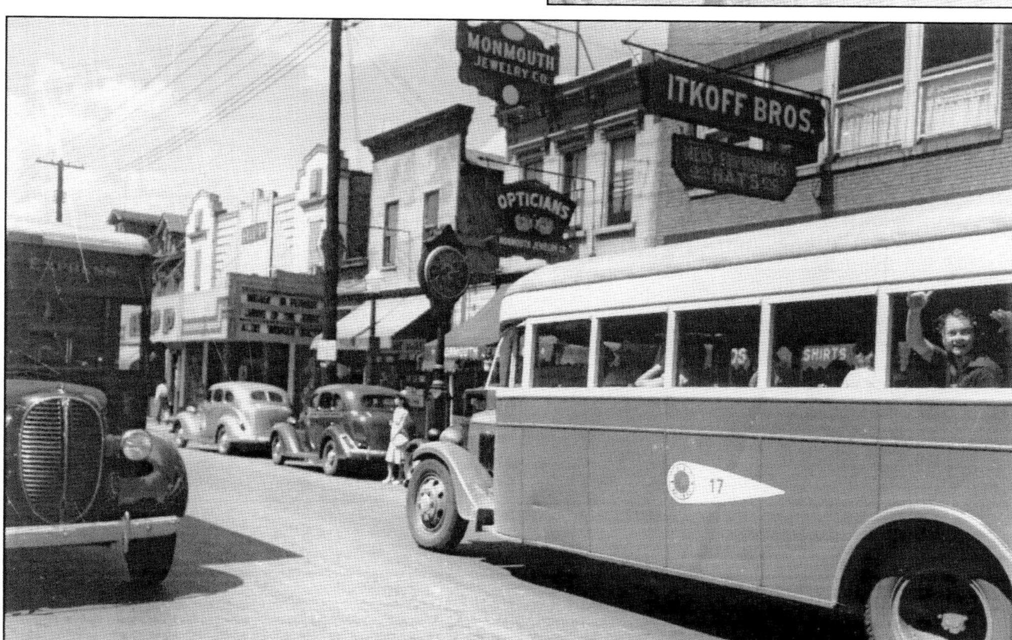

This view of the 700 block of Monmouth Street in 1941 gives us a glimpse of the Hippodrome Theatre at the far left. (Courtesy Special Collections and Archives, University of Kentucky Libraries.)

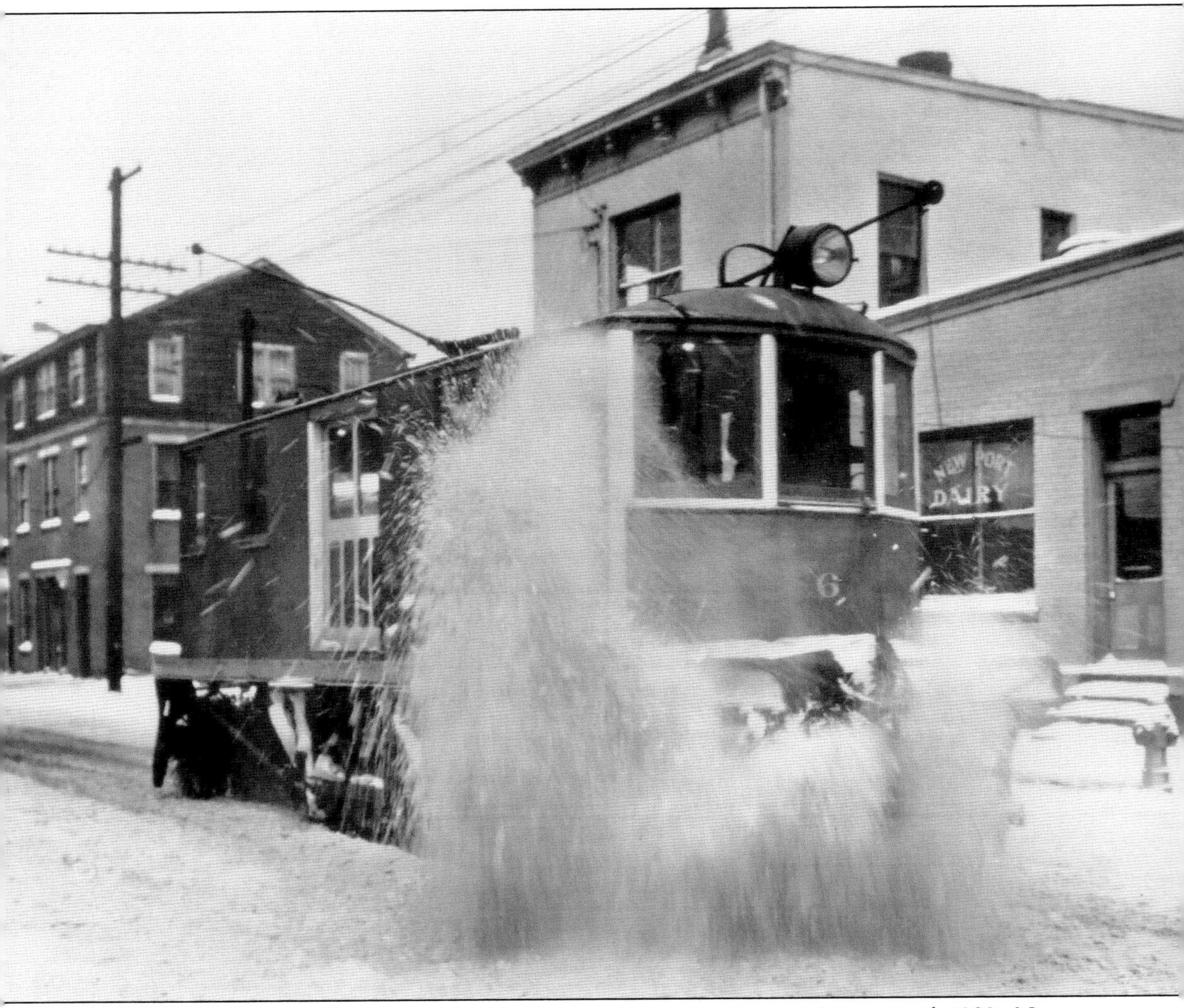

A snow sweeper endeavors to keep the streetcars running in January of 1939. Newport Dairy is seen in the background. (Courtesy Special Collections and Archives, University of Kentucky Libraries.)

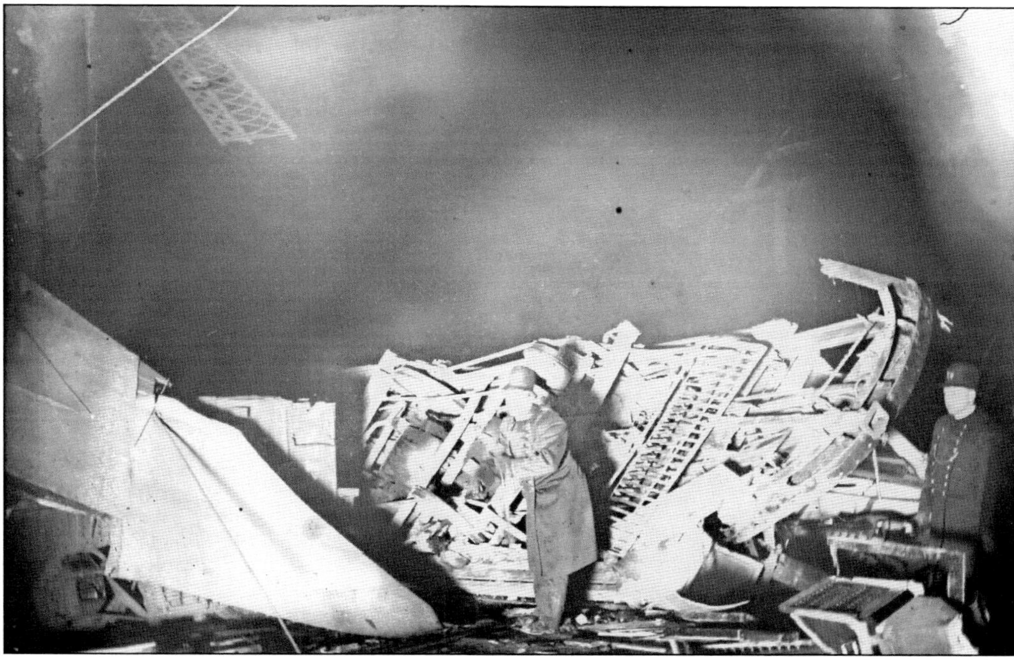

Two policemen investigate the wreckage of Cincinnati, Newport & Covington (CN&C) Street Railway Company streetcar No. 104. The streetcar originated in Bellevue and had traveled through Newport onto the Central Bridge when it derailed on January 5, 1912. Derailment occurred on the Cincinnati side of the bridge. The five men aboard the car included motorman Henry Finan, conductor Harry Wessling, and passengers Benton Schroll, Edward Hampel, and Samuel Hollow. Finan died two days later as a consequence of his injuries. The mangled bridge railing can be seen hanging in the upper left corner of the photo. (Courtesy Peter Garrett.)

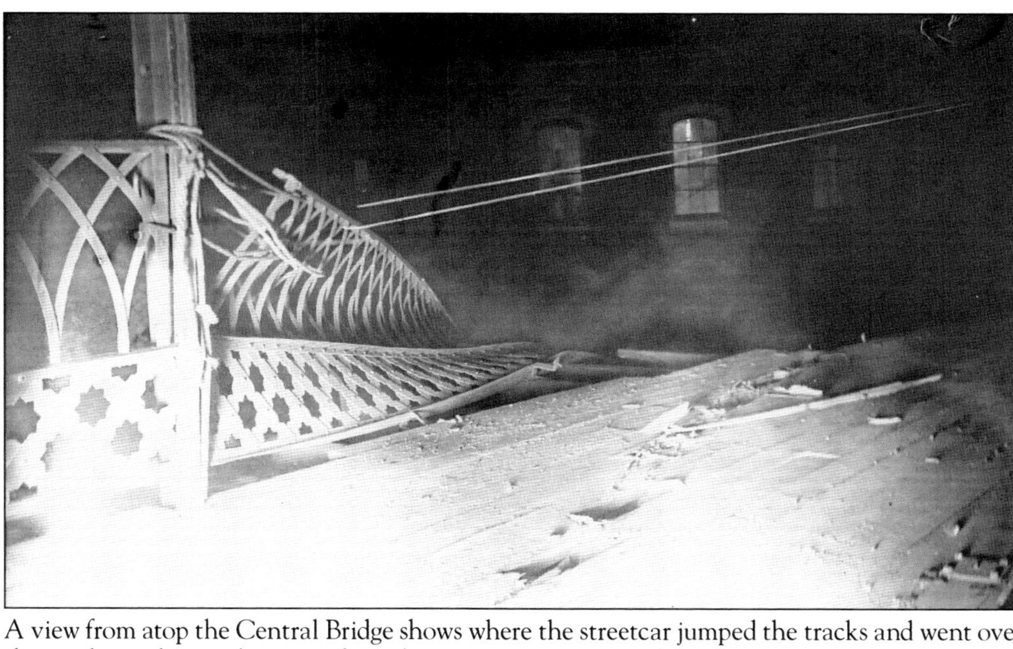

A view from atop the Central Bridge shows where the streetcar jumped the tracks and went over the perilous edge to plunge 40 feet . (Courtesy Peter Garrett.)

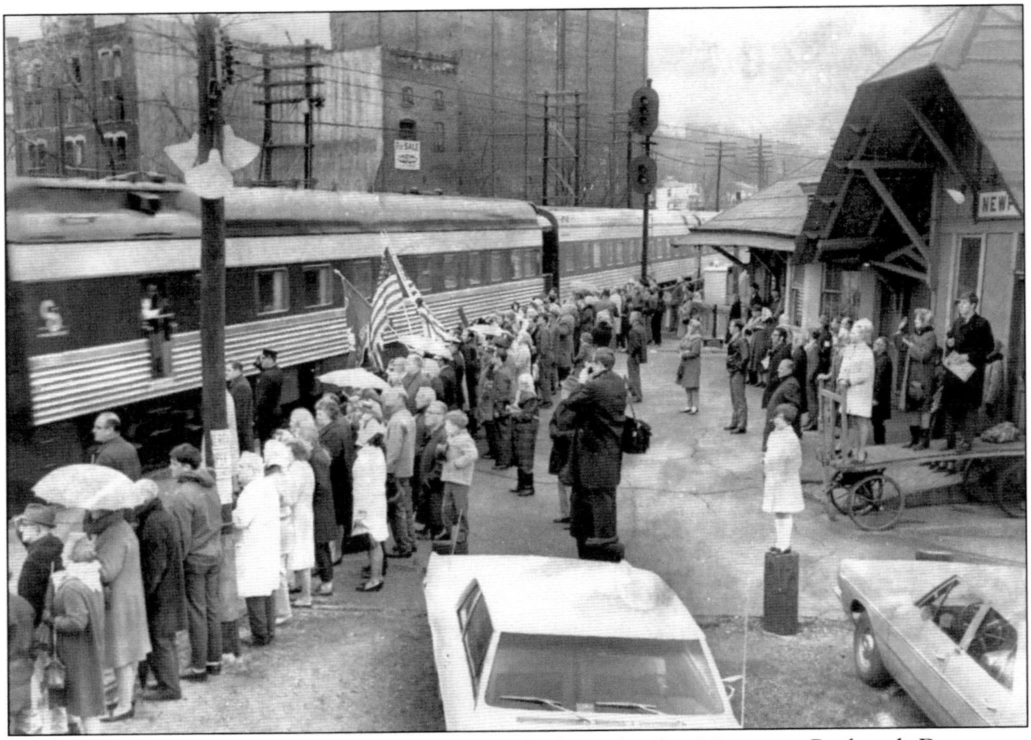

The Dwight Eisenhower funeral train passed through the Newport Railroad Depot on April 1, 1969. (Courtesy Kenton County Public Library.)

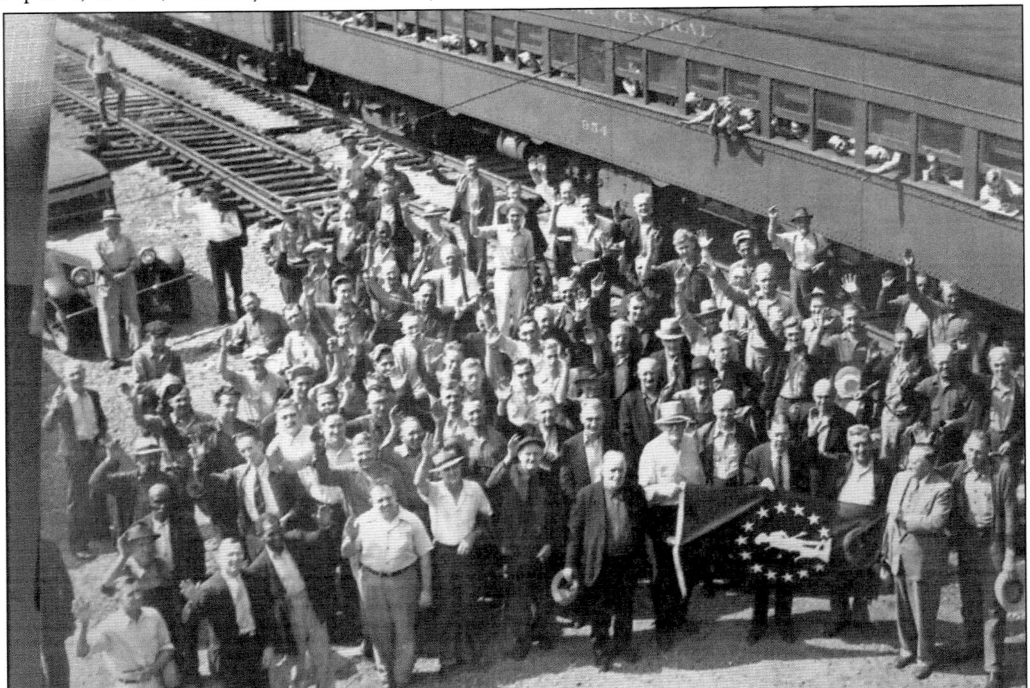

A crowd gathered at the Newport Railroad Depot in the 1940s to send-off servicemen as they departed for duty. (Courtesy Campbell County Historical Society.)

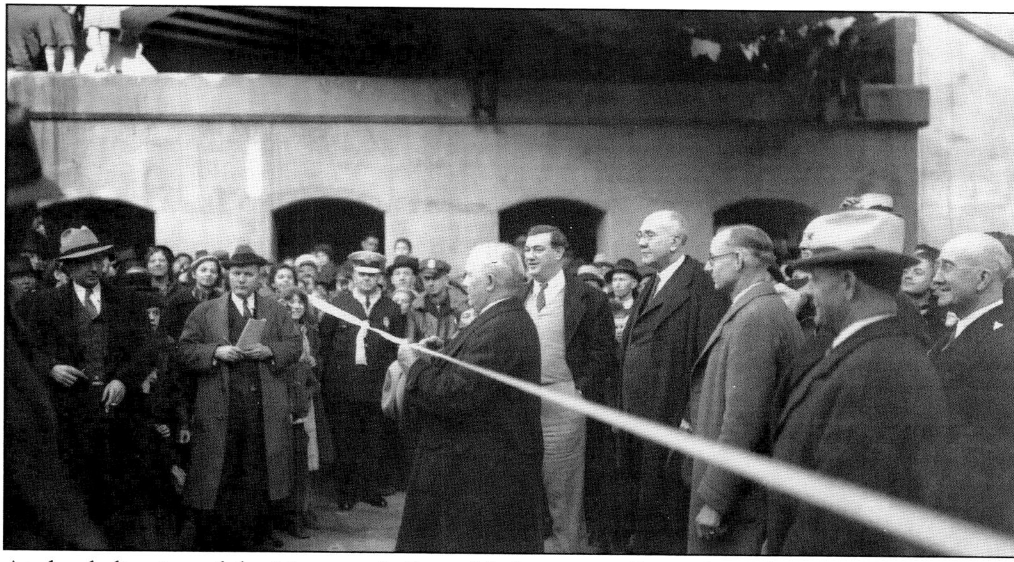

At the dedication of the Monmouth Street Underpass on December 15, 1936, are O.M. Rogers (state highway commissioner), Joseph Heman, Brent Spence, and John Rawlings. Brent Spence was born in Newport in 1874. Initially practicing law in Newport, he served in the Kentucky State Senate from 1904 to 1908 and in the U.S. House of Representatives from 1931 to 1963. He lived to be 92 years old. (Courtesy Kenton County Public Library.)

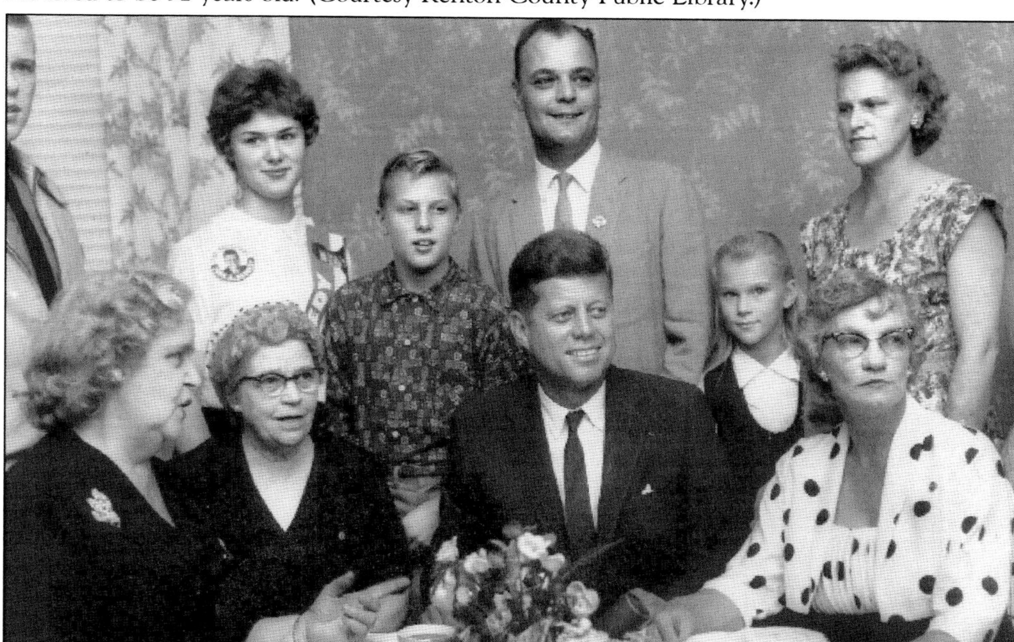

President John F. Kennedy visited Newport in October 1960. One of his planned visits was to 1168 Park Avenue, home of Mrs. Ethel Steil, president of the local chapter of the Gold Star Mothers. The American Gold Star Mothers, an organization of mothers whose sons or daughters served and died in the line of duty in the U.S. Armed Forces, was founded in January 1929 by 25 mothers. Its name is derived from the tradition of a blue star representing each person serving in the U.S. military, with a gold star substituted when a member died. President Kennedy is pictured here with Mrs. Steil (far right) and her family. (Courtesy Linda Ziegler.)

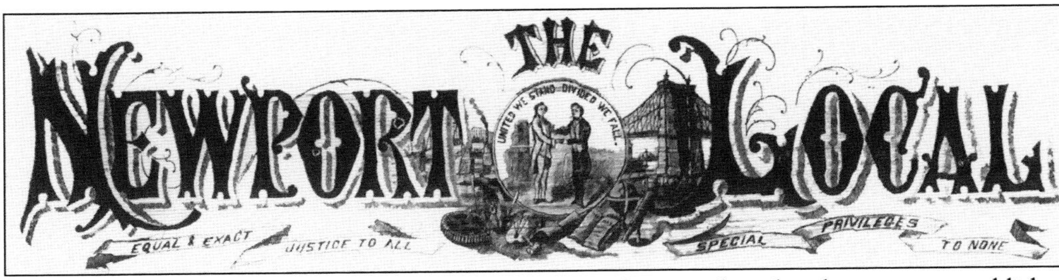

Inaugurated on September 5, 1876, *The Newport Local* was a short-lived newspaper published three times a week. Subscription cost was $4 per annum or 10¢ per week by carrier. The editor was George M. Dittoe; offices were located at 19 and 21 Jefferson Street. In September of 1879, *The Newport Local* ceased to exist and became the *Kentucky State Journal.* (Courtesy Kenton County Public Library.)

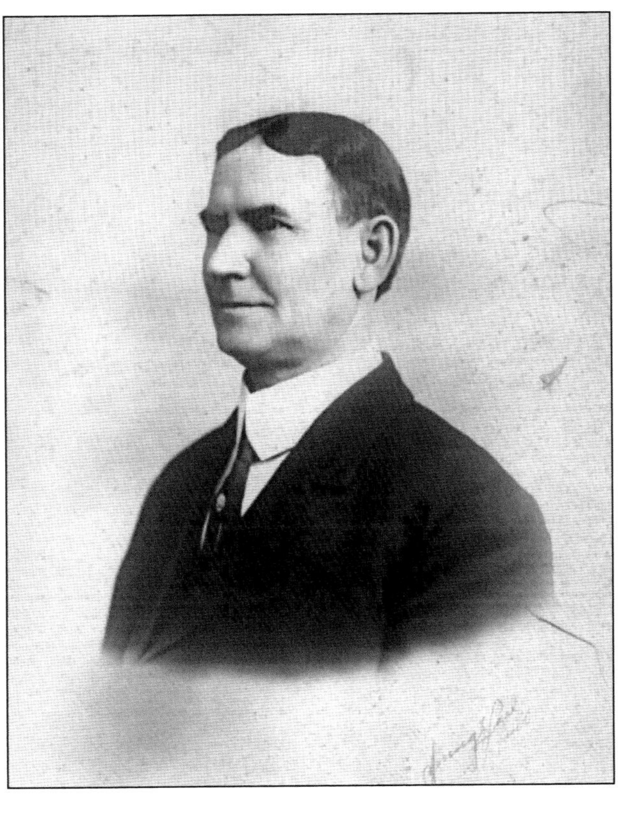

Jule Plummer was sheriff at the time of the legendary Pearl Bryan murder and trial in 1896. Pearl Bryan was a young girl found in Fort Thomas after being murdered and beheaded. Her head was never found. The highly publicized trial took place in Newport and dental students Scott Jackson and Alonzo Walling were sentenced to hang for her murder. Regarding his role at the hanging, Sheriff Plummer was quoted by *The Kentucky Post* as saying "It will be my painful duty to spring the traps . . . mine will be the hand to adjust the rope and open the traps . . . one must not shrink from his duty, however unpleasant it may be." (Courtesy Detective Keith A. Aulick.)

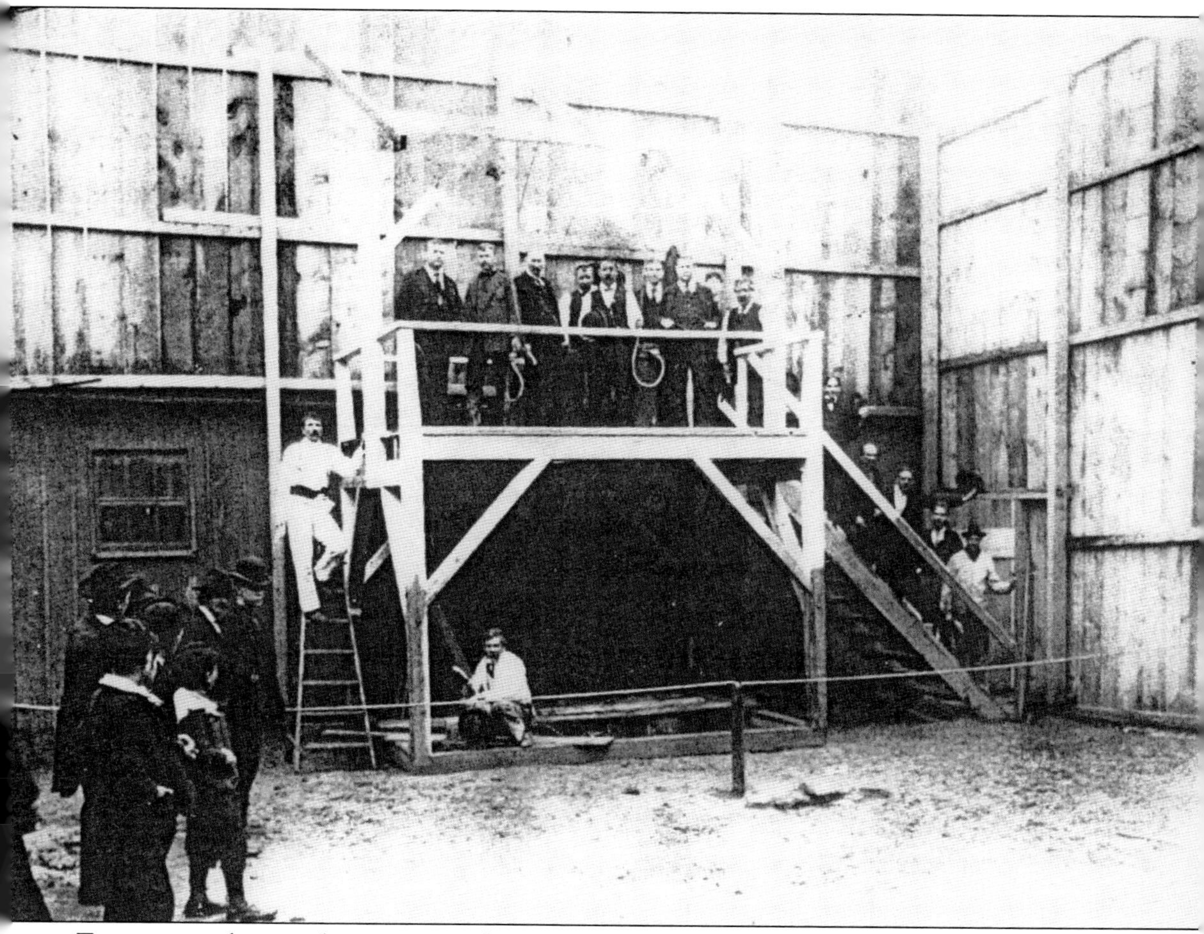

To carry out the punishment imposed on murderers Scott Jackson and Alonzo Walling, plans were made for an uncommon double hanging. Sheriff Plummer was reportedly pleased with this arrangement because he "dreaded two ordeals." An Ohio man offered to pay $25 for the privilege of building the scaffolding, provided he could keep the structure following the hanging to sell pieces of it as souvenirs. Instead, the job was given to Newport carpenter Horace Allen who specially designed the scaffolding so that one lever would drop both traps simultaneously. After the expiration of their appeals, the double hanging of Jackson and Walling took place on May 20, 1897, in the Newport jailyard. This was the last hanging Campbell County residents would witness. Currently, Washington is the only state where hanging is still a potential mode of execution. Washington inmates may choose hanging as an alternative to lethal injection. (Courtesy Campbell County Historical Society.)

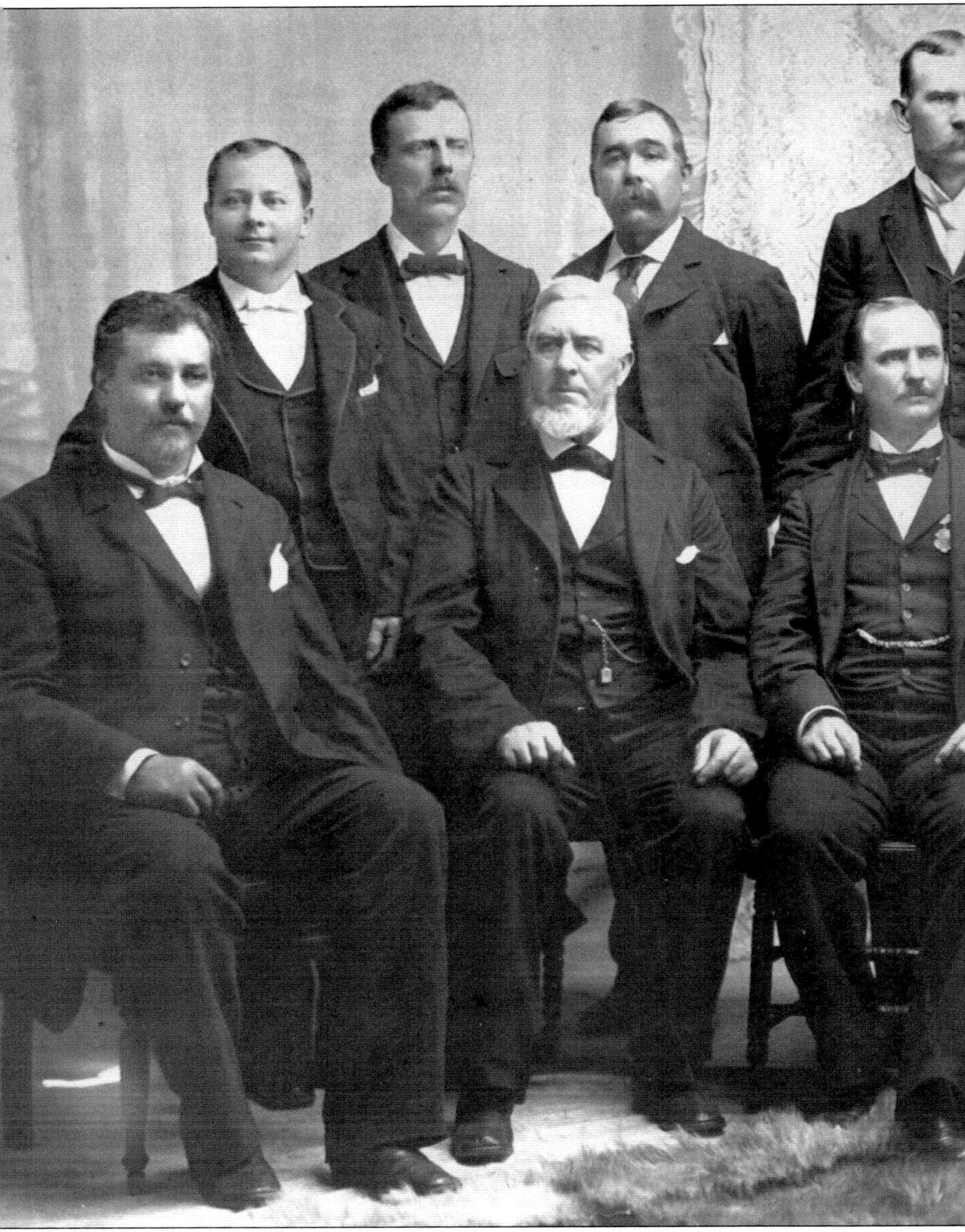

The jury of the 1896 Pearl Bryan trial found Scott Jackson guilty of her murder. Jury foreman was George Peter Stegner, who is seen in the back row, fourth from the left. Alonzo

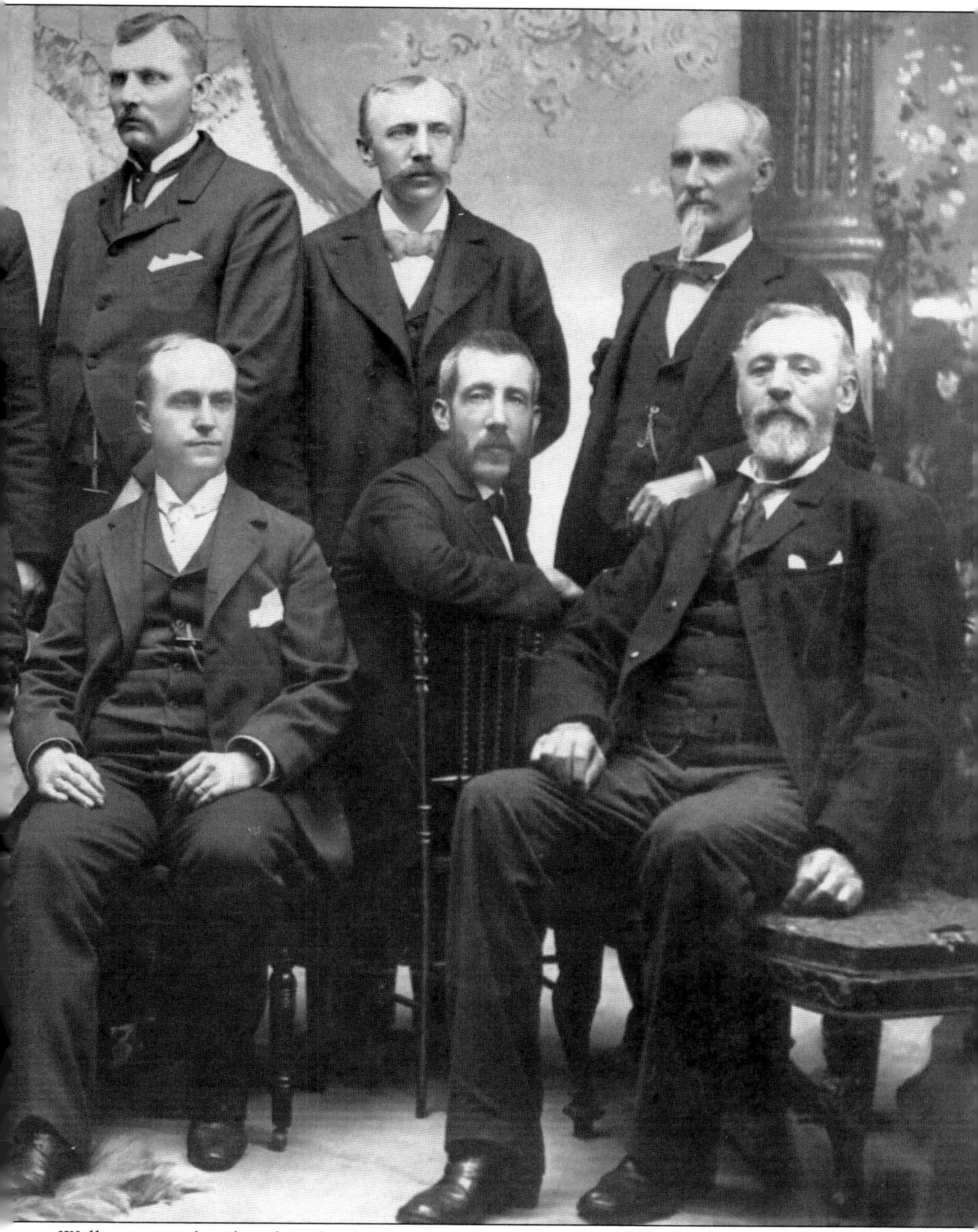

Walling was also found guilty by a separate jury one month later. (Courtesy Campbell County Historical Society.)

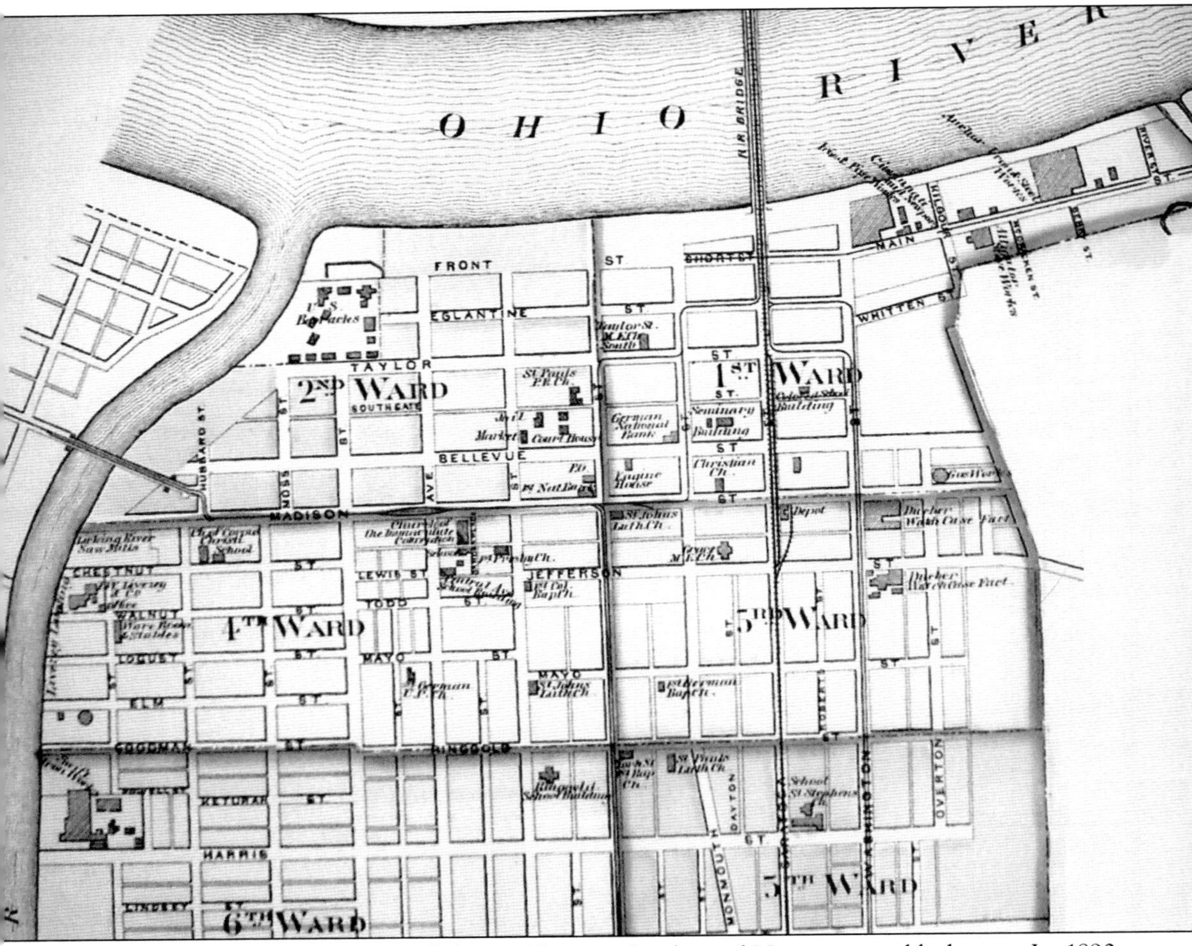

Not long after the making of this 1883 map, the face of Newport would change. In 1890, many street names changed as well as the numbering system for some addresses. The following changes were instituted: Front Street became First Street, Eglantine became Second Street, Taylor became Third Street, Bellevue became Fourth Street, Madison became Fifth Street, Jefferson became Sixth Street, Mayo became Seventh Street, Ringgold became Eighth Street, Harris became Ninth Street, Tibbatts became Tenth Street, Williamson became Eleventh Street, and Liberty became Twelfth Street. (Courtesy Special Collections and Archives, Northern Kentucky University.)